THE
CENSORSHIP
PAPERS

Also by Gerald Gardner:

Who's In Charge Here?

All the President's Wits

The Watergate Follies

THE CENSORSHIP PAPERS

*Movie Censorship Letters
from the Hays Office,
1934 to 1968*

by
Gerald Gardner

DODD, MEAD & COMPANY   New York

Copyright © 1987 by Gerald Gardner
All rights reserved
No part of this book may be reproduced in any form
without permission in writing from the publisher.
Published by Dodd, Mead & Company, Inc.,
71 Fifth Avenue, New York, N.Y. 10003
Manufactured in the United States of America
Designed by Mike Cantalupo
First Edition

1 2 3 4 5 6 7 8 9 10

Library of Congress Cataloging-in-Publication Data
Gardner, Gerald C.
    The censorship papers.

    Includes index.
    1. Moving-pictures—Censorship—United States.
2. Moving-pictures—United States—Editing.   3. Hays,
Will H. (Will Harrison), 1879–1954.   4. Breen, Joseph E.
5. Motion Picture Producers and Distributors of
America.   I. Title.
PN1995.62.G37   1987   302.2'343   87-19927
ISBN 0-396-08903-8

To Harriet,
with love

CONTENTS

AUTHOR'S NOTE

Censorship is a dark and dirty business.

Most people don't even like the word—even the censors. At the TV networks the censors call the censorship department "Standards and Practices." In Hollywood the censors called their censorship group the Production Code Administration, and their censorship rules, the Production Code. Censors have a flair for euphemism in their appellations and in the objects of their censorship.

Censors are uneasy about the exercise of their function. Like the natural functions they keep off the screen, they look on censorship as a necessary process of elimination, but one that should be exercised with prudence and secrecy.

Thus, when the Hays Office was first established, one of the provisions of its creators was that all correspondence that flowed between the censors and the studios would not be open to public scrutiny.

Film censorship ended in 1968—not with a bang but a whimper—to be replaced by the more civilized and flexible film rating process. Then, a year ago, the parent body of the Hays Office opened the secret files to the examination of authors and historians.

There were over five thousand files, one for each produced film, and they were turned over to the Academy of Motion Picture Arts and Sciences, which welcomed the gift with becoming gratitude. From this bountiful treasure trove, the Academy selected one thousand film files that were the most famous of the vast Hollywood output; from this thousand, I have excerpted letters and reconstructed events from threescore of the most memorable movies.

Mind you, some famous films will not be found here, for the simple reason that they did not engage the attention of the censors. Even the Hays Office could find little that was blasphemous or corrupting in *The Wizard of Oz* or *National Velvet*. Here one will find only the famous films that ran afoul of the moralists.

Where the files contained the information, I have indicated which of the censors' demands were met and which were successfully thwarted by the studios. Often the file did not yield these facts. The reader will not be often wrong if, lacking data to the contrary, he assumes that the lion's share of the censors' demands were satisfied.

I have tried to give the reader a moral or creative context within which to consider the censorship correspondence for each film. To appreciate the importance—and the audacity—of the censors' letters, one needs to know something of the film's roots and the author's intentions. I have tried to provide this perspective in my introductory remarks for each movie.

Virtually all of these letters are signed by Joseph E. Breen, the likable, protean head of the censorship board. Breen's boss was Will H. Hays, architect of the code that Breen enforced. Doubtless many of the letters that bore his signature were written by one of his assistants—the erudite Geoffrey Shurlock, who would one day succeed him, the witty Jack Vizzard, who would one day write an incisive memoir of his censoring days, and the rest. The censors wanted to imply that they spoke with one voice, and so Breen signed all correspondence. In a larger sense, the voice was that of Will Hays, the Hoosier politician who had come to Hollywood to keep the government off the filmmakers' backs.

Hays succeeded; and, with the help of Joe Breen, he did his job not wisely, but too well. He saw his duty and he overdid it. Breen and Hays were dedicated men, and an examination of their correspondence shows what they were dedicated *to*.

Because the Hays Office acted as a conduit for the deletions of both state boards and foreign censors, I have included the eliminations made by those worthies as well. It is fascinating to find the Hollywood censors warning the filmmakers of the excesses of the state censors. Spiro Agnew said, "When you've seen one ghetto you've seen them all," but when you've seen one censor you have *not* seen them all. State censors were often more virulent and bizarre in their protests than were their Hollywood counterparts, and the foreign censors, each with its own indigenous bias, were odder still.

There is humor in these censorship letters, because nothing is quite as funny as yesterday's taboos. Doubtless the congressmen's wives who deplore the vulgarity of today's rock lyrics will someday laugh at their present outrage—if their husbands remain in Congress long enough.

Along with the humor and nostalgia—since these are the most beloved films of our time—there is a sense of outrage. Behind closed doors, a group of men had the power to lay their hands on the creations of artists, to twist them this way and that, to satisfy the mandates and morals of a pious little group who feared for the souls of their fellow men. It was all done in the name of public morality and the greater good; but the film censors were always a step behind the public and were doomed to fight a rear-guard action against maturing tastes, until they were forced, kicking and screaming, into a long retreat.

Here then, for better or worse—usually the latter—are the secret censorship letters that were used to mold and manacle the most famous films of our century.

INTRODUCTION

Psychiatrists tell us that we pay a price when we turn our back on truth and embrace illusion, that we are healthiest and safest when we look at life as it is, not as we would wish it to be. For half a century America boasted an organization whose function it was to protect us from the truth and to saddle us with comfortable illusions. That organization was called the Hays Office.

Reality seldom reared its head in films for many years, since the guardians of public morality at the Hays Office were vigilant and thorough. They would root out all signs of the disagreeable facts of life, and many of the agreeable facts, as well.

Today, when our films commonly offer us scenes of fornication, frigidity, adultery, incest, prostitution, homosexuality, rape, cannibalism, voyeurism, and necrophilia, it is difficult to visualize a gentler time when cinema presented beautiful movies about beautiful people.

As long as we have had movies, there has been a struggle over what could properly be projected on the big screen, which has so profoundly affected our culture and perceptions. The members of the Hays Office—Hollywood's self-imposed board of censors—seldom had doubts on the matter. They were guided by the gamily explicit rules of their censorship code, and, as they reviewed each screenplay and every foot of film, they knew what was acceptable and what was not.

The letters in this volume are the instruments that carried their demands for deletions to the filmmakers, expressed with the certitude of papal decrees.

It is interesting to examine the genesis of the Hays Office, since the operation of censorship in films is like a social history of America, as well as a cautionary tale of folly committed in the name of virtue.

Censorship was a painful pill for Hollywood moguls to swallow. When one reads the letters from the Hays Office to men like Louis B. Mayer, Jack L. Warner, and Harry Cohn, one can picture these autocrats thrashing about like hooked marlin, as the censors gutted the most dramatic ingredients from their most prized and profitable pictures.

It was a fascinating contest of wits and wills. Some like Cecil B. De Mille were able to evade the censors—by telling tales of the Bible that made sin acceptable to the pious—but most had no such escape and had to toe the censor's line.

Movie censorship is nearly as old as the movies, and the industry had only itself to blame. It was the victim of its own exploding popularity and its own humble beginnings. Movies began, after all, in the sleazy ambience of the penny arcade and the peep show, not in the elegance of the concert hall. The poor, impressionable public had to be protected from its own gullibility by those whose morality was of a superior breed. No era has ever been short of smut-minded censors, high-minded reformers, sanctimonious critics, and self-promoting politicians who could find in films the perfect outlet for their pieties and ambitions.

It was a scant four months after the Stock Market Crash that Hollywood sold short on its artistic future. The major studios adopted a formal censorship code under the leadership of Will H. Hays, a man with impeccable religious and political credentials. If George Bernard Shaw and Eugene O'Neill had written the code, it might have been a defensible document; but alas, it was written by a Jesuit priest, Father Daniel Lord, and a prominent publisher and Catholic layman, Martin Quigley.

The creation of the code and the appointment of Hays as the guardian of movie morals were not without provocation. The artists and fast-buck experts who comprise the filmmaking community have always known that the right button to push to bring out the multitudes was marked "Sex," and so, as the economy sank like a stone into depression, the movies rode a rising tide of sex and sensation. There was already a list of dos and don'ts—mostly don'ts—that Hollywood acknowledged in their breach, but, for the most part, Tinseltown's producers were putting images on the screen that were very nearly as titillating as their titles implied. The code of commandments was adopted with

all the enthusiasm of a tax bill in an election year. The producers swallowed their misgivings, because they feared the alternative. It is said that democracy is the worst form of government except all the rest. Self-regulated movie censorship was
the worst form of control except all the rest—censorship im-
posed by the federal government, the states, and the church.

The public had always been ambivalent about Hollywood. It
adored the movies and loved the stars, but deplored the sexuality on the screen and the ugly scandals off it. Hollywood had
always struggled to maintain a decent public image. The appointment of Will Hays and the adoption of a censorship code
was intended to give the town and its product a face lift.

Hays was a Republican politician from Indiana with the impatient look of a postman whose paycheck has been sent by
mail. Indeed Hays was an employee of the postal department—
he had been Postmaster General under the most corrupt administration of the century, that of President Warren G. Harding.
Will Hays had friends in high places, and he had large funds
available from the plush film industry. His immediate task: to
stifle the threat of government censorship. How to do it? Well,
stars could be persuaded to avoid scandal (which was like asking rabbits to eat less lettuce); movie titles could be made less
suggestive (no more *What the Butler Saw*); and Hays could lobby
legislators and civic groups about Hollywood's new leaf.

Hays had his hands full. This was an era of two vamps in
every garage, women smoking cigarettes and performing other
"unnatural" acts, men carrying hip flasks and playing sheik.
Churchmen were decrying Hollywood as the center and the
stimulus of all this libertine behavior. The Hollywood scandals
always seemed more savory and well publicized than the rest
because they involved famous names like Charlie Chaplin and
Mary Pickford. Newspaper publishers like William Randolph
Hearst rode these scandals to new heights of circulation, even
as he dallied with his own movie mistress, Marion Davies, and
privately referred to her genitalia as "Rosebud." The fan magazine, Hollywood's company press, ran open letters to the stars,
pleading with them to abandon their sinful ways.

Public fury reached a feverish pitch with the indictment of
fun-loving film star Fatty Arbuckle. According to witnesses, the
corpulent comic had done something to an aspiring actress in a

hotel room with a soda bottle. The girl died, along with Arbuckle's career, and Hollywood's reputation reached a new low. All over America, the cry went up for the movies to reform.

The fact that some of these screen libertines were earning five thousand dollars a month, at a time when a quarter of America's work force was jobless while the rest found twenty dollars a week an ample wage, did little to endear Movieland to the public.

Like so many leaders mired in chaos, Hays had a formula. His was called the Law of Compensating Values. The Hays Office suggested that filmmakers could put as much sex as they wished in their films, but warned that the sex must never be condoned. Men could sin, so long as the sinner paid for his sinful ways. Evil must be punished. Give the moviegoer eighty minutes of delicious vice and in the last ten minutes deplore it.

With Hays's solicitude and the deepening of the Depression, Hollywood served up the dollops of sex that the censorship code was designed to inhibit. Occasionally, some bombastic congressman would make a speech attacking this Sodom in the sun, and a state or two might set up a censorship board; but the moneymen of Hollywood paid little attention. The profits were good and their tans were becoming. They should have known it was too good to last, but then they believed in happy endings.

The willingness of the movie industry to ignore its responsibilities to public morality, ignoring its own censorship code in its pursuit of private profit, finally drove the Catholic Church to act. The first shot was fired by Cardinal Dougherty of Philadelphia who, enraged at Hollywood's on-screen and off-screen sins, declared all movies in Philadelphia off limits to Catholics. W.C. Fields's famous comment in a moment of pain that "on the whole, I'd rather be in Philadelphia" was inspired by this quarantine.

In April of 1934, the Roman Catholic Church convened a committee of bishops which brought forth its aptly named Legion of Decency. Parishioners across the country were commanded at their Sunday mass to recite an oath of obedience not to patronize any movie that had been condemned by the Legion. Stalin once derisively inquired, "How many battalions has the Pope?" In 1934 there were no battalions, but there was one Legion, and that was too much for Hollywood. It promptly settled for a negotiated peace.

It should be noted that the Catholics had no monopoly on virtue. Though they led this attack on cinema sin, Protestants and Jews held their flanks. For example, the Federal Council of Churches admonished moviemakers to clean their skirts or face federal legislation.

Say what you will about the taste and avarice of Hollywood moguls, they were not stupid. After fifteen years of warnings and millions of Catholics vowing to shun their films, the magnates knew it was time to act.

It was time to heed the warnings of Will Hays and put some teeth in the Hays Office.

The vision of millions of unsold movie tickets spurred Hollywood to action. A new censorship code was adopted in June of 1934—and this time there was a machinery with which to enforce it. The instrument was called the Production Code Administration (PCA) and it was given a power over the creation of films that would distort the perceptions of filmgoers for a generation.

A tough-minded but genial Catholic journalist named Joseph Breen was put in charge of the office. He ruled it for many years, placing the stamp of the new code on every film—from the pedestrian to the inspired—that sprang from the fantasy factories.

This time there would be no avoidance or evasions, because this time there was "the seal." What brought the producers to heel was the fact that the studios agreed never to distribute a film that lacked the Hays Office's Seal of Approval. All the best movie theaters in America were owned by the major studios, and so, a film that had been denied a seal was dead in the water. When Joe Breen wrote to a producer that a film based on this book or that play could not hope to receive a seal, a vaultlike door slammed shut. The power of the Hays Office, with Joe Breen at the helm, had suddenly become formidable, and it would be decades before any producer—such as the doughty Otto Preminger—would challenge the threat of the seal.

The Hays Office seal, and the possibility of its being withheld, was such a potent weapon that self-censorship in Hollywood finally took root. It made the Production Code, as the new censorship rules were called, the immutable commandments of the movie business. From that point onward, all the sex in Hollywood ended up on the cutting-room floor. "It may sound un-comfortable," said Fred Allen, "but that's Hollywood!"

The code became the Bible of Joe Breen and his disciples at the Hays office. After reviewing a screenplay for a forthcoming film—which they always referred to as a "proposed" film to gently imply that its fate was still in doubt—Breen would cite the code as holy writ. In its name ministers would be turned into laymen, fade-outs would be turned to dissolves, lines of dialogue would disappear, scenes would be moved from bed-rooms to patios, prostitutes would be turned into dancers—all in the name of adherence to the code. The apostles of Orwell did not intone the rules of Big Brother with half the obedience of the employees of the Hays Office.

The Production Code was a document so thorough and ex-plicit in its prurience that Will Hays would have forbidden its reading on a movie screen. Not surprisingly, three quarters of the code was devoted to those manifestations of sex that were forbidden to the screen. The subclassifications under the stark heading of "Sex" read like a contents page of *Penthouse* maga-zine. They included Adultery, Seduction, Rape, and Sexual Per-version. Other sections of the code dealt with such matters as Profanity, Vulgarity, Obscenity, Blasphemy, and Costume De-sign. The denizens of the code viewed their films through a pu-ritanical prism indeed.

Much of the correspondence flowing from the Hays Office to the studios was preoccupied with lines of dialogue that, in spirit or in specifics, were in violation of the code. The authors of the articles listed several words and phrases that were taboo on the screen. Like most censorship, this tawdry lexicon looks rather charming in retrospect. The forbidden words honored by inclu-sion included: "chippie," "fairy," "goose," "madam," "pansy," "tart," "in your hat," and "nuts." "Hell" and "damn" managed to sneak in in the early sixties, but only for discreet use. The code said that traveling salesmen stories were forbidden, and singled out "children's sex organs" to be denied exposure. Few producers inferred from this that the sex organs of adults might be shown.

Obscenity in songs was expressly proscribed and this taboo deprived moviegoers of the sophisticated wit of Cole Porter, Larry Hart, and Stephen Sondheim.

An expressive "Oh God" was considered blasphemy, and a

generation of screenwriters ground their teeth as they typed "Oh boy!"

Costumes and wardrobe were a perennial preoccupation of the Hays Office. The code commanded that undue exposure of the female body was forbidden, and Breen's letters often reminded producers this codicil applied most specifically to women's breasts. The code added, with racist sensibility, that this did not include natives in foreign lands.

The code precluded electrocutions, which cut the opening scene from *Double Indemnity*; childbirth, which forced Scarlett and Melanie into silhouette in *Gone With the Wind*; social disease, which made Claire Trevor a victim of tuberculosis in *Dead End*; prostitution, which turned Donna Reed into a bar girl in *From Here to Eternity*.

The authors of the Hays Office code evidently felt that movie audiences were extremely susceptible to suggestion—that once shown an evil act, they would feel impelled to emulate it. Hence, moviemakers were forbidden to show the techniques of murder in any detail. The word "arsenic" was struck from many scripts on the theory that, deprived of this information, the moviegoer would never realize that arsenic was a lethal substance.

As will be observed in the letters that follow, the Hays Office exercised prior restraint to accommodate their fellow censors in England. Pointing out that the British usually deleted scenes of married couples in double beds, Breen would commonly ask producers to put their couples in twin beds. Thus, a generation of American filmgoers grew to maturity believing that all married couples slept in twin beds—and that's all they *did* in twin beds.

The code fostered a number of other numbing myths that distorted our perspective of life. Since the major activity of honeymoons could not be displayed or alluded to—an entire series of scenes in Hitchcock's *Rear Window* show the effects of this edict—audiences grew up believing that a honeymoon night consisted of a series of farcical happenings.

Other myths to flourish under the Hays Code were the belief that divorced couples invariably remarried one another, the conviction that all criminals are punished, that war is a glorious adventure in which American boys are impervious to harm, and that women probably have no navels, since none could be exposed on the screen.

The Hays Code showed more solicitude for the feelings of foreign nations than it did for the intelligence of Americans. It insisted that the biases and sensitivities of foreign countries be respected. This led Joe Breen to delete barefoot Mexicans from *The Treasure of the Sierra Madre* and an obtuse Brazilian cab driver from *Now, Voyager.*

The Hays Office code threw a blanket of myths and distortions over the making of American movies, and, for a third of a century—from its adoption in 1934 to its replacement by the rating system in 1968—every writer, director, and producer of films squirmed under its suffocating embrace.

Directors like Alfred Hitchcock, John Huston, Billy Wilder, and William Wyler had to devote a good deal of their gifts to circumventing the code and bringing an extra bit of truth to the audience. Playwrights like Tennessee Williams, Lillian Hellman, and George Bernard Shaw had to fume as they saw their dialogue deleted and their characters distorted. Producers from David O. Selznick to Darryl F. Zanuck had to maneuver and compromise, rant and reason, to keep their films from being too badly gutted.

The Hays Office injected itself into every phase of the production. When a studio considered optioning a best-selling book or a hit Broadway play for the screen, the Hays Office would often step in—as they did with *Pal Joey* and *Tea and Sympathy*—and assert that no film made from such fetid source material could ever be approved in a finished film.

Once a screenplay was completed, the Hays Office would read it and dispatch a lengthy list of deletions and eliminations, and once the film itself was completed and edited, the Hays Office would screen it to be sure that nothing objectionable—a dress or a dance, an undulating hip or a vile gesture—had been slipped in by an aberrant director.

Often, the Hays Office employees would check the film in local theaters to be sure that the cuts agreed to by the producers had actually been made in the distributed prints. Sometimes, as in the case of one Mae West epic, they discovered that the film they had been shown was not the film that was sent out to the theaters.

Like Thomas More and Marie Antoinette, the producers had the right of appeal. If the Hays Office denied their finished film the coveted Seal of Approval, or, if the producers felt a ruling of the Hollywood censors was unjust, they could protest to a higher authority. Jack Warner wanted to preserve a "dammit" in *Life With Father* and a whole string of expletives in *Who's Afraid of Virginia Woolf,* and availed himself of the appellate machinery of the code. To do so, the protesting filmmaker would notify the appeals board in New York of a desire to appeal. The hearing was called in New York's St. Moritz Hotel. The appeals board consisted of the presidents of all the major movie distributors, four independent film producers, and six theater owners. The movie was screened for the board members, who then listened to the anguished appeal of the studio involved and the rebuttal of the Hollywood censors. Censors and producers then left the room and the board remained to reflect in Solomon-like dignity. Fifteen mature men would sit around a long table and discuss whether Elizabeth Taylor could say "Screw, sweety." (They decided she couldn't.)

Since the Hays Code was at heart a rigid and repressive document, and its architecture a basically unyielding one, there were few reversals. Indeed, there were very few appeals, reflecting the studios' knowledge of the odds. From 1954 to 1964 there were only six appeals, and only one in all of 1962 and 1963.

The pariah whose appeal had been denied had two alternatives. He could cut his negative into banjo picks, or he could release his film without a seal. Neither alternative was appealing. Most theaters would not touch a movie that had been denied a seal; military bases barred them; and the producer was certain to run into a barrage of virulent attacks, boycotts, and harassments from religious groups and women's clubs. His film would also be cut to pieces by the puritans of the state and local censor boards.

There was, of course, a third alternative, which was universally adopted by any filmmaker whose appeal had been rejected. He could bow to the wishes of the censors and make all the changes they demanded, right down to the mildest expletive and the gentlest pat on the posterior.

One of the major miracles of the twentieth century, to stand beside the Salk vaccine and the election of Harry Truman, is the fact that so many memorable movies were produced within the suffocating restraints of movie censorship. It is a tribute to the ingenuity of America's filmmakers that they were able to work within the confines of such a strangling system.

This book offers the epistolary voice of the censor, sharp and clear, as it was heard by the creators of some of America's most celebrated films. There are few pedestrian films in this volume. They represent the most enduring achievements of Hollywood in its most luxuriant years. As one examines the carps and admonitions of the censors as expressed in these letters, and one sees how producers yielded to them, one is left with a sense of awe at the cinematic marvels the producers wrought.

Like the Jews of the Warsaw ghetto, who, despite domination and humiliation, managed to live their lives and even create "a theater in a graveyard," Hollywood's filmmakers turned out a succession of films that belie the conditions of their creation—films that are often brilliant and sometimes superb.

It leads one inescapably to ponder what marvels they might have produced—or how much more splendid these films might have been—had there been no Hays Office to hamper and harass them.

THE CENSORSHIP PAPERS

Chapter 1

ADVENTURES

CASABLANCA

When Julius and Philip Epstein adapted to the screen for Warner Brothers an undistinguished play called *Everybody Comes to Rick's*, they could not have dreamed that history would catch up with their clattering typewriters. They called the film *Casablanca*. Just a few days after the movie opened, the attention of the world was focused on that North African town, when Allied forces landed there.

General Eisenhower's green troops ran into some unexpected roadblocks in French Morocco, and the Epstein brothers ran into some roadblocks of their own with the Hollywood censors.

Rick (Humphrey Bogart) runs a café in Casablanca that is a center of intrigue. Free Frenchmen are plotting the liberation of their country, while refugees scamper to arrange visas to America. A key figure in the Epsteins' plot was Captain Renault (Claude Rains), a Vichy police official, deliciously corrupt. The authors conceived Rains selling visas to desperate women in exchange for their sexual favors. The censors blanched at this, and tooled out every indication—subtle or heavy-handed—of such an arrangement. The barter system is time-honored, but not in *Casablanca*.

The steamy romance of the story was likewise toned down by the Hollywood censors. Victor Laszlo (Paul Henreid), leader of the European underground, is passing through town. With him is his wife Ilsa (Ingrid Bergman). Ilsa, it seems, was Rick's lover in days past. The Epsteins created a flashback in which Rick and Ilsa cuddled in a bedroom above a Paris bordello, while her unsuspecting husband was off at his labors. The censors bridled

1

at the brothel and the husband, moving one and killing the other. Widows do not commit adultery.

As the Epsteins jousted with the censors, the government of Sweden was nimbly sidestepping the bellicose Germans, who had gobbled up the rest of Europe. It was thus not surprising that the Swedish censors removed from *Casablanca* any lines that might give offense to their pugnacious neighbors.

The wariness with which the Hollywood censors sought to disguise the sexual appetite of the Vichy captain, and the care of the Swedish censors to disguise the warlike appetites of the Nazi officer, are in retrospect as amusing as the original casting of the role of the hero. Rick, the career-making role in this triumphantly popular film, was originally assigned to a Warner Brothers contract player with a rather monotonous style. His name was Ronald Reagan.

In a letter dated May 19, 1942 to Jack Warner, president of Warner Brothers Studios, Joseph Breen, chief honcho of the Hays Office, wrote:

> We have received one of the incomplete scripts for your proposed picture *Casablanca*. While we cannot give you a final opinion until we receive the balance of the script . . . going through the material so far submitted, we call your attention to the following:
>
> *Page 5:* The following lines seem unacceptably suggestive . . . : "Of course, a beautiful young girl for Monsieur Renault, the Prefect of Police."
>
> *Page 14:* . . . The following lines seem unacceptably suggestive: "It used to take a villa in Cannes . . . and a string of pearls. Now all I ask is an exit visa."
>
> *Page 28:* The following dialog seems unacceptable: "How extravagant you are, throwing away women like that. Some day they may be rationed."

On May 19th Joe Breen received the second part of the scenario for Casablanca *from Warner Brothers and wasted no time in dispatching these censorious notes:*

> The present material contains certain elements that seem to be unacceptable. . . . Specifically, we cannot approve the suggestion that Captain Renault makes a practice of seducing the women

to whom he grants visas. Any such inference of illicit sex could not be approved. . . . Going through this material we call your attention to the following:

Page 76: The following dialog is unacceptable: "By the way—another visa problem has come up." "Show her in."

Page 86: The suggestion that Ilsa was married all the time she was having her love affair with Rick in Paris seems unacceptable. . . .

On June 5th Joe Breen wrote to Hal B. Wallis, the producer of Casablanca, to confirm an understanding they had reached the day before, regarding Captain Renault's lechery and Rick's love affair with Ilsa:

With a view to removing the offensive characterization of Renault as an immoral man who engaged himself in seducing the women to whom he grants visas, it has been agreed with Mr. Wallis that the [several] references to this particular phase of the gentleman's character will be materially toned down.

Page 5: The line in Scene 15, "The girl will be released in the morning," will be changed to, "The girl will be released later."

Page 73: Delete [Rick's] line, "They went along with the sound of the tinny piano in the parlor downstairs." The purpose here is to get away from the quite definite reference to a bawdyhouse.

Page 75: The word "enjoy" in Renault's line is to be changed to "like": "You like war. I like women."

Page 76: Renault's line, "At least your work keeps you outdoors" is to be changed to ". . . gets you plenty of fresh air."

Page 105: Rick's line, "Captain Renault is branching out" is to changed to "Captain Renault seems to be getting broadminded."

On June 18th, Joe Breen had received additional pages of the script for Casablanca, including pink pages that reflected changes demanded in his previous letters. The new pages contained a hint that Rick and Ilsa had gone beyond kissing in Paris. Wrote Breen:

The present material seems to contain a suggestion of a sexual affair [between Rick and Ilsa], which would be unacceptable if it came through in the finished picture. We believe this could possibly be corrected by replacing the fade-out . . . with a dissolve, and shooting the succeeding scene without any sign of a bed.

The following note refers to the memorable moment when Rick suddenly hears Sam (Dooley Wilson) playing "As Time Goes By" on the cafe piano:

> Page 60B: Please rewrite the line, "What the —— are you playing?"

Sentimentalists might have felt that Rick was entitled to an unstated expletive, but not the Hays Office. Not only was the word "hell" on the code's forbidden list, but it could not even be implied by a pause.

The Other Censors

Sweden, one of the few European countries to remain neutral throughout World War II, was careful to delete from the film any lines, shots, or scenes that might present the Germans in an unfavorable light. The Swedish censors eliminated the following dialogue:

"Some Germans gave this check."
"Is it good?"

"The Mayor is one of the Third Reich's ablest aides."
"You emphasize Third Reich. Do you expect others?"

"Will you divulge them?"
"If I didn't do so in that camp where you used force, I won't give you the names now."

"What if you killed these men? If you killed us all? From all parts of Europe thousands would replace us. Even Nazis can't kill so fast."
They also eliminated the shooting of Colonel Strauser (Conrad Veidt) and the kicking of the Vichy water bottle.

THE TREASURE OF THE SIERRA MADRE

Critics have placed this Humphrey Bogart film—directed and written by John Huston from a novel by B. Traven—in the small repertory of Hollywood's enduring achievements. They admire its compelling honesty, its ironic twists, its grisly look at greed and gold. They find it a crucible of human conflict about the corruptibility of the human soul.

Hollywood's censors took a more narrow view of this brutal, bitter film. They saw it as offensive to the Mexican censors. The Hays Office responded with Pavlovian regularity to scenes of Mexican poverty. When they saw a sleeping Mexican riding a donkey, they ordered him awakened. When they saw a barefoot Mexican trodding a dusty street, they put shoes on his feet and dispelled the dust. The Mexican censors had to be appeased. Though Americans who ventured south of the border may have seen shoeless or sleeping Mexicans, the Hays Office was saying in effect, "Are you going to believe us or your own eyes?"

There was more at stake than the Mexican market in a film like *Sierra Madre*, which depicted the raw elements of the Mexican ambience. Hollywood had learned that Latin censors were most empathetic. A film that insulted Mexico would also give grave offense to Mexico's neighbors to the south. The barefoot Mexican, a flophouse, saloon, or lady of easy virtue might cause the film to lose the entire Latin American market. When Mexico caught cold, Venezuela got the flu, and Honduras caught pneumonia.

On July 2, 1942, the Hays Office's Latin American adviser, Addison Durland, wrote to Jack L. Warner to warn him of trouble to the south:

We have read the undated screenplay for your proposed production titled *The Treasure of the Sierra Madre*, bearing in mind the possible reaction of Latin American audiences, and regret to report that this material in its present form seems to be unacceptable.

This unacceptability is due to: the sordid locales, such as the Mexican saloon and gambling joints, the Mexican flophouses; the extremely derogatory presentation of Mexican nationals, such as the "floosies," the cruel Mexican bandits, the barefooted Mexicans . . . and the derogatory statements about Mexico, its people, and its institutions made by the American characters.

The presence in the screenplay of all this . . . seems to violate Article X of the Production Code that reads, "The history, institutions, prominent people, and citizenry of other nations shall be represented fairly."

. . . We also wish to call your attention to the regulations recently issued by the Department of Motion Picture Supervision of the Government of Mexico. According to these regulations, motion pictures authorized for public exhibition in Mexico must not contain scenes in which the country is affronted or defamed . . . or scenes that incite wickedness, exemplified by cruelty, perversity, hatred, revenge, and vice. . . .

On June 30, 1942, Joe Breen wrote to Jack Warner. This was three days before the Latin American expert dispatched his letter. He had other things on his mind besides Latin sensibilities:

We have read the first draft script of your proposed picture *The Treasure of the Sierra Madre*. . . . Going through the script in detail we call your attention to the following . . .

Page 20: In handling these Mexican girls, please avoid any direct suggestion that they are prostitutes.

Page 44: In this sequence, please make it clear that the bandits are attempting to rob the woman and nothing more. There should . . . be no suggestion of attempted rape.

THE AFRICAN QUEEN

Humphrey Bogart and Katharine Hepburn, under the direction of John Huston, created a film about a daring jungle odyssey made by a prim missionary sister and a dissolute adventurer. It is a brilliant job of writing (Huston and James Agee adapted the C. S. Forester classic), and an exciting and stimulating job of acting. Yet what the apostles of the censorship code found in *The African Queen* was an unacceptable tale of an immoral relationship, without a trace of what they referred to as "a voice of morality"—that is, there was no spokesman to declare that this endearingly odd couple was cohabiting among the reeds without benefit of clergy, and this was *wrong*.

The film is incisive in its characterizations and witty in its dialogue, as the appealing love story unfolds. The sequences are vivid, the action riveting in its details. The censors, however, were mostly concerned with the possibility that portions of Miss Hepburn's elegant body might be exposed.

On April 2, 1951, Joe Breen wrote to producer Sam Spiegel. He had read the screenplay by John Huston and James Agee, the former cinema critic for Time magazine, and he was not pleased:

We have read the script dated February 14, 1951 for your proposed production *The African Queen* and regret to have to tell
you that, in its present form, this basic story is not acceptable. . . .

The reason for this basic unacceptability rests with the immoral relationship which exists between Rose [Katharine Hepburn]
and Allnutt [Humphrey Bogart] . . . an immoral relationship
which is treated quite as a matter of course, with not the faintest
voice of morality or indication of compensating moral values.

Before this basic story can be approved, it will first be necessary for you to correct this fundamental problem.

With respect to the characterizations of Brother [Robert Morley
as a missionary] and Rose, it will be essential that they not be
caricatures. Any suggestion of caricature with respect to Brother
would further render your story unacceptable. There is, of course,
no objection to the proper portrayal of a devout missionary, but
there must be no suggestion of lampooning his devotion.

. . . It will be necessary that you make certain [their scenes]
contain nothing likely to give offense to people of serious religious conviction.

Page 2: None of the children should be naked.

Page 3: Please eliminate any suggestion of effeminacy with respect to one of the male characters.

Page 5: There must be no suggestion whatever of nudity, either
on the part of the man or the women. . . .

The Production Code makes it mandatory that the intimate parts
of the body—specifically the breasts of women—be covered at all
times.

Page 7: It might be well to change the word "hell-fish" . . .

Pages 9, 10, and 12: The sound of . . . stomach growlings seems
in rather questionable taste. . . .

Page 31: In the reading of the burial service, there must be no
suggestion of ridicule. . . .

Page 81: The undergarments shown should not contain any
intimate items of underwear.

Page 103: It is quite likely the British Board of Film Censors
will delete "Our Father who art in heaven."

Page 108: The fade-out on this page unmistakably indicates a
sexual affair. . . . Some means will have to be found for correcting this basically unacceptable situation.

Page 114: There must be no unacceptable exposure of Rose's
person as "she tucks her skirt up into her underclothes." We
assume the intention here is to tuck the skirt under the knees of
her bloomers.

Page 115: Allnutt should not strip to his drawers.

Page 122: The word "Lord" seems not used with the full reverence required by the code.

Two weeks later, on April 16th, Joe Breen again wrote to Jack Warner. Revisions had been made in response to Breen's first letter, but the Hays Office was still not altogether appeased:

We have read with considerable interest a temporary script dated April 11, 1947 for your proposed production *The African Queen* and are happy to say that this basic story seems to comply with the requirements of the Production Code.

However, we call your attention to the following . . . :

At the outset, we direct your particular attention to the need for the greatest possible care in the selection and photographing of the costumes to be worn by Rose.

As to the . . . treatment of religious elements and the selection of hymns . . . we request that you secure properly technical advice. . . .

Page 18: The British Board of Film Censors may delete the expression "bleedin' noses."

Page 20: We recommend that Allnutt's line be amended to read "my two <u>native</u> fellers . . ." Negroes seem to resent the appellation "black."

Page 35: Please delete the expression "hymn-singin' Methodists."

Page 51: It will not be acceptable that Rose and Allnutt are nude in this bathing scene. . . .

Page 55: The use of the underscored word in the line "<u>Lor'</u> love a duck" is unacceptable.

Page 77: Please omit the expression "on our behinds."

Page 80: . . . None of the kissing here or elsewhere should be passionate, lustful, or open-mouthed.

Page 96: Rose and Allnutt should not be lying down half-embraced. Please refrain from putting them into any questionable positions.

Page 109: Were Allnutt to be shown wearing a pair of Rose's linen drawers, we feel there would be an unmistakable implication of undue intimacy between the two. . . .

Chapter 2⸻

MUSICALS

42ND STREET

Busby Berkeley did to the censors what the censors would not permit men to do to women in the movies. In staging the dance numbers in *42nd Street* and a dozen other Depression-era musicals, he seemed to have had a license for lechery. Exploiting the Broadway tradition of the underdressed chorus girl, Berkeley succeeded through attireless efforts. He breached virtually every clause of the Hays Code, yet the Hollywood censors just kept tapping their toes. The Berkeley camera insinuated itself through the legs of lines of lissome chorus girls. Often they would shed their diaphanous costumes to reveal lace brassieres and gartered panties. Sometimes Berkeley would place his nubile nymphs in pageantlike production numbers: bare-breasted on the wings of airborne planes, or naked in silhouette as a lascivious dwarf looked on, or supporting a line of six-foot bananas from their pelvises, lifting them in improbable erection and then letting them droop, as in some herculean orgy.

Foreign censors banned many of these production numbers, including the notorious banana dance from *The Gang's All Here*, but Berkeley's voracious appetite for eroticism found few critics among American censors. The Hays Office correspondence on *42nd Street*, a film that starred Dick Powell and Ginger Rogers, seems like mere carping when one considers the sex and sin that characterized Berkeley's titillating camera work.

On September 28, 1932, Jason S. Joy, head of the Production Code in those early days, wrote to Darryl F. Zanuck, production chief of Warner Brothers Studios:

We have read with great interest your script of 42nd Street and believe it to be satisfactory under the code. . . . There are, however, several individual lines which we would like to call to your attention.

   1. Such profanity as "Good Lord!" in Scene 34 . . .

   2. *Scene 62:* You may lose the reference to "Any Time Annie—she only said 'no' once, and then she didn't hear the question."

   3. *Scene 65:* Some [state] censors will undoubtedly take out this close shot of the sign on the door reading "Men."

   4. There are several times in which the phrase "on the make" is used. Some of the [state] censors are becoming a little sensitive about this phrase. . . .

   5. *Scene 166:* One of the difficulties we are running up against is the fact that injected sex scenes such as this, not essential to the story, have been making it difficult for us to deal with the [state] censors when it comes to really necessary sex scenes.

By the end of December, 42nd Street had been filmed. James Wingate of the Hays Office wrote to Darryl Zanuck on December 27th to report his reaction to the finished film:

We enjoyed very much seeing your picture 42nd Street, and in our opinion it is satisfactory under the code.

   With regard to [the state censor boards] we suggest that you give some further consideration to the following . . .

   1. The reference to "Any Time Annie". . . . [Berkeley had clung to the line despite the censors' misgivings.]

   2. The shot of the party sequence in the hotel room in which the girl is slapped on the posterior. . . .

   3. The song about the traveling man and the farmer's daughter seems entirely innocuous. However, it is the custom of . . . the state boards to eliminate any "traveling salesman song or story." However, we suggest you take a chance on this.

In 1936 Warner Brothers wanted to reissue 42nd Street, but by then the Hays Office had become far less acquiescent—even to Busby Berkeley. With the creation of the Legion of Decency and the Seal of Approval, Hays Office demands were more enforceable. In August, 1936 Jack Warner applied for a code seal so that he might reissue 42nd Street. Joe Breen replied with none of the solicitude and tolerance of his predecessors:

We have had the pleasure today of reviewing your picture titled *42nd Street* for which you have requested a Production Code certificate. . . . We regret to inform you that, in its present form, the picture is not acceptable. . . .

This objection is based upon the fact that there is throughout the picture a general flavor of suggestiveness. If you will inform us when the following objectionable elements have been eliminated, we shall be pleased to view the picture again.

Reel 1. Eliminate the following dialog and action:

A girl says "First door to the left." Ruby Keeler goes over to door and man comes out of door marked "Men."

Reel 2. Where chorus girls are lined up for inspection of their legs. Eliminate following dialog:

    FIRST GIRL: "Afraid I gotta run."

    SECOND GIRL: "First door to your left."

After girl says that her address is on Park Avenue, eliminate remark by Ann: "And is her homework tough!"

Eliminate underlined portion of following dialog:

    FIRST MAN: "Just trying to make her . . . "

    SECOND MAN: "Make her is right."

Eliminate remark by Ann: "You know she makes forty-five dollars a week and sends her mother a hundred of it!"

In number where girls are . . . being carried by two men, eliminate remark by Lorraine: "You got the busiest hands."

Reel 6: Eliminate scene where [Guy] Kibbee slaps girl on posterior.

Reel 7: Eliminate business of Bebe Daniels being lifted off floor . . . where there is undue exposure of her breasts.

Reel 9: Eliminate view of Peggy putting slippers out through curtains of [upper] berth, of her saying "Oh!", of her hand flying up in the air and then dropping slippers, and of her hand hanging limp between curtains of berth.

Warner Brothers obediently deleted all the material to which the Hays Office now objected. In a letter from H. J. McCord of Warners' film editing department to Joseph Breen, the chief censor was assured that all the eliminations had been made in all prints of the movie. Today Manhattan's 42nd Street is a tawdry avenue along which pornographic movie houses elbow one another like dirty street urchins. In 1936 the cinematic *42nd Street* had been scrubbed clean.

THE FRENCH LINE

The filmmaker who caused the greatest number of instant coronaries among the censors was an industrialist named Howard Hughes with his nineteen-year-old discovery from Van Nuys, California, Jane Russell. In the early forties Hughes starred her in an assertively sexual, tastelessly inept Western called *The Outlaw*, which turned censorial fury into box-office gold. (See Chapter 3, "Westerns.") Then, in 1953, concurring with Oscar Wilde that nothing succeeds like excess, he returned his big-bosomed protégée to the screen in a trivial musical called *The French Line*. The Hays Office file on the film is one of the most voluminous in cinema history.

Today it is hard to see what all the shouting was about—and the torrid dances and sensual contortions provoked quite a lot of shouting and volcanic memos from the Hays Office. Of course, when screening *The French Line* today, it is well to bear in mind that the marathon letters that Joe Breen dispatched to Howard Hughes about its erotic elements managed to tool out a great deal of what our moral guardians found objectionable.

The song in which Jane Russell wears a peekaboo outfit that focuses attention to her genital region and remarkable bosom was edited into a single long shot that looked like the camera had been placed in Pasadena. All the close-ups landed on the cutting-room floor. The stills that were distributed to newspaper editors displayed the costume in all its prurient glory and sent censors' temperatures soaring, along with those of the newspaper editors.

The French Line capitalized on the notoriety that Hughes's battles with the censors produced. The advertising campaign, filled with risqué headlines and noisy ballyhoo, filled the theaters. Jane Russell's image for sexuality prospered along with Howard Hughes's balance sheet, and no one besides the critics seemed to notice that *The French Line* was a tired concoction of anemic dialogue, tuneless songs, and predictable misunderstandings.

On March 11, 1953, Joe Breen received a copy of the screenplay for The French Line *from an executive of RKO-Radio Pictures named William Fieder. Fieder was RKO's director of public relations, which seems fitting in that Howard Hughes seemed determined to show Jane Russell having relations in public. Breen wrote to Fieder:*

> We have read the script . . . for your forthcoming production *The French Line* and wish to report . . . there is one important element present in this material which is unacceptable . . .
>
> The element to which we refer is found in the early portions of the story. Pierre is characterized as some sort of eminent roué and decides to embark on a tour as a "professor of love." These sequences, which include his demonstration with a model dressed in a negligee; being arrested for putting on an indecent show; and overall suggestive dialog and situations; all indicate that he is teaching the fundamentals of seduction, and this is unacceptable. . . . [This entire element was eliminated from the script.]
>
> Going through the script in detail, we will point out the [following] difficulties . . . :
>
> *Page 1:* We cannot approve photographing the girl's breasts and [seeing her] dressed in intimate articles of underwear. . . .
>
> The censor gag seems objectionable and we would recommend it be eliminated. [Hughes fought unsuccessfully to retain it.]
>
> *Page 3:* The utmost care will be required regarding the characterization of Farrell Firelle in order to avoid any indication he is a "pansy." . . . [Hughes agreed to this.]
>
> *Page 36:* The line "I have never had any complaints before . . ." is unacceptable. . . .
>
> *Page 42:* We cannot approve gags based on the Kinsey Report. [Hughes agreed to this.]
>
> *Page 76:* Please bear in mind that we cannot approve the bikini-type bathing suits. [Hughes stuck to his guns.]

On April 1st, Breen wrote again to RKO's Fieder, listing objections to additional parts of the script that had reached him.

> *Pages 17–18:* This bathing scene seems to be overly suggestive and, as presently described, it goes too far. Mary's [Jane Russell] legs should not be photographed suggesting that she is completely nude. . . .
>
> In addition, the utmost care will be required when Mary emerges from the tub.

In a letter dated April 24th, Joe Breen continued his cautionary correspondence:

Page 31: The "lay of the land" gag is offensive and we ask that it be eliminated. [It was removed.]

Page 42: The line "can't wait to get home nights" could come through as offensively suggestive. . . .

Page 47: The line ". . . which won't be hard on our honeymoon" is unduly pointed. . . .

On May 14th, Joe Breen dispatched a letter to William Fieder. He had read Parts 3, 4, 5, and 6 of The French Line and issued the following caveats:

Page 57: The "diapers gag" is unacceptable toilet humor and must be eliminated. [It was killed.]

Page 72: The final line of dialog is unacceptable . . . : "See, there are other things than money a guy can be after."

Page 81: The following dialog is overly pointed . . . : "I bet you could teach a guy a lot." "And he does mean everything."

Page 83: In our opinion, the entire speech by Annie about "putting the L in lech" is unacceptably suggestive. . . .

Page 86: The expression ". . . all but sold tickets" has a vulgar connotation.

The correspondence that preceded the filming of The French Line is much more temperate than that which followed its production. Once the Hollywood censors actually saw the film, their fury knew no bounds. The censors' rage turned on the thirty-eight-inch bust of Miss Russell. In February of 1953, Jack Vizzard, a representative of the Hays Office, filed a combative report for the files under the grim headline: "List of Unacceptable Items—The French Line":

Reels 1–2.
1. Abbreviated housecoat worn by Jane Russell for entering bathroom.
2. Breast shots in bathtub.
3. Red costume worn by Jane Russell at bar; assorted shots of breast exposure.
Reels 3–4.
1. Same red costume at beginning of reel; cleavage and breast exposure.
Reels 5–6.
1. White dress worn by Jane Russell with yellow brassiere. Effect about the breasts . . .

Reels 7–8.
   1. Same dress, assorted shots.
   2. Costume worn by Jane Russell with black tight pants . . . various breast shots.
   3. White dinner dress worn by Myrtle Brown . . . excessive breast exposure.
   4. Gymnasium costume worn by Jane Russell on shuffleboard decks . . . too much cleavage.
Reels 9–10.
   1. . . . Costumes worn by Jane Russell and Mary McCarty in "Girl From Texas" routine . . . particularly at the end of routine where girls are bowing.
Reels 11–12.
   1. "Lookin' For Trouble" production number, costume, and dance; many troublesome elements.
   2. White dress worn by Jane Russell when Gilbert Roland picks her up and carries her out. . . .
   3. Girls in panties and brassieres.

When he saw the film of The French Line, Joe Breen's politeness deserted him. He was a likeable man, but the exploitation angered him, and Hughes's film was nothing if not exploitive. Breen was denying the film a code certificate of approval. He wrote to James Grainger, the nominal producer of The French Line, though Hughes was calling the shots—in every sense of the word:

Following our review and discussion last evening of *The French Line*, I am sending you this formally to advise you that it is the considered unanimous judgment of the staff . . . that this picture is definitely and specifically in violation of the Production Code. . . .

This unacceptability is indicated by the indecent and undue exposure of the character portrayed by Miss [Jane] Russell. . . .

We feel also that some of the dancing in this picture is likewise unacceptable because of the costuming and the emphasis on indecent movements. . . .

I regret to have to send you this unfavorable report, but under the circumstances we feel compelled to do so.

The film was denied the censors' Seal of Approval, and like *The Outlaw* a decade before, profited from the censors' fulminations. The denial is something of a puzzlement, since the code seal had been granted to many films with an equal degree of torrid contortions. One explanation of the censors' sensitivity might be its 3-D presentation, which tended to thrust Miss Russell's endowments far out over the orchestra. A more likely explanation of the furor was the arrogance of Howard Hughes who challenged the censors' right to regulate sex and morals in film.

The Other Censors

The Legion of Decency gave the film a "C" rating, its lowest, which meant that American Catholics were admonished to avoid it. The sight of Miss Russell's bust, it was implied, might turn one into a pillar of salt. The legion found that the film contained "grossly obscene, suggestive, and indecent action, costume, and dialog." In addition, the legion proclaimed the movie's incidents "gravely offensive to Christian standards of morality" and warned that it could exercise a baleful influence on those who viewed it, especially the young.

PAL JOEY

It was a challenging enterprise when Columbia Pictures tried to transfer to the pristine movie screen a Broadway musical about a group of people, none of whom had even a nodding acquaintance with decency. The Hays Office had struggled to keep the facts of life off the flickering screen for years and with considerable success, and some hoofer named Joey in a Chicago dive was not about to undo their good work.

Pal Joey began as a series of pieces in *The New Yorker* written by John O'Hara, whose stories tended to revolve around the genitals. When Richard Rodgers and Lorenz Hart, the Stephen Sondheims of their time, transferred it to the stage, Brooks Atkinson, the venerable critic of *The New York Times* had concluded his chilling review with the rhetorical question, "Can you draw sweet water from a foul well?"

The Rodgers and Hart score was among their finest, and, given the subject matter—an attractive heel and the wealthy woman who keeps him—the sophisticated lyrics were encrusted with bawdy, naughty wit. The Hays Office laundered lines galore, and Columbia ended up yanking most of the songs entirely, replacing them with Rodgers and Hart "standards" that pictured a romanticized, rather than a raunchy, love and that were sweet enough to decay the teeth at twenty paces.

The original songs highlighted a story of a punk who romances an ex-stripper turned Nob Hill society. He becomes her paid lover, but the basic relationship was blurred by the censors and the situations in the boudoir were camouflaged. Hollywood was drawn to this sharp, witty material and then, under the admonitions of the censors, softened and sanitized it. Nowhere is this process clearer than in the laundering of Larry Hart's lyrics. The following lines were removed from "Bewitched, Bothered, and Bewildered":

> "Vexed again
> Perplexed again
> Thang God I can be oversexed again . . . "

> "Romance finis
> Your chance finis
> Those ants that invaded my pants finis . . . "

> "I'll sing to him
> Each spring to him
> And worship the trousers that cling to him . . . "

> "He's a laugh but I love it
> Because the laugh's on me . . . "

Frank Sinatra played Joey on the screen and it is ironic that a celebrity whose love life has not been that of a choirboy, should portray a singer whose romances had to be carefully laundered. If life sometimes imitates art, there are times when art dares not imitate life.

Joe Breen wrote his first discouraging letter to Harry Cohn, President of Columbia Pictures, in 1941. A measurement of Breen's success may be seen in the fact that Pal Joey did not reach the screen till 1957, On February 14, 1941, Breen wrote to Cohn to say he had read the book of the Broadway musical Pal Joey, "written in acid" by novelist John O'Hara. Like Queen Victoria, Breen was not amused. He wrote:

We have read the play script . . . that you submitted for our consideration and regret to report that this material is in violation of the Production Code on a number of points. . . .

In preparing a screenplay on this subject, the following thoroughly unacceptable items will have to be removed entirely from the treatment:

Omit all suggestion of the adulterous affair between Joey [Frank Sinatra] and Vera [Rita Hayworth].

Omit all references to sexual perversion, all profanity, all suggestion of double-meaning dialog.

Omit all suggestions of loose sex on the part of your hero with various women.

A number of lyrics are entirely unacceptable, specifically "Happy Hunting Horn," "Bewitched, Bothered, and Bewildered," "In Our Little Den of Iniquity." A number of the others contain unacceptable lines which will have to be changed.

The wheels of God grind slowly, yet they grind exceeding fine. Sixteen months later, on June 30, 1942, Joe Breen again wrote to Harry Cohn. By now, a first-draft screenplay based on the O'Hara musical had been written by Dorothy Kingsley. Said the censor:

We have read the first draft script dated June 16, 1942 for your proposed production titled *Pal Joey*. While the basic story seems to me to meet the requirements of the Production Code, the present version still seems to contain the suggestion of an illicit sex affair between Joey and Vera. . . . Going through the script in detail, we call your attention to the following . . . :

Page 24: There must be no suggestion . . . that the woman is on the way to the toilet.

Page 57: There must be no exposure on the part of the chorus girls when Joey enters the dressing room.

Page 88: Please change Joey's line, "I'll be in—really in" as possibly sex suggestive.

Page 111: Please eliminate the underlined words "It was nice to have known you—three or four times."

Kindly submit to us all lyrics that will be used in this production.

Thirteen more years elapsed before Joe Breen wrote to Harry Cohn with further cautionary remarks on the revised screenplay for Pal Joey. On May 1, 1954, Breen wrote to review the changes the Hays Office had exacted from Columbia at a meeting that had taken place the day before:

Page 41: Vera will be characterized as a divorced woman. The reference here will be to her ex-husband.

Page 57: The line "Until I could sleep where I shouldn't sleep" [in the song "Bewitched"] will be changed. [It was changed to "Till love came and told me I shouldn't sleep."]

Page 77: The following dialog, "You know what you've got to do to get Joey?" "Say, she probably doesn't know" will be changed or omitted.

Page 79: The line "I must be what they call frigid" must be changed.

Page 80: The line in the lyric "I don't like a deep contralto or a man whose voice is alto—Zip! I'm a heterosexual" will be changed. [This was from the witty song "Zip" that is sung about intellectual stripper Gypsy Rose Lee.]

Page 81: The expression "struck out" will be omitted.

Page 86: The line ". . . is all you've got left to lose" will be rewritten.

Page 100: The lyric "Take him—pajamas look nice on him, but how he snores . . ." will be rewritten. [This is from the brittle duet "Take Him," sung by the two women in Joey's life who are jointly dismissing him.]

By July 1956 Joe Breen had retired and been replaced by the erudite Geoffrey Shurlock, his longtime assistant at the Hays Office. Still the changes poured down upon Pal Joey, the pig's ear that was being transformed into a nylon pocketbook through the wonders of censorship. In a letter to Harry Cohn on July 17th, Shurlock wrote:

We have read the second estimating draft, dated June 27, 1956, for your forthcoming production *Pal Joey.* . . .

Page 41: The two "elegant-looking escorts" seem to be characterized as sex perverts. . . .

Page 43: Under the same heading, we ask that you eliminate the following line of dialog . . . : "Hardly! We're interior decorators."

Page 51: The expression "flat work" has an objectionable double meaning.

Page 58: The following line is unacceptable: "Two years, Vera, that's a long time between drinks."

We kindly ask that you eliminate the following line of dialog: "I know! You'll take your clothes off anywhere."

GUYS AND DOLLS

The plot of *Guys and Dolls*, the smash Broadway musical written by Abe Burrows and Jo Swerling from a Damon Runyon story, deals with seduction and gambling, two subjects that in earlier years were anathema to the Hollywood censors. By 1955, when Sam Goldwyn decided to move it to the screen, these subjects had lost much of their stigma. Unfortunately for Goldwyn, *Guys and Dolls* contained another ingredient that was still taboo: the "mockery" of religion. Runyon's story is about the unpredictable fraternizing between some Times Square gamblers and a Salvation Army mission group. Sky Masterson (Marlon Brando) is willing to bet on anything. Nathan Detroit (Frank Sinatra) operates a floating crap game. Detroit bets Masterson that he cannot seduce a Salvation Army lass (Jean Simmons). The Hollywood censors feared that this musical fable might offend some pious folk in the audience, and most of their efforts centered on this aspect of the story.

Samuel Goldwyn had acquired the motion picture rights to Guys and Dolls, set Joseph L. Mankiewicz to work adapting it to the screen, and dispatched a copy of the Burrows/Swerling book to the Hays Office, along with the lyrics of Frank Loesser's score. On October 1, 1954 Joe Breen responded:

We have read the original Broadway script for your picture *Guys and Dolls* and are sending you a few . . . suggestions to be incorporated into the motion picture script that you are preparing. . . .

Page 1: There should . . . be no streetwalkers in your screen version.

It will be most important that the portrayal of the "Save a Soul Mission" be free from any offense to religious-minded people. Those engaged in this work should be portrayed properly and free from any attempt to burlesque them or their activities. . . .

Page 1.8.67: Throughout the script, Sarah [Jean Simmons] should not be portrayed as actually drunk. . . . When Sarah imitates the Cubans, there must be no bumps or grinds or any offensive body movements.

Page 1.10.73: We suggest changing Adelaide's [Vivian Blaine] line [regarding a hotel's bridal suite], "I've tried all the other rooms" possibly to "I've tried most of the other rooms."

Page 2.1.2: We feel the line "Now when I think of what you

want in exchange" [in the song "Take Back Your Mink"] is unacceptably suggestive. [This song has been carried into millions of living rooms on the original cast album. It is sung in the show by a line of chorus girls, and burlesques the innocent damsel being seduced by furs and jewels.]

Page 2.5.31: The "Bronx cheer" is forbidden by the code.

By January 1955 Geoffrey Shurlock had taken over the censorship reins from Joe Breen. Joe Mankiewicz had completed a screenplay for Guys and Dolls *and it had been submitted to the Hays Office. On January 19th, Shurlock wrote to Sam Goldwyn:*

This goes to you in confirmation of our conference yesterday with . . . Mr. Joseph Mankiewicz with regard to the script . . . for your picture *Guys and Dolls.*

We discussed with Mr. Mankiewicz the advisability of toning down some of the references to "sin" and "sinner," which in some of the sequences sounds like ridicule. . . . In this connection, it would also be well to bear in mind that the expression "Hallelujah" has a rather serious import for a great many people. . . .

Scene 58: In as much as Sarah is a mission worker, this scene of her drunk may be very offensive, unless it is handled with great delicacy. . . . [She sings Loesser's song, "If I Were A Bell."] . . . Also, it would be well to reconsider the comedy use of our "Star Spangled Banner," as well as the Cuban National Anthem, as a gag to stop the fight. . . . The use of these anthems may cause a great deal of protest, and we suggest replacing them with some other tunes.

Sequence 88: It is important in this scene that the Mission General not be portrayed in any stupid or derogatory light. . . .

With regard to the lyrics in "Adelaide's Lament," we suggest the reconsideration of the lines, "If she's tired of getting the fish-eye from the hotel clerk" and "The female remaining single just in the legal sense."

In the number "Take Back Your Mink," the following agreements were arrived at: This will be done without any of the objectionable flavor of a mass striptease. The girls will take off no more than is indicated in the lyric. After the dresses come off, they will be dressed in a proper dancing costume, shorts, and an adequate bodice or bra. . . .

In a letter to Samuel Goldwyn dated March 1, 1955, Shurlock wrote:

We have read the new "opening number" for your picture *Guys and Dolls*. Some of the action indicated seems to be unacceptable. . . . [This is the number that presents a Broadway tableau with cropshooters, horseplayers, cops, gangsters and other Times Square habitués on display.]
   . . . The action of the two hostesses with their "tired slither" seems to be suggestive of prostitutes soliciting. . . . The gag of the Rockettes going into the lingerie shop and "coming out wearing falsies" is also unacceptable. . . .

HIGH SOCIETY

When MGM set out to create a musical version of Philip Barry's play, *The Philadelphia Story*, and commissioned Cole Porter to write the songs, they might have anticipated trouble with the censors. Porter's wit often leaned to subjects that were not readily discussed in Main Street living rooms. When Hollywood made a movie of Porter's Broadway hit *Anything Goes*, the line "I get no kick from cocaine" had been turned into "I've heard of perfume from Spain." When they moved *Kiss Me, Kate* to the screen, several deliciously bawdy songs suddenly turned innocent and humorless. In "Where is the Life That Late I Led," this line evaporated:

> And lovely Lisa
> Where are you, Lisa?
> You gave a new meaning to the Leaning Tower of Pisa.

Porter's saucy wit emerged in *High Society*—as the musicalized *Philadelphia Story* was called—with Bing Crosby, Frank Sinatra, and Grace Kelly replacing Cary Grant, James Stewart, and Katharine Hepburn; and Porter's salaciousness was predictably suppressed by the guardians of the public's morals.

On December 28, 1955, Geoffrey Shurlock wrote to Dore Schary, head of production at MGM:

We have read the lyrics from the song entitled "Well, Did You Evah" used in your forthcoming production *High Society*.
   Confirming our conversation of today . . . we find these lyrics to be acceptable with the exception of the line sung by Mike [Frank Sinatra]:

Have you heard
Professor Munch
Ate his wife and divorced his lunch.

With the censors' attention momentarily captured by the antics of Professor Munch, Cole Porter was able to slip the following line past them in the same song:

Have you heard
That Mimsy Starr
She got pinched in the Ass-tor Bar.

GOING MY WAY

It is not surprising to find the censors' hackles rising at the calculated cleavage of *The French Line* or the prostitution and adultery of *From Here to Eternity*. It is more perplexing to encounter the reformers' dismay at a wholesome, inspiring film like *Going My Way*. It is somewhat like finding the censors carping about Disney's *Three Little Pigs* or *Fantasia*, which indeed the Hays Office did protest.

In addition to the Hollywood censors' complaints about *Going My Way*, certain circles in the Catholic community objected vehemently. Sharply worded criticism appeared in *The Catholic Worker* as well as the *Pittsburgh Catholic*. The Reverend Paul J. Glenn, Professor of Philosophy at St. Charles Seminary in Columbus, Ohio, reproved the Legion of Decency for approving the film for general patronage. In a lengthy analysis, Father Glenn articulated no fewer than five major objections to the movie:

1. In picturing two Catholic priests (Bing Crosby and Barry Fitzgerald) it stressed worldly works alone and gave no time to questions of faith.

2. A ubiquitous bottle of whiskey, from which the elderly pastor took a swig, seemed to imply that to be Catholic and Irish also meant "to be a drinker."

3. The film presented a young woman who had run away from home and thus established a poor example for young America.

4. The film was awash in sentimentality, and at its core was pure mush.

5. It suggested that Catholicism was just social work, and ignored the basic issue of personal sanctity.

Another theological critic, Father John J. Hugo, attacked the film in *The Catholic Worker*, but acknowledged that he had not seen the film.

The protests of these religious leaders demonstrate the scrutiny to which the Catholic Church subjected the products of Hollywood. If such an ode to virtue as *Going My Way* could be attacked as anti-Catholic, filmmakers were indeed in the religious bull's-eye.

Going My Way ran into trouble with the Hollywood censors as well. It told the story of a young priest who is put in charge of a debt-ridden church in a tenement district, that has grown shabby in the years since it was built by Father Fitzgibbon (Barry Fitzgerald). So the Bishop dispatches Father O'Malley (Bing Crosby), a cheerful and progressive young paster, to take charge. The older cleric is bewildered by and hostile to Crosby's penchant for golf, tennis, and pop music.

On May 12, 1943, Joe Breen of the Hays Office wrote to Luigi Luraschi, Paramount Pictures' liaison for censorial matters. Breen had read an incomplete script of Going My Way and had certain admonitions. He wrote:

> While this basic story appears to be acceptable . . . the material in its present form seems to us to need very special handling and possibly some considerable revamping against the possibility it may give serious offense to Catholic patrons. As I presumed to suggest to Mr. [Leo] McCarey [the producer/director] yesterday, we strongly urge and recommend that you get in touch with Father Devlin . . . the technical adviser appointed by Archbishop Cantwell. . . .
>
> It is our judgment that a number of the details of this picture are not quite orthodox—from a technical standpoint—and it is much to be desired that they be straightened out before you actually go into production. We think, too, that the characterization of the three priests might well be reexamined and possibly raised considerably in general tone and flavor. For example, both Father O'Malley and Father Timony [Frank McHugh] appear to us to be thoroughly undignified in both their general conduct and language; and both, we are sure, would not conduct themselves [in real life] as they do in certain scenes in this picture. Father Timony appears at certain times to be definitely obnoxious.
>
> Then, too, there is considerable dialog set down to be spoken

by the priest which likewise is not only questionable, but possibly likely to give offense. For example, on page 22, in response to the aged priest's question [to Father Timony], "How did you ever come to be a priest?" Father O'Malley replies, "We blind-folded him and he thought he was joining the Elks." Such a speech would, of course, give serious offense to Catholics everywhere.

Page 32: Father Fitzgibbon should not conclude a prayer before meals with "a jerk."

Page 37: We think it might be well to delete entirely the scene with the two old ladies who go to the Rectory to make a confession.

Page 52: The expression, "Ah, pig-dust!" is questionable. . . .

Page 56: Father Fitzgibbon's remark, "I will not permit Three Blind Mice to come between me and my God" is likely to give offense. . . .

Page 98: We would like to suggest that, whenever you show Jenny in the company with the priest, she have a companion with her. . . . It might be well if she were never shown associating with the priests unchaperoned.

The Hays Office acted as a defender of Hollywood against those who were even more sensitive than themselves. On August 20, 1943, Joe Breen wrote to the Most Reverend Joseph T. McUcken, the Auxiliary Bishop of Los Angeles, to say:

I beg respectfully to acknowledge receipt of your letter . . . in which you tell me of the concern of certain dramatic teachers visiting here from Chicago with regard to a proposed picture in which Bing Crosby is characterized as a "crooning priest who is the author of a number of popular ditties." I also note that the ladies inform you "that running through the background of the picture is the vision of a love affair which the crooning Padre is said to have experienced before he became a priest and which provides the inspiration for his various songs."

I note also that the ladies have related to you "that there is such a priest on whose life the film is based, and, if he knows about the picture, if he is getting royalties, and if he is aware of the love angle that is woven into the film. . . ."

Breen ably defended the film against the schoolteachers' charges of blasphemy and plagiarism. He pointed out that *Going My Way* was a creation of the exuberant imagination of Leo Mc-Carey and was not adapted from the life of any crooning priest in Chicago.

Chapter 3

WESTERNS

THE OUTLAW

It is fortunate for the forces of Hollywood censorship that Howard Hughes's aircraft business and the Second World War occupied so much of his time and attention. Had he been free to indulge all his exploitive talents and his obsession with the mammary glands, there is no telling what might have happened. Hughes's titillating Western, *The Outlaw*, enraged the censors and captivated the country. The Hays Office file on the movie threatened to burst free of its folder, just as the well-promoted bosom of its star, Jane Russell, threatened to rupture the flimsy blouses in which Hughes bedecked her.

Since Hughes was first an aeronautical engineer and only second a filmmaker, he used his former talents to design a special cantilevered bra that circled Miss Russell's breasts and thrust them—and their owner—into the limelight. This brought exposure and prominence to both Jane Russell and the inept vehicle that displayed them. Unlike David O. Selznick's *Duel in the Sun*, which offered some pretensions of art and serious conflict, *The Outlaw* had little to commend it but Jane Russell's ample girth, an anemic screenplay by Jules Firthman, and its director's ingenuity in finding dozens of occasions for the star to bend over, revealing a maximum of cleavage.

Joe Breen's background as a journalist conditioned him to keep emotion out of most of his correspondence, but his feelings about *The Outlaw* spilled out over the Production Code letterhead. Once he screened the finished picture, Breen fired off an irate letter to his boss, Will Hays, that was virtuous and vituperative. For years, Breen had been holding his finger in the dike against a flood of cleavage, and now, in one film, Howard Hughes was

26

trying to break the barriers. Breen opposed issuing a Seal of Approval to *The Outlaw* unless all the scenes in which Jane Russell was bending, stooping, kneeling, and genuflecting were reshot. The movie provoked every kind of censorship one could imagine: its steamy screenplay, its lurid advertising, its controversial billboards, and, of course, the movie itself. Yet, despite the furor it created, the Hays Office finally granted its imprimatur. When the dust settled, Howard Hughes had cut a mere forty feet of film and a few lines of dialogue from his salacious epic.

On December 27, 1940, Joseph Breen wrote to Howard Hughes at United Artists. He had read the final script for The Outlaw. At this stage Breen knew nothing of Hughes's plans for Jane Russell and her ample bosom. He wrote of the scenario:

The present version seems to contain various elements which seem to be in violation of the Production Code and whose inclusion in the finished picture we believe would render it unacceptable. . . . These unacceptable elements are briefly as follows:

First, Billy [the Kid] is characterized as a major criminal who is allowed to go free and unpunished. . . . Second, there are also two sequences suggestive of illicit sex between Billy [Jack Buetel] and Rio [Jane Russell]. . . . Third, certain scenes are suggestive of undue brutality. . . .

Page 34: Great care will be needed in this scene of the struggle between Billy and Rio in the hayloft to avoid any questionable angles or postures.

Page 35: There must be no exposure of Rio's person in the scene when her dress gets torn.

Scene 34: These scenes of Rio in her nightgown should be fully covered and, if possible, [she should] be wearing a bathrobe throughout the picture.

Page 70: Care will be needed in this scene of Rio putting the hot stones in the bed. There must be no scene . . . of her putting them against Billy's thighs. . . .

Pages 82–83: Care will be needed in this scene of Billy pulling Rio down on the bed and kissing her, to avoid sex suggestiveness.

Page 93: Taken in connection with the suggestion of sexual intimacy, this dialog about trading the girl for the horse is unacceptable. . . .

Breen and Hughes struggled over this line of dialogue. At Doc Holliday's (Walter Huston) request, Rio is looking after the wounded Billy. She ends up sharing his bed to provide the requisite warmth. Meanwhile, Doc has borrowed Billy's horse. On his return, Doc is furious at Billy's liberties with Rio. Billy observes the equity of the situation—Doc has had the use of Billy's horse; Billy has had the use of Doc's girl. "A fair exchange is no robbery," says Billy in a profound display of logic. Breen bridled at the line. Hughes replaced it with another: "You borrowed from me, I borrowed from you." Breen found this even less acceptable. Hughes requested an alternative and the censor obliged. "How about tit for tat?" suggested Breen. Hughes hastily agreed.

On March 28, 1951, Joe Breen saw a screening of the finished film. His temperature rose abruptly. What he saw was a film with few artistic merits; one that defied all the canons of the censorship code. He promptly wrote to Howard Hughes:

As you know we had the pleasure this afternoon of witnessing the projection room showing of your production titled *The Outlaw*. . . . The picture is definitely and specifically in violation of our Production Code, and, because of this, it cannot be approved.

The specific and basic objections are twofold:

1. The inescapable suggestion of an illicit relationship between the "Doc" and Rio, and between Billy and Rio.

2. The countless shots of Rio in which her breasts are not fully covered.

Before this picture can be approved . . . *all* the shots of the girl's breasts where they are not fully covered must be entirely deleted from your picture.

The following day, Breen dashed off an angry, breast-beating note to The Honorable Will Hays, former Postmaster General of the United States and Breen's superior at the censorship board:

In recent months we have noted a marked tendency on the part of the studios to more and more undrape women's breasts. In recent weeks the practice has become so prevalent as to make it necessary for us, almost every day, to hold up a picture which contains these unacceptable breast shots. With a view toward focusing attention on this recent trend, we sent to all our [studio] contacts a week ago a special letter about this matter. . . .

In the last few days we have again had to hold up a Universal picture in which there was a shocking display of women's breasts. We also found it necessary to withhold approval on a Columbia picture in which, scattered throughout the entire picture, there were a large number of "sweater shots"—shots which emphasized women's breasts by means of tight close-fitting garments.

Yesterday, we had the exhibition of breast shots in Howard Hughes's picture *The Outlaw*, which outdoes anything we have ever seen on the motion picture screen. . . .

Ten days later, on April 8th, Breen again wrote to Hughes. He had studied the film carefully and was ready to read Howard Hughes chapter and verse on the cuts that would be required to bring a semblance of decency to The Outlaw:

. . . We submit to you our thoughts as to how best you might bring your picture *The Outlaw* acceptably within the provisions of the Production Code. I suggest the following:

With a view to cutting down the quantity of the objectionable-to-us breast shots, we would like to have your cutter carefully examine Reels 5, 6, 8, and 10, which are the reels in which most of the unacceptable shots appear, and see just how many of these he can delete without seriously interfering with your story line.

Reel 5: The three or four shots of the girl leaning over the bed, we think, should be deleted. In this same reel, and subsequent to these shots, there are three breast shots—two of them in our judgment quite bad. . . .

Reel 7: In this reel there appear to be eleven or twelve breast shots, which, if they are not definitely bad, they are . . . very objectionable. These are the shots beginning with the breast shot in the mirror. . . .

Reel 8: In this reel there appear to us to be eight or nine unacceptable breast shots. We think all the material showing the girl with her arms extended as she is suspended from the tree might be acceptable, if some of the other breast shots could be deleted. . . . Specifically, we direct your attention to the long and sustained scene where the girl is sitting on the stump of tree; the bad shot is as she leans over the fire [and] the shot where she leans down to pick up the stone. . . .

Reel 9: We recall the breast shots of the girl as she begins to serve food to the men sitting at a table, and the particularly bad shot of the girl talking to Billy. . . .

In April 1941, having been denied a Seal of Approval, Hughes availed himself of his right of appeal. On May 1st, Breen informed the millionaire of the disposition of his appeal. He wrote:

The board of directors of the Association screened *The Outlaw*, a print of which you forwarded to New York in accordance with your appeal. The decision of the Production Code Administration declining to issue a Certificate of Approval [was weighed]. After further conference with your representatives . . . it was finally agreed that the Certificate of Approval would be issued for this film [if] the following agreed changes would be made in all prints of this picture . . . :

1. In Reel 5 delete approximately eight feet, so as to eliminate the business of Rio bending over the bed and exposing her breasts.

2. In Reel 5 delete approximately nine feet, so as to eliminate [from] the scene between Billy and Rio, her remark to Billy, "You are not well enough," as he sits on the bed and draws her to him.

3. In Reel 6 it is agreed that Billy's line "tit for tat" is to be deleted. [Ironically, as has been noted above, this line was originally suggested by Breen himself.]

4. In Reel 7 delete approximately sixteen feet, so as to eliminate the shots of Rio at the mirror, where she bends down and fully esposes her breasts.

5. In Reel 8 delete approximately three feet, so as to eliminate the close-up of Rio seated, the camera moving from Billy to Doc to this close-up of the girl . . . in which her breasts are unduly exposed.

After two years of battles with the Hollywood censors, the beleaguered film finally appeared in public in San Francisco's Gaiety Theatre. Despite the tumultuous conflict that had lavished tons of newsprint on the film, *The Outlaw* turned out to be something of a bust. The millionaire industrialist had sought to catapult two unknowns—Jane Russell and Jack Buetel—into the ranks of the stars. Miss Russell never achieved lasting stardom in the manner of such full-bosomed imports as Sophia Loren, and Jack Buetel passed from obscurity to oblivion.

The Other Censors

State censors savaged the film.

Maryland banned the film, and when Hughes fought the case in court, a Baltimore jurist upheld the ban, declaring that Miss Russell's breasts "hung over the picture like a thunderstorm spread out over a landscape." The film would have profited from such colorful writing.

Ohio deleted the dialogue between Doc and Billy after Rio had warmed the latter's bed.

New York deleted the line, "Cattle don't graze after sheep."

Massachusetts banned the film on the Sabbath.

British, Australian, and Canadian censors decried the film as obscene, Canadians going so far as to censor the film's trailer.

Sweden rejected the film in its entirety.

Denmark did likewise, which is amusing when one considers that two decades later, Denmark would be the leader in legitimatizing pornography and becoming a home to adult films.

Though Howard Hughes's motives were more pecuniary than artistic, *The Outlaw* brought a breath of fresh air to the public perception of the female body. Like Mae West, who laughed at the repressions of the censors, Howard Hughes, with a little help from a sensual Van Nuys receptionist, had forced the censors into their first important retreat.

DUEL IN THE SUN

David O. Selznick foresaw that the opening line of his obituary would read, "David O. Selznick, producer of *Gone With the Wind*, died today"; and so, he set out to turn Niven Busch's novel, *Duel in the Sun*, from an artistic little Western into a glorious masterpiece of the primitive. Everything had to be overscaled—the sets, the landscapes, the cast, and the budget. Only Selznick's stockholders could object to the extra money poured into the film—and they would be assuaged when it became a great box-office success—but when the protean producer poured in the sex, the censors were at his throat. Personal emotions may have led Selznick to add an excess of steamy sex for the film's heroine, Pearl Chavez, the fiery half-breed Indian girl, played by Jennifer Jones, whom Selznick loved. As he surrounded her with a blue-chip cast, he also plunged her into scenes and dialogue that crackled with sin and sex. The censors were doubtless surprised to find Jennifer Jones, whose greatest previous success had been as the spiritual Bernadette in *The Song of Bernadette*, cast as a bobcat half-breed in a tempestuous romance.

The girl's love affair with the despicable Lewt—played by Gregory Peck in a shocking bit of reverse casting—brought the censors out of their chairs. Indeed it drove them to pursue the company out to the desert heat of Tucson, where Selznick did his location work, to examine Jennifer Jones's costumes and observe her dances. Both were found to be too suggestive.

Selznick's preoccupation with sex in *Duel in the Sun*—wags called the film "Lust in the Dust"—extended to its musical score. Detailing his wishes to composer Dimitri Tiomkin, he called for various musical themes for the movie, including "a love theme, a desire theme, and an orgasm theme." Tiomkin's orgasm theme, when it finally satisfied Selznick, was the only sexual aspect of the film that the censors failed to cleanse, probably because the Production Code failed to cover music.

In August 1944, before Selznick had entered the picture, RKO-Radio had optioned Niven Busch's steamy Western novel and commissioned a screen adaptation. On August 2nd, Joe Breen wrote to William Gordon of RKO. He was not sanguine about the film's possibilities:

> We have read the script for your proposed picture *Duel in the Sun* and regret to reply that in its present form it seems to be unacceptable. . . . This unacceptability arises from the fact that it is the story of illicit sex [and] murder for revenge. . . .
>
> In addition . . . the present version contains a number of unacceptable sequences . . . :
>
> *Page 3, Scene 7:* Showing the hanging man's legs kicking in the air . . .
>
> *Page 4:* To avoid any possible suggestion of incest, we suggest changing the letter to read, "As her father was your cousin *by marriage* . . ."
>
> *Page 50:* The scene as written in a bedroom suggests attempted rape on the part of Lewt. . . .
>
> *Page 19:* Please omit the following dialog: "I get that kind of service from my studs . . ."
>
> *Page 130:* Pearl's mouthing of a prayer as she shoots Lewt is unacceptable.
>
> *Page 133:* This scene of Pearl pumping shot after shot into Lewt's body [is unacceptable].

The film now passed into the eager hands of David Selznick and his Vanguard Films. Joe Breen wrote to Margaret McConnell, a Selznick executive:

> We have read the script for your proposed picture *Duel in the Sun*. . . . The present script contains a number of scenes which

are unacceptable. . . . [Breen cited a number of scenes he had previously mentioned to RKO. Since Selznick had added numerous scenes to the film in attempting to give it epic proportions, there was more material to capture Breen's attention.]

Page 2: All action suggestive of prostitution or a brothel should be removed from this opening sequence. We refer specifically to the line reading, "Women in soiled kimonos lean invitingly out of windows."

Page 8: With regard to this character, The Sinkiller [Walter Huston], it will be necessary to make it quite clear that he is in no sense an ordained minister. [There is] the flavor of a travesty of religion. . . .

Page 41: As written, this bathing sequence, suggesting that both your male and female leads are swimming in the nude, is unacceptable.

Page 46: In this scene in the bedroom, please omit any suggestion that Pearl is nude in bed. She should be wearing her nightgown.

Page 49: Please omit the line, "Let it lie where you're softest."

Pages 54–56: This sequence suggestive of rape is unacceptable. As you know, the code states that seduction or rape should never be more than suggested. . . .

Page 61: Scene 228 is too sex suggestive. Please show these two characters [Jennifer Jones and Gregory Peck] in some less suggestive situation than with Lewt stretched out on Pearl's bed.

Page 124: Please change the dialog, "And that's how a fella feels on his weddin' night, so let's hurry up with the drinkin' and eatin' so's the groom and his bride can get upstairs where they belong."

As the revisions piled up—first by screenwriter Oliver H. P. Garrett, then by the producer himself—Breen wrote once more to David O. Selznick:

We have read the script of February 12th of your proposed picture *Duel in the Sun.* We call your attention to these individual items . . . :

Page 81: The sequence of the mating of the horses, taken in connection with other elements in the story, is unacceptable.

Page 91: Please eliminate the line, "Except that love to him was nothin' more than what takes place in the barn."

Page 117: Please omit the underlined words, "It's got to be you and right now."

Page 164: Please omit the action of Pearl kissing Lewt as he is dying in order to get away from any flavor of a glorification of their illicit relationship.

On April 4th, Geoffrey Shurlock, the Hays Office official who would ultimately replace Breen on his retirement, was assigned to monitor Duel in the Sun *and sent the following memo to his boss:*

> G. S. visited the studio to check on the costume worn by Miss Jennifer Jones in the scene where she gets out of bed and goes before the Sinkiller. Miss Jones was wrapped in a serape which, however, did not adequately cover her breasts. I stated to Mr. Selznick and Mr. Vidor, the director, that it would be necessary to have her breasts properly covered. . . . They said they would do this.

On July 13th, as the Duel in the Sun *company moved to location in Arizona, Breen wrote to Selznick:*

> Mssrs. Shurlock and Lynch of this office consulted with Miss Woodbury regarding the dance sequences for Miss Jones. . . .
> It was agreed that certain portions of the dance were dangerous from the point of oversuggestiveness. . . . Parts of the dance . . . had to do with the hip movements particularly, that might be interpreted as sex movement in connection with the tree in symbolism. . . .

A typewritten list prepared by an official of the Hays Office on January 17, 1947, indicated a surprising degree of acquiescence by the usually strong-willed Selznick.

Notes in Chronological Order of the Debatable Items in *Duel in the Sun*

> [Some of these items were preceded by an emphatic check, indicating Selznick's agreement; others bore a cross, indicating Selznick's defiance.]
> 1. [The Lionel] Barrymore speech to [Gregory] Peck advising him to "take your fun where you find it." [Selznick agreed to eliminate.]
> 2. Jennifer Jones' low-cut blouses okay, excepting her first

entrance where cleavage and bosom are overexposed. [Selznick agreed.]

3. The characterization of the Sinkiller definitely evades the code on the handling of men of the cloth. . . . [Selznick would not agree.]

4. The seduction of Jennifer Jones by Gregory Peck can more rightly be termed rape . . . in violation of . . . the code. The scene is further unduly emphasized by the lustful open-mouthed kissing and the symbolism of the storm and lightning. . . .

5. The red blouse worn by Jennifer Jones was too low-cut . . . [Selznick disagreed.]

6. The scratches on Peck's face are further evidence of the rape.

7. There is something immoral about the manner of the conversation by the two brothers while Jennifer Jones is crying her heart out after being raped. . . .

8. . . . There is no mistaking the following action wherein [Jennifer Jones] goes to the window and calls Peck, obviously to have another affair with her.

9. Jennifer Jones wears a low-cut blouse . . . in which the top of the sleeve is worn on the arm instead of the shoulder. [Selznick agreed.]

10. The stallion-mare conversation seems altogether too pointed. [Selznick agreed.]

11. Jennifer Jones "I'd like to take a swim" with the suggested business goes way overboard. [Selznick agreed.]

12. The scene between [Lionel] Barrymore and Peck in which the former not only condones but encourages his son's illicit relationship is wrong. . . . [Selznick agreed.]

13. [Walter] Huston appearance at the funeral is again an offensive caricature of religion. [Selznick agreed.]

14. For the *Duel in the Sun* climax, this is correct as a payoff on what has preceded it, except at the very finish, wherein Peck kisses Jones and dies. In this way, they both not only get what they deserve, but what they want, and [it] actually amounts to a scene of sublimation and exaltation. . . . [Selznick agreed.]

HIGH NOON

At first glance, *High Noon*, with its minute-by-minute excitement, does not seem the sort of Western that would engage the attention of the censors. It had none of the mountainous mammaries of *The Outlaw* or the steamy sensuality of *Duel in the Sun*, but it did have at least two ingredients that the Hays Office found reprehensible. There was the chilly Grace Kelly as a Quaker bride, who climaxes her little homilies on brotherhood by killing a gunman, and there was the exotic Katy Jurado as the former mistress of two of the townsmen and the present mistress of our hero's Judas.

High Noon relates the story of the marshal of a small Western town who is menaced by the imminent arrival of the men he sent to prison. In describing how the lawman is deserted by the entire town to face the crisis alone, *High Noon* is something of a morality play, and, since morality was within the jurisdiction of the censors, it was perhaps inevitable that they would stick in an oar.

Intriguingly, the entire action of the film is staged identically in the same time that it takes to project the picture on the screen—just over eighty minutes. The Hays Office took somewhat longer to straighten out what they viewed as the moral kinks in the story.

On August 14, 1951, Joseph Breen wrote to George Glass of Stanley Kramer Productions:

We have read the script . . . for your proposed production of *High Noon.* . . . We think it is essential that you secure adequate technical advice concerning the characterization of Amy [Grace Kelly], who is established as a Quaker, in order to avoid offending the religious sensibilities of the Society of Friends. In this connection, we are particularly concerned . . . with her action of taking up a gun and killing one of the men attacking her husband [Gary Cooper].

There is also in this present version of the story an unacceptable characterization of Helen Ramirez [Katy Jurado], . . . [who is] currently the mistress of Harvey [Lloyd Bridges].

We feel it will be necessary to establish that she was perhaps engaged to marry these several men in the past, is currently the beloved of Harvey—eliminating the definite indication that, with each of these men, she had been engaged and is engaging in an illicit sex affair.

In this connection, we suggest that the entire sequence between Helen and Duane and Harvey be removed to some locale other than her bedroom, and that she, of course, be fully dressed.

At present she is described as in a negligee and the indication is unmistakable that Harvey spent the night with her.

Page 25: The same would apply to here where she and Harvey are having breakfast in her room.

Page 41: Along the same line, please eliminate the clerk's dialog to Duane: "Think you can find it all right, eh?" referring to Helen's room.

Chapter 4

CRIME

THE MALTESE FALCON

Just as Brutus was Shakespeare's first draft of Hamlet, Dashiell Hammett's first draft of the characters in *The Maltese Falcon* were sketched in the short stories he wrote for *Black Mask* magazine in the twenties. They were a colorful, profligate lot, and, when they were drawn together in *Falcon*, and Warner Brothers set out to make the movie, the censors went on red alert. There was a satanic detective who was sleeping with his partner's wife; there was a homosexual Armenian who kept making advances to a psychotic young killer; there was a heroine who bedded down with men in order to use them; and the chief heavy, in every sense of the word, was a gluttonous gentleman whose favorite exclamation was "By Gad," which to the censors sounded uncomfortably close to blasphemy. There was also a great deal of violence and the consumption of gallons of liquor.

On top of all this degeneracy and brutality, there was a gratuitously insulting speech on the corruptibility of district attorneys. The Hays Office had no desire to enrage America's district attorneys—the censors were too pusillanimous to offend dentists, let alone the men who wielded the power to ban movies in America's cities and towns.

Ted Turner recently raised a firestorm of protest when he colorized *The Maltese Falcon*, as a sop to TV audiences that like their colors from palettes rather than from personalities. Interestingly, forty-five years before, the Hollywood censors had prepared for Turner's color enhancement by bleeding much of the color out of the film.

On May 23, 1941, Joe Breen dispatched a letter to Jack L. Warner at Warner Brothers. John Huston had written a screen-

play from the riveting detective novel The Maltese Falcon. *If a possibly apocryphal story is to be believed, Huston had his secretary write the screenplay by simply transcribing the very cinematic novel into script form. Wrote Breen:*

> We have read the temporary script dated May 16, 1941 for your proposed production of *The Maltese Falcon*. . . . Going through the script page by page, we call your attention to these points:
>
> *Page 15:* . . . Some other business besides drinking must be substituted on Pages 15, 20, 21, 47, 57, 58, 76.
>
> *Page 24:* It is essential that [Sam] Spade [Humphrey Bogart] should not be characterized as having had a sex affair with Iva [his partner's wife]. Accordingly . . . the following lines must be deleted or changed . . . "You shouldn't have come here today, darling" . . . and Iva's line "Could you come tonight?" . . .
>
> *Page 40–41:* We cannot approve the characterization of [Jeol] Cairo [Peter Lorre] as a pansy, indicated by the lavender perfume, high-pitched voice, and other accoutrements. In line with this, we refer you to Page 48, where Cairo tries to put his arm around the boy's shoulder and is struck by the boy [Elisha Cook, Jr.]. . . .
>
> *Page 78:* This fade-out of Spade and Bridget [Mary Astor] is unacceptable because of the definite indication of an illicit sex affair. . . .
>
> *Page 81:* The boy's line " —— you!" and his soundless repetition of the same words will not be acceptable. . . .
>
> *Page 96:* Gutman's [Sidney Greenstreet] use of the interjection "By Gad" here and [elsewhere] seem to be offensive, if only by the number of times he uses it. . . .
>
> *Page 111:* The action of the boy kicking Spade's temple should be masked [unseen]. . . .
>
> *Page 135:* Spade's speech about the district attorney should be rewritten to get away from characterizing most district attorneys as men who will do anything to further their careers. This is important.

The Other Censors

Sweden rejected the film in its entirety.

British Columbia eliminated the view of Bogart being kicked in the head while lying on the floor.

Australia did the same, as did Ontario.

Kansas, New York, and Maryland approved the film without deletions.

THE POSTMAN ALWAYS RINGS TWICE

There are some books, observes a character in a Jean Kerr comedy, that are unsuited to production on the Broadway musical stage, and one of these is *Twenty Thousand Leagues Under the Sea*. According to the Hollywood censors, there were some books that were unsuited to production as motion pictures, and one of these was *The Postman Always Rings Twice*. The Hays Office exercised all its formidable power and persuasive skills to keep Columbia Pictures and RKO-Radio Studios from optioning the book for the screen. Warner Brothers made the same decision without the coercion of the censors. Thus, Joe Breen felt himself betrayed and embarrassed, when MGM, without soliciting the censors' advise, optioned the James M. Cain book and set to work making the film.

Postman is a rather unwholesome narrative that violates the code commandments in numerous ways. In it a pair of lovers, who fail in their first effort to murder the girl's husband, succeed in their second attempt and, thanks to the venality of an insurance adjuster, are acquitted of murder. Their mutual love and trust suffer and, just when they have adjusted more happily, the girl is killed and the boy is unjustly convicted of her murder.

The long hesitation of the Hays Office in permitting the film to be made seems an exercise in unnecessary caution. The movie, which starred John Garfield and Lana Turner as the murderous, adulterous pair, turned out to be a sternly moral film and was faithful to the story and spirit of the Cain book. When director Bob Rafelson created a more recent version of *Postman*, without the constraints of the censorship code, it was still pretty much what it had been in the forties version—a sordid story of two weak and sordid people.

The tale of censors hampering the filming of Postman *began in 1934, when the Production Code and Joe Breen's strict stewardship were young. On February 16th, Breen wrote to Merian Cooper of RKO-Radio Studios:*

We have read the synopsis of the story Bar-B-Q [The Postman Always Rings Twice]. . . . It is our considered judgment that this story . . . is definitely unsuited to motion picture production, and we strongly recommend that you pass it up. . . .

Three weeks later, Breen encountered another flurry of interest in Postman, this time coming from another source. His letter to RKO had inhibited their interest, but now, Harry Cohn, the autocratic ruler of Columbia Pictures, had discovered the gritty novel. Wrote Breen in a memo to the files:

> Talked with Mr. Lewis Milestone, Harry Cohn, and Mr. Sam Briskin about the story, which Columbia was anxious to buy, *The Postman Always Rings Twice*. This story is a very dangerous one, which has been presented heretofore by RKO-Radio.
>
> As in the case of RKO-Radio, we persuaded the company not to buy the story on the grounds that this was a difficult one for screen portrayal.
>
> It is interesting to note that, in the course of the conversation with Mr. [Eddie] Mannix [of MGM] this afternoon, he advised us that, within the hour, he had purchased for $25,000, the screen rights to the book *The Postman Always Rings Twice*. This information was a shock to us. Not two hours previously . . . I had succeeded, after an hour's conference, in persuading the Columbia company not to buy the story. A fortnight back we had done the same thing with RKO-Radio . . . and it has recently come to our attention that Warner Brothers had turned the story down, fearful that any attempts to get a screen story out of it would end in disaster [a disaster orchestrated by the Hays Office].
>
> It is to be noted that Mr. Mannix did not consult this office in any way previous to his buying the story. He merely announced to us that he had made the purchase in the course of the conversation.
>
> It is not unlikely that two companies at least [Columbia and RKO-Radio] will set up a squawk the minute they discover that Metro has purchased a story that we persuaded them not to purchase. . . .

The Hays Office was eager to act in good faith with the studios that paid their salaries. It was one thing to infuriate them by gutting their movies; that was business, ordained by the code. It was quite another to seemingly favor one studio over another. Six days later, Will Hays wrote to Nicholas Schenck, president of MGM, in an attempt to get him to drop the project and spare the Hays Office blushes and reproach. Hays wrote:

> Information reaches me just now indicating the purchase by Metro of the recently published novel by James M. Cain entitled *The*

Postman Always Rings Twice. I am worried about this, because the story is such, both by reason of the details presented and the general atmosphere, [that] its picturization would be fraught with the gravest dangers to the company and to the industry as a whole. . . .

In all sincerity, it is difficult to conceive a more unwholesome narrative or one which more surely will violate many of the provisions of the Production Code. I understand that three other companies considered the book for possible purchase . . . that two of these companies decided after consultation with our office on the coast that they were not interested in the material because of the general tone and the nature of the events related; a third company reached the same conclusion of its own volition. . . .

I'm sure the seriousness of the matter warrants your personal attention and I will be gratified if you will advise me.

Hays's mixture of cajolery and threat had its effect. Faced with a vow of intransigence by the censors, MGM dropped its plans to film Postman. *Fade-out, fade-in nine years later. Paramount Pictures now joined the ranks of studios drawn to the siren song of the postman. Paramount's liaison to the Hays Office, Luigi Luraschi, inquired gingerly of the censors about the book. Responded Breen:*

With regard to the novel *The Postman Always Rings Twice* by James M. Cain, concerning which you requested our opinion, we regret to have to report that this novel as published seems to be thoroughly in violation of both the letter and the spirit of the Production Code. . . .

The story seems to be a thoroughly unwholesome and objectionable one. . . . The grossness of the numerous sexual irregularities; the detailed methods of crime; the gruesomeness surrounding the murder and the attempted murder; the brutality visited on at least one of the characters; the emphasis on the dishonesty of the lawyers and the representatives of the insurance companies, whose actions allow murder to go unpunished—all these but add to the general offensive character of the story and make its production, in our judgment, a very dangerous undertaking. . . .

Breen's letter was as successful in squashing Paramount's interest as Hays's letter had been in demolishing Metro's, nine years before. But MGM's appetite for the story was not dead, only dormant. Perhaps they were waiting for Lana Turner to grow up. In 1945, two years after Paramount dropped Postman, and eleven years after Columbia, RKO, and Warners had abandoned it for good, MGM's passion for the property resurfaced. On April 20th, heaving a ponderous sigh of resignation, Joe Breen wrote to Louis B. Mayer:

We have read with considerable care the . . . script for your proposed production *The Postman Always Rings Twice*. . . . In its present form this picture appears not to be acceptable. . . . We feel, however, that this story can be made acceptable with some careful rewriting. . . .

The unacceptability of the script in its present form is suggested by the overall flavor of *lust*, which in our reading, is inescapable. . . . This flavor could be substantially reduced if we could cut out . . . all scenes of physical contact—hugging and kissing—between Cora [Lana Turner] and Frank [John Garfield]. . . .

We also feel that the scene indicating the illicit sexual relationship between this pair should be merely suggested and not emphasized in any way. [In the eighties version of *Postman*, Frank and Cora couple on the kitchen table. So much for merely suggesting an illicit relationship.]

MGM ordered a revised screenplay for Postman, and twenty-seven days later, it reposed on Breen's desk at the Hays Office. On May 17th Breen wrote to Mayer:

We have read with great interest the revised temporary script . . . for your proposed production *The Postman Always Rings Twice*. . . . In going through the script page by page, we respectfully direct your attention to the following . . . :

Scene 72: We suggest that in the playing of this scene with Cora and Frank in Frank's bedroom, that Frank be attired in something more than a pair of swim trunks. [The swim trunks stayed.] It would be better if Frank were attired in a bathrobe. [Several years later, Breen tried to put a bathrobe over Burt Lancaster's swim trunks in the famous beach scene in *From Here to Eternity*, with an equal lack of success.]

Page 55: It might be good to eliminate the expression "ball bearings." . . .

The Other Censors

Indonesia banned the film.

Switzerland banned the film, calling it "indecent and immoral." Thus spoke the nation of laundered bank accounts.

Spain banned the film "due to the spirit of adultery perceived throughout the film."

South Africa shortened the sequence showing the hitting of the blackmailer, reflecting South Africa's well-known sensitivity to violence. The film was passed for exhibition only to whites over sixteen.

Trinidad passed the film on appeal, subject to the shortening of the murder sequence.

Sweden required the deletion of the assault on the blackmailer.

Ireland banned the film, calling it "a base, sordid picture."

In Iowa, Cora's response to Frank's line, "But they hang you for something like that" was eliminated. The next line had been: "Not if we do it right—*and plenty of people have.*" Iowan husbands could rest easy.

DOUBLE INDEMNITY

On March 15, 1943 Joe Breen wrote to Paramount Pictures to discourage them from making a movie about a pair of adulterous lovers who kill the woman's husband to collect his insurance. The film was called *The Postman Always Rings Twice*, and Paramount was persuaded to drop it.

On the very same day, Joe Breen wrote another letter to Paramount Pictures about another movie dealing with still another pair of adulterous lovers who kill the woman's husband to collect his insurance. The film was called *Double Indemnity*, and, with this property, Paramount plunged ahead.

Both stories were based on novels by James M. Cain, and both provoked the same objections and threats by the censors. Both were clearly in violation of provisions of the Production Code; both films were likely to be unapprovable, which meant no major theater chains would exhibit them. Both—warned the censors—would end in costly fiascos—the forties equivalent of *Heaven's Gate.*

A policeman's lot is not a happy one, observed W.S. Gilbert, and this is especially true of a policeman of the public morals. On *Double Indemnity*, Joe Breen marshalled all the force of his office and the taboos of the code in trying to discourage Paramount's interest. Yet, as with *Postman*, the adultery and murder of *Double Indemnity* managed to reach the screen and, as with *Postman*, *Double Indemnity* became a splendid melodrama, packed with many moments of gripping suspense.

Of the two films, whose censorship history offer striking parallels, *Double Indemnity* rested in the hands of somewhat more gifted artists. Its screenplay was written by the creator of Philip Marlowe, Raymond Chandler, and its director was Billy Wilder. Both men would struggle against the censors' whims throughout their years in Hollywood, Wilder in *Some Like It Hot* and *Sunset Boulevard*, and Chandler in *Strangers on a Train*, but none of these censorial conflicts, past or future, would match their problems with the Hays Office on *Double Indemnity*.

Joe Breen's less successful letter of March 15, 1943, went to Luigi Luraschi of Paramount Pictures, just as his matching letter on Postman *did. Paramount had requested a report from Breen on the Cain novel,* Double Indemnity, *to see how serious were the roadblocks to its production. Wrote Breen:*

With regard to the novel *Double Indemnity*, I regret to inform you that, because of a number of elements, the story is in violation of the provisions of the Production Code and, as such, is almost certain to result in a picture which we would be compelled to reject. . . .

As we read it, this is the story of the murder of a man by his wife and an insurance agent who is apparently her lover. The motive of the murder is to collect insurance on the dead man, which the murderous couple had conspired to place upon his life. At the end of the story, the crime is confessed by one of the murderers to the auditors of the insurance company, who proceed thereupon to withhold this information from the proper legal authorities and successfully effect a gross miscarriage of justice by arranging for the escape of the two murderers. [The film did not end in this manner.] . . . The first part of the story is replete with explicit details of the planning of the murder and the effective commission of the crime, definitely violating the code provisions, which forbid the presentation of "details of crime." . . . The second part of the story has to do with the successful efforts of the criminals to avoid arrest and punishment and culminates in the decision of the man to kill his accomplice. The attempt is frustrated when the woman shoots him, whereupon the wounded man, with the stepdaughter of his accomplice, confesses the crime to save the girl he loves, against whom a mass of circumstantial evidence has piled up.

The story violates the provisions of the Production Code in that:

1. The leading characters are murderers who cheat the law and die at their own hands. . . . Though they commit suicide . . . one of these criminals is in a sense glorified by his confession to save the girl he loves. [Note the harsh morality of the code: It is not sufficient that a criminal die for his sins; he must have no redeeming qualities.]

2. The story deals improperly with an illicit and adulterous relationship.

3. The details of the vicious and cold-blooded murder are clearly shown. . . .

The general low tone and sordid flavor makes it, in our judgment, thoroughly unacceptable for screen presentation. . . . It is most important in consideration of material of this kind to avoid "the hardening of audiences, especially those who are young and impressionable . . ." [This story doubtless would have a hardening effect on younger members of the audience, especially once they were exposed to Barbara Stanwyck in her tight white sweater.]

It is our considered judgment that the story under discussion is most objectionable. Unless it can be materially changed, both in structure and in detail, all consideration of it for screen purposes should be dismissed.

Undismayed by Breen's pronouncements, Paramount proceeded with a script. About six months later, on September 24th, Breen had received a part script/part treatment for Double Indemnity. *He wasted no time in writing to Paramount to detail his objections:*

We have read the [script] for your proposed picture *Double Indemnity*. . . . Going through this material in detail, we call your attention to the following . . . :

Page 6: This bath towel must properly cover Phyllis [Barbara Stanwyck] and should certainly go below her knees. . . .

Page 8: These "flimsy house pajamas" must also be adequate, otherwise these two scenes cannot be approved. [The point of this scene was the seduction of the insurance man. By turning the towel into a bath sheet and the flimsy pajamas to flannel, the censors were frustrating the author's intentions.]

Page 43: In line with Association's regular policy re fingerprints, please omit the following line, "And listen, don't handle that policy without putting gloves on." [The Hays Office wished to conceal from the general public the fact that miscreants could be traced by their fingerprints. They reasoned, no doubt, that if they could conceal the method by which life is reproduced among mammals, they could conceal the method of identifying felons by their fingerprints.]

Page 47: Please omit the underlined words in the line "To park your south end."

Pages 62–63: We feel that the whole sequence of the detailed disposition of the corpse is unacceptable as a too detailed exposition of the crime.

By December 1st, Breen had received the remainder of the script and wrote again to Paramount:

We read the balance of the script for your proposed picture *Double Indemnity.*

As we advised you before, this whole sequence in the death chamber seems very questionable in its present form. Specifically, the details of the execution . . . seem unduly gruesome . . . [The scene was shot, but eliminated from the film and never appeared on a movie screen.]

ANGELS WITH DIRTY FACES

It would be a distortion to imply that the Hays Office was always devoted to suppression and that moviemakers were always devoted to art. During the Depression years, film producers filled their gangster movies with as much sex and violence as possible and reached new lows in coarseness and vulgarity—anything to keep the public lined up at the box office.

There was a special formula to the explosive gangster film of the thirties. Warner Brothers was the studio that mastered the genre, and James Cagney was the actor who personified it. Together, Warners and Cagney played recklessly with the flames of censorship that were licking at the film colony. The Warner cameramen, set designers, screenwriters, and actors seemed to have the knack for realistically portraying crime and violence. Indeed, so many gangster films poured out of the Warner Burbank studio that the censors and the church groups were alarmed as never before.

Though Cagney was the prototype—in *Angels with Dirty Faces* and *Public Enemy*—there were also Edward G. Robinson, Paul Muni, and Humphrey Bogart, making gangsterism appealing to the public in such crime epics as *Scarface* and *Little Caesar*. The public embraced these sensational films. Some critics praised the naturalism of the dialogue and the superior quality of acting, but the censors perceived the gangster films with more clarity. What Hollywood was peddling to the moviegoer, they said, was sadism and sexuality, wearing the mask of tough, topical fiction.

Clerics and censors—who were often one and the same—deplored the coarsening effect the gangster films were having on the average moviegoer, and it must be acknowledged that the male members of the audience were probably identifying with James Cagney as he mashed a grapefruit into the face of Mae Clarke in *Public Enemy*. After all, for twenty years, the male moviegoer had seen members of his sex degraded by a colorful variety of vamps. Turnabout was fair play, and, if men enjoyed Cagney's sadism, perhaps he appealed equally to the masochistic tendencies of some women. The only group to disapprove of the excesses of Cagney, Robinson, and their Prohibition-era group were the censors.

In January 1938 Jack Warner sent Joe Breen a screenplay for a new Cagney vehicle called Angels With Dirty Faces. *On January 19th, Breen responded:*

This goes to you . . . with regard to the script *Angels With Dirty Faces*, which you submitted for our consideration. . . . While it might be possible to make a picture from the basic story which would meet the requirements of the Production Code, the script, in its present form, is not acceptable on a number of counts. I list these briefly below:

It is important to avoid any flavor of making a hero and sympathetic character of a man who is, at the same time, shown to be a criminal, a murderer, and a kidnapper. In order to achieve this, great care will be needed both in the writing and actual shooting of the picture. . . .

The present script also violates the Association's ruling re "Crime in Motion Pictures" on a number of points, as follows:

The successful kidnapping for ransom.

The gun battle with the police, in the course of which a policeman is shown dying at the hands of the criminal.

The unpunished gangster murder of the man in the telephone booth.

It is our understanding that you intend to rewrite this script very considerably. However, just for the record, we set down the following . . . items, in addition to the above-mentioned major difficulties:

Page 49: [State] censor boards will probably delete all suggestion of a strip poker game. We suggest that you change it. . . .

Page 74: There should be no machine gun in the hands of the gangsters, and this killing should not be shown in such detail, but merely suggested.

Page 79: This scene of Rocky [James Cagney] manufacturing a bullet-proof vest should be omitted.

Page 87: There should be no scenes of policemen dying at the hands of Rocky.

Page 94: [State] censor boards everywhere will delete these details of the preparation of the electrocution.

Page 101: This flippant reference by Rocky to God should be changed.

Chapter 5_____

WAR

FOR WHOM THE BELL TOLLS

The Hays Office met the challenge of fine literature the same as it met the carpentry of Hollywood hacks—with a myopic devotion to dogma. The essential mood and texture of Ernest Hemingway's triumphant novel, *For Whom the Bell Tolls*, was somehow lost in the thickets of Joe Breen's carping letters. In the filming of Hemingway's controversial novel, the bell tolled for Ernest. The compromises that one might have expected in a translation of this brilliant account of the Spanish Civil War all occurred on schedule. The eloquence and meaning of the book, the complex characterizations, the message that democratic doctrine is irresistible—all were somehow lost in the mountains.

One of the memorable scenes in the novel had the American saboteur, Robert Jordon (Gary Cooper), sharing a sleeping bag with Maria (Ingrid Bergman). When the Hays Office was through, the scene had all the eroticism of a laundromat. Joe Breen demanded such circumspection in the photography of Cooper and Bergman embracing under the Spanish sky that the famous sleeping bag could have held nothing but air. The sleeping bag obsessed the censors, and much of their correspondence focused on the "illicit sex" being performed within its folds.

The censors were determined to present Pablo (Akim Tamiroff) and Pilar (Katina Paxinou) as married, and Jordan and Maria as just good friends—relationships that Hemingway's novel and the chemistry of the performers resisted.

For Whom the Bell Tolls was destined to become a prim, bloodless, studio-bound, mock-Spanish rendering of Heming-
50

way, which was a pity, given its literary bloodline, its stars, and supporting cast.

The final struggles over the screenplay for *For Whom the Bell Tolls* occurred in March of 1942. There was an irony in the efforts to sanitize this classic work at this particular time. Three months before, the Japanese had attacked Pearl Harbor and America had declared war on Japan and Nazi Germany. Hemingway's novel was a tough, honest work that celebrated the valiant struggle of free people against fascism. It was a tale of an American who, along with a Spanish waif who has been raped and orphaned by fascists, goes behind the nationalist lines to blow up a bridge. It is perhaps not too pointed to observe that Hemingway was raped and his novel was orphaned.

Paramount optioned the Hemingway novel for the screen and messengered a copy to Joseph Breen at the Hays Office for his reflections on its vulnerability to movie censorship. On October 21, 1940, Paramount received his reply:

> We have read the novel *For Whom the Bell Tolls* by Ernest Hemingway, which you submitted for our consideration, and regret to report that it contains one element which is in violation of the Production Code and, hence, is not acceptable. I refer to the illicit sex affair carried on by your two sympathetic leads, Robert [Gary Cooper] and Maria [Ingrid Bergman]. This will have to be eliminated if the finished picture is to be acceptable. . . .

By the following October, Dudley Nichols had completed a screenplay for the Hemingway novel, and Paramount had sent it to the Hays Office. Joe Breen met with the filmmakers and then, on October 17, 1941, wrote a letter summarizing their points of agreement:

> As was discussed with you, it will be vitally important that in the finished picture there be no suggestion whatever of an illicit affair between . . . Jordon and Maria. In order to make certain of this, we venture to make certain suggestions . . . . :
> We strongly urge that you omit *entirely* from the picture the sleeping bag. This we believe will go far to remove any possible suggestion of a sex affair. We also recommend that some of the dialog between Pilar and Jordan be changed or omitted to get away from any possible suggestion that Pilar is trying to bring the two together for sexual purposes.

We also strongly urge that you endeavor to remove entirely from this picture the suggestion that Maria was raped [by army troops]. . . .

Furthermore, the greatest care will be needed in the shooting of all the scenes between Jordan and Maria to avoid any posture . . . that could in any way be interpreted as suggesting . . . a sexual affair.

Going through the script in detail, we call your attention to the following. . . :

Page 25: Some [state] censor boards may delete the expression "lying on her belly."

Pages 2–29: Here begins the dialog between Pilar and Jordan concerning Maria referred to above. . . . We suggest you change the expression "Be careful with this girl," because of its connotation and connection with the fact that Maria has been raped. . . .

Page 45: The expression "she-dog" is unacceptable.

Page 52: As discussed with you, we recommend getting in on this page a line definitely indicating that Pablo and Pilar are man and wife.

Page 61: In the scene where Jordan is preparing for bed, there must be no suggestion that he is expecting Maria.

Page 63: We question the advisability of the following dialog: "I am glad you came. Did Pilar send you?" "I wanted to come, but she sent me, too."

Page 108: The expression "And nuts!" must be omitted.

Page 112: The expression "Slut!" is unacceptable.

Page 146: The British Censor Board will delete the scene of Pablo and Pilar in the bed together.

Page 160: The following is unacceptable: "Yes . . . yes . . . it is too late."

On February 11, 1942, Dudley Nichols had revised the screenplay of For Whom the Bell Tolls in accordance with the censors' wishes. Paramount sent the altered script to the Hays Office and, on March 20th, received a reply listing the following additional problems:

Page A-30: The line "Not fifteen minutes? Not even a quarter of an hour?" is unacceptably sex suggestive. . . .

May we call your attention to the advisability of making it evident in your picture that the word "woman" used throughout the script means "wife." . . .

Page 32: The expression, "Unspeakable son of an *unmarried gypsy*" is unacceptable.

Page 47: We suggest changing the expression "seed bull."

Page 69: The dialog "Ten o'clock tonight" and the accompanying wink are unacceptably sex suggestive. . . .

Page 138: These scenes of the slaughter of town officials will have to be handled with great care. . . . [The Hays Office was concerned about gruesomeness, rather than possible emulation by American audiences.]

Page 215: We suggest omitting the line "Where they put me on the couch" as being unduly pointed.

Page 216: The same applies to the line "when things were done to me." . . .

The file copy of the above letter from Breen to Paramount contains marginal notations that indicate which of the censors' demands were accepted and which were not.

"Not fifteen minutes, not a quarter of an hour" remained in the script.

"Son of an unmarried gypsy" remained.

"Seed bull" was eliminated.

The wink remained.

The slaughter of the town officials remained.

The expression "slut" was eliminated.

The expression "things were done to me" remained.

FROM HERE TO ETERNITY

Literary critics lauded James Jones's gritty novel of prewar army life in Hawaii, *From Here to Eternity*. Some paid it the exorbitant compliment of calling it an extension of the Hemingway mystique. If Jones was not quite up to Papa Hemingway in economy and style, there was one measurement by which Jones's work was comparable to the best of Hemingway: the rage of the censors. When Columbia Pictures optioned *Eternity* for the screen, it caused every bit as much chagrin at the Hays Office as did *For Whom the Bell Tolls* and *A Farewell to Arms*.

Joe Breen was especially galled at Jones's taste for four-letter words and deftly struck out all profanity from the script, giving the barrack scenes the ambience of a Scout meeting. Breen was shocked at the sexual affair between a top sergeant (Burt Lancaster) and his captain's wife (Deborah Kerr). The Pentagon may have been outraged at the violation of rank; Breen was concerned that the pair had failed to suffer for their sins.

Another disturbing element of the story (which the sanctimonious and family-oriented *Life* magazine referred to as "From Here to Obscenity") was the locale of the novel's second sexual affair—a Honolulu house of prostitution. The censorship code was explicit in denying the existence of call girls and brothels, which brings to mind the man who looked at a camel and declared, "There's no such animal." The lovers in this sanitized liaison were a lonely GI (Montgomery Clift) and a whore (Donna Reed). The censors invited the moviegoers to believe that soldiers would pay money to young women for the privilege of chatting with them in private rooms. "If you believe that," said one Hollywood wag, "there's a bridge in Brooklyn I want to show you."

Eternity was one more in the string of controversial movies that Columbia's hard-headed Harry Cohn had chosen to film, in defiance of predictable protests from the censors. Though he won an occasional battle with the Hays Office in this yarn of soldiers and sex, the film lacked the depth, anger, and compassion of the original novel.

The battle was joined on August 4, 1952, when, having received a copy of the first-draft screenplay for Eternity *from Harry Cohn, Joseph Breen dictated a pointed letter that declared the fundamental problem he foresaw in filming the smoldering novel:*

> We feel that the adulterous relationship between Karen [Deborah Kerr] and Warden [Burt Lancaster] in this present version of the story is handled without any recognition of the immorality of this relationship.
> . . . We feel it will be necessary to have a strong voice of morality by which their immoral relationship can be denounced. . . . [Screenwriter Daniel Taradash suggested that Karen might wear a scarlet "A" throughout the movie.] . . . In all likelihood, that can be done by Karen in that part of the story where she and Warden are parting, she to go back to her husband.
>
> In this regard, we feel that it is extremely important to indicate that Karen does not return easily from her lover to her husband, but rather that, because she has been involved in an adulterous affair, she has created a formidable barrier in any future relationship to her husband, a barrier which, it should be indicated, may

be overcome, but will nonetheless present her with serious future difficulties. [Breen would make the same demand of another character played by Deborah Kerr in *Tea and Sympathy*. As the headmaster's wife who adulterously gives herself to a student to prevent his suicide, her marriage had to be shattered.]

The second important element which will need extreme care will be the portrayal of the New Congress Club. . . . We feel that this club has all the appearances of a house of prostitution. We feel that it is of greatest importance that the stage setting, as well as all the activities of this club, be clearly and thoroughly established as a legitimate business enterprise. . . . It should be quite clearly and affirmatively established that [the girls] are not prostitutes.

We would also like to call your attention to the following . . . :

Page 14: Please eliminate Leva's line, "She knows what it's for."

Page 57: . . . We think it would be well to have these girls state exactly what it is they do at the club; that is, to say that they are paid to drink and dance with the men there.

Page 58: Lorene [Donna Reed] and Pru [Montgomery Clift] should not be lying down in this scene. . . .

Page 64: It would be well to have either Karen or Warden put on a beach robe or some other type of clothing before they go into the embrace. [This was an attempt to launder one of the most famous love scenes in cinema history. Harry Cohn's objection to this bit of censorship was as loud as the crashing waves, and the censors retreated.]

Page 86: The action of Warden breaking the beer bottle and using it as a weapon will undoubtedly be widely deleted by [state] censor boards. For this reason we would suggest you find some other bit of business not quite so startling.

Page 109: Pru's line, "This is just like bein' married, ain't it?" and Alma's reply, "It's better" are unacceptable.

Page 134: Please eliminate the line, "That girl had blowed my fuse."

Page 176: . . . Eliminate the word "even" from Alma's dialog, "We can even get married."

On December 4th, Messrs. Shurlock and Dougherty of the Hays Office met with Buddy Adler, Daniel Taradash, and Fred Zinnemann, the producer, writer, and director of the film, concerning the screenplay. Next day, Joe Breen sent Cohn a summary of the concessions his aides had wrested from the filmmakers:

Page 43: Stark's line, "They said she took up with nearly every man and his brother back there" would be changed.

Page 55: Something to the effect of "I'll ask Mrs. Kipfer if we can use her suite," would be inserted in Lorene's speech. [This was to indicate that the room that the couple was using was not a brothel bedroom, but the club owner's parlor.]

Page 57: The door leading from the room in which we find Lorene and Pru would not be shown as opening into a bedroom.

Page 58: The reference to "working for Mrs. Kipfer" would be eliminated.

Page 83: Some weapon other than a beer bottle will be substituted at this point. [Their agreement notwithstanding, the beer bottle remained.]

Pages 108–9: Pru's line, "This is better than bein' married, ain't it?" and Alma's answer, "It's even better" will be played in such a way as to avoid any suggestion of sex suggestiveness.

Page 156: The important problem remaining in the story from the code's standpoint is the lack of proper compensation for the immoral relationship between Warden and Karen. . . . [The matter was resolved by having the adulterous wife tell Burt Lancaster that what they had been doing with such joy and exhilaration was evil and that she and her corrupt officer husband "deserve each other."]

The Other Censors

The Legion of Decency assigned a "B" class to *Eternity*, calling it "morally objectionable" and asserting that it reflected "the acceptability of divorce" and tended to condone immoral actions."

Egypt cut a portion of the Lancaster/Kerr kiss on the beach.

British Columbia deleted the following dialogue: "I've had another key made for you, and you can use it any time, even if I'm not here."

Australia reduced the embrace on the beach and eliminated the sound of Sergeant Fatso releasing the blade of his spring knife.

Indonesia banned the film in its entirety and listed the following reasons:

1. Unallowed lover relations between the sergeant and the captain's wife.

2. Fightings between the private and his superiors.

3. Pester of the private by his superiors.

4. Bombardments and destructions.
5. Inadmissable scenes in bars of soldiers and women; . . .
not in accordance with our ideas; the more so as we have not
reached yet the desired perfection in our army.

A FAREWELL TO ARMS

Here was Ernest Hemingway's finest novel turned to film, but it
set the censors' stomachs turning. To the Hays Office, David O.
Selznick, the man who was famous for his fidelity to famous
novels— from David Copperfield to Gone With the Wind—had
not provided a faithful rendition of this classic novel. This was
simply a tale of an American ambulance driver and an English
nurse who paw, fondle, clasp, nuzzle, and bed down. The censors saw the script through an enormous keyhole.

Out of respect to Ernest Hemingway—and in response to the
drop in movie attendance caused by the incursions of television—chief censor Geoffrey Shurlock permitted more frank sensuality than his predecessors would have countenanced. Shurlock was a man of taste and moderation. Other censors of the
time found a string of scenes that left an unclean feeling, each
with a gratuitous "dirty detail." State censors deplored the fact
that, when the lovers go to a mirrored hotel room, Jennifer Jones
surveys the room and says, "I never felt like a whore before."
They complained of "an obstetrical orgy" that might send women
screaming from the theater.

When not viewed through the distorted prism of the censor,
Hemingway's classic love story of World War I had been trans-
posed into a powerful and absorbing film. Paramount had made
a version in 1932 that starred Gary Cooper and Helen Hayes,
but the Selznick version was far superior, more faithful to the
book. In retrospect, the sexual angle seems to have been managed tastefully and inoffensively.

Ernest Hemingway had little patience with Hollywood censorship—the epic struggles between bosoms and boycotts, the
unflinching cowardice of the filmmakers, the nonsense and
foolishness that governed movie production. Writing of novelist
William Faulkner, who occasionally labored as a screenwriter,
Hemingway said: "There is a question whether a nation can

survive half slave and half free. There is no question whether a writer can survive half whore and half straight."

On November 2, 1955 Geoffrey Shurlock, now head of the association, wrote to David O. Selznick to confirm a phone conversation regarding the producer's plans for a screen adaptation of A Farewell to Arms:

> In preparing a screen version of this novel which would meet the requirements of the code, the following elements should be taken into consideration:
> There should be a definite voice for morality condemning the action of the two leads living together outside of marriage.
> We have an uneasy feeling that the intimate and protracted affair played in a hospital room where the man lies seriously wounded in the leg will introduce a question of flavor that might make the whole sequence unacceptable. . . .
> A good deal of the dialog referring to the affair, while reading very well between the covers of a book, would, we feel, be objectionably graphic if presented to audiences from the screen. . . .
> With regard to the impossibility of the couple getting married, we would like to suggest that the plausibility of this might be reinforced if it were indicated that they asked the priest to marry them and he was the one to advance the impossibility in view of military regulations. . . .

By October 29, 1956, Ben Hecht had written a screenplay based on the novel, and Selznick had submitted it for Shurlock's scrutiny. He wrote the producer to say:

> This goes to you in confirmation of our conference . . . with regard to the screenplay for your production of *A Farewell to Arms.*
> During this discussion, the following points were considered and agreed to as follows:
> *Page 12:* You will consider dropping or rewriting the line "or just givin' myself to him."
> *Page 16:* Here and throughout, please make certain that none of these embraces and kisses are too prolonged. . . .
> *Pages 23–24:* We will consider dropping the reference to "Virgin" and "nonvirgins." . . .
> *Page 26:* The following dialog will be modified or possibly dropped as too blunt: "Do you want me, darling?" "I don't want anything else. Tonight."

Page 51: We discussed rewriting the reference to "the illegitimate son of President Wilson."

Page 65: Consideration will be given to omitting or rewriting the following lines . . . :
"You mustn't—you're not well enough."
"Yes I am—please."
"You shouldn't. You're sick."

Page 67: We suggest omitting the underlined words in the line: "I used to think that <u>when it happened</u> I'd want to cry."

Page 94: The suggestion that Renaldi has suffered from venereal disease could not be approved. . . .

Page 128: . . . Please eliminate the action of Henry kneeing the officer in the groin.

Page 180: We recommend discretion in the portrayal of Catherine's [Jennifer Jones] labor pains. . . .

Page 185: It is agreed that in this scene Henry will again express his regret that he and Catherine have never been married.

Selznick demanded obedience from his subordinates, and his marathon memos kept them on a short leash. In the case of the Hays Office, Selznick was at the other end of the leash. The producer's abject surrender to the Hays Office suggestions will be seen in Geoff Shurlock's letter to Selznick on February 4, 1957:

We have read the final script of your picture A Farewell to Arms and are happy to note the changes and improvements therein in line with the various discussions we had before your departure [for location work in Italy]. However, there is one element in this story which still gives us real concern. In the letter from Miss Schiller [Lydia Schiller, a Selznick aide], she indicates that you feel that you have gone beyond our requests in regard to the "voice of morality" . . . so we have read the script very carefully with this in mind, but we regret to report we found not much difference in this respect. . . . There is no feeling of guilt or condemnation on the part of Catherine. . . .

Going through this new script in detail, we call your attention to the following:

Page 1: We suggest not doing anything that would stress the Casa Villa Rosa as a house of prostitution. It would be well to omit any showing of a red light. . . .

Page 48: There seem to be here some rather pointed references to sexual intercourse. . . .

Page 60: The following lines by Catherine seem to be pretty strong justification of their illicit sex relationship. "I'm a very honest woman. Very happy. And very proud."

The forbidden word "damn" had triggered an acrimonious dispute for Selznick in Gone With the Wind. *The word "whore" catapulted Selznick into another clamorous battle in* A Farewell to Arms. *In July, having read the revised final shooting script, Shurlock wrote to the producer:*

> . . . We are concerned about a possible bad reaction to the use of the word "whore." While it is absolutely valid in context, it is our impression that this expression has not been used on the screen before. Possibly, it may sound too shocking to be heard on the screen before mixed audiences.
>
> We are, therefore, urging that you take a protection shot of this particular dialog, substituting either "harlot" or "prostitute." In this case you would be protected if, at the preview, you learn that our above-mentioned fears are justified.

When *Arms* was released with the word "whore" on its sound track, Hal B. Wallis, chief producer at Warner Brothers studios, wrote the Hays Office. He was outraged. He said sardonically that he had tried to arrive at a comparison between the scenes he witnessed in *A Farewell to Arms* and the letters he received from the Hays Office about "childishly inoffensive scenes" in his own movies. He protested that these censorial letters warned him of open-mouthed kissing and the exposure of women's breasts "and all the other silly nonsense." Then, said Wallis, he sees *A Farewell to Arms* with its "dirty jokes about rectal thermometers" and a nurse climbing in and out of bed with a wounded man who hurriedly buttons his pajamas.

In short, Wallis was not affronted by the purported immorality of *A Farewell to Arms*. Rather, he was saying "How do I get in on it?" Hal Wallis was especially irate over the girl saying she never felt like a whore before. He was doubly resentful, he said, in noting how the bars were down for Selznick, while the Hays Office continued to delete "inconsequential things" from his own scripts.

It was clear that the Hays Office censorship operated with

great flexibility in the case of different pictures, and produced extraordinarily varying results on the screen.

The Other Censors

The British changed "venereal disease" to "imaginary disease." In the hotel room scene, they removed the clerk's line, "Our mirror room, very popular," plus two shots of the clerk leering. They removed the shot of the baby feeding at its dead mother's breast, and they reduced shots of Catherine in labor. They changed "whore" to "wanton."

Chapter 6————————————

MONSTERS

DR. JEKYLL AND MR. HYDE

Dr. Jekyll, as lovers of this Robert Louis Stevenson shocker will recall, was experimenting with a drug that would so alter man's soul as to separate the good from the evil within him. The censors of the Hays Office had much the same task—separating the good from the evil in a film script and removing the latter. It was a simplistic approach on the part of both Dr. Jekyll and Mr. Breen; good and evil are inextricably mixed in most characters and most lives and do not lend themselves to easy separation.

Nonetheless, in this third filming of the Stevenson thriller—John Barrymore and Fredric March had played the role before—the Hays Office censors sought to separate out the evil shots, scenes, and lines.

Most particularly, in their meditations on modern morals, they focused on Dr. Hyde (Spencer Tracy), his sadism and his lechery, and on Ivy (Ingrid Bergman), turning her from a prostitute into a flirt. Miss Bergman was originally offered the anemic role of Dr. Jekyll's fiancée, with Lana Turner cast as Ivy. Bergman sensibly opted for the latter role and endowed the film with all its moving, erotic interludes, while giving the censors most of their troubles. Bergman is presented as a barmaid who—under the censors' strictures—is essentially a kind, well-meaning girl who attempts an innocent flirtation with Dr. Jekyll and suddenly finds herself the terrified object of Mr. Hyde's attentions. Lana Turner was dismayed to find herself in the unobjectionable role of the sweet, adoring fiancée.

Dr. Jekyll encounters strong opposition from his own profession, which prevents him from continuing his experiments. MGM and Louis B. Mayer encountered strong opposition from the censors, which prevented them from being as graphic as they would have liked. Dr. Jekyll decides to try the drug on himself and finds to his delight that he can change from one character to another. His evil deeds grow worse and he discovers that the drug does its work too well. It could be said of the drug of movie censorship that it, too, did its job too well.

On November 12, 1940, Joe Breen wrote to MGM's Louis B. Mayer to say:

We have read the temporary complete script for your proposed picture *Dr. Jekyll and Mr. Hyde*. . . . The present version contains certain . . . items that are not acceptable and which must be changed in the finished picture. . . . We call your attention to the following . . . :

Page 17: The line "wives and sweethearts are far at home" gives the whole speech an unacceptably sex suggestive flavor. . . .

Page 25: In this sequence of montage shots [in the lab], please avoid any suggestion of vivisection on the part of Dr. Jekyll. . . .

Page 33: Care will be needed with the characterization of the girl Ivy to avoid characterizing her as a prostitute. . . .

Page 35: Please change the shot of the landlady looking suggestively after the couples.

Page 38: The scene of the girl taking off her stocking must be done inoffensively and without any undue exposure. Please also do not overemphasize the garter. . . .

Page 39: This action of the girl falling back on the bed swinging her bare leg must be changed. . . .

Page 47: The line "I want you—want you every minute" is not acceptable. . . .

Page 49: Omit the underlined words in the expression "The little white-breasted dove."

Page 63: The following broken line must be changed: "Underneath I'm as soft as your white—"

Page 56: The dialog that ends the scene beginning "I'm hurting you because I like to hurt you—" is *unacceptable* by reason of containing a definite suggestion of sadism. . . .

Page 65: Great care will be needed . . . to avoid any suggestion of rape. . . .

By February 4th, a revised screenplay had been written by John Lee Mahin and sent to the Hays Office. It produced the following letter from Joe Breen to Louis B. Mayer:

Page 6: There must be no exposure of Ivy in this scene, where she takes off her blouse.

Page 60: The broken line, "You said it wasn't evil for us to—" is unacceptable. . . .

Page 68: This action of Hyde poking the landlady in the backside is not acceptable. . . .

Page 76: The British Board of Film Censors will probably delete this reference to Buckingham Palace.

By June, principal photography had been completed and the rough cut was screened for the Hays Office. On June 3rd, Joe Breen wrote to Mayer:

. . . Before we can approve this picture under the code, the following eliminations will have to be made:

In the scene where Jekyll carries Ivy up to her room, delete the large close-up where Ivy's breasts are unduly exposed. . . .

In the first montage, delete all scenes [of Hyde] lashing the two girls.

In the second montage, delete all scenes having to do with the swan and the girl, and the stallion and the girl.

In the scene in the cabaret, delete the crotch shot of the dancing girls.

If you will inform us that these changes have been made, we will be happy to review the corrected reels and to send you the Association's certificate.

As will be noted, the censorship board did not operate on the honor system. The studio chief's assurance that the changes had been made was insufficient. The censors had to see for themselves.

The Other Censors

Spain demanded the deletion of the second and third kiss in Reel 2 and a shortening of Ivy's bedroom sequence.

Sweden eliminated part of the fight in the bar and the pursuit of the frightened Ivy.

In the Union of South Africa, children under sixteen were not permitted to see the film.

Chicago, which was home to the oldest local censor board in America and which is famous for its devotion to peace and tranquility, eliminated the scene were Dr. Jekyll is shot and falls down stairs.

Ohio required the deletion of "all scenes showing chairs being crashed over men's heads" during the fight in the cafe.

THE BRIDE OF FRANKENSTEIN

When moralists discuss the excesses of movies and television, they speak of "sex and violence" as the twin sins of the mass media. Yet the attention lavished on sex in the Hollywood censorship code is much more comprehensive than that applied to violence. Under the category of "Sex," the censors proscribe adultery, passion, lustful kissing, seduction, rape, abortion, prostitution, perversion, and indecent dances. Under "violence" are listed suicide, murder, brutality, kidnapping, mercy killing, and the flaunting of weapons.

Brutality and gruesomeness were more the focus of the censors in monster movies such as *The Bride of Frankenstein*. There was a small sexual ingredient—the perverse chemical attraction of a monster for its mate—but the Hays Office's chief concern was the level of brutality.

One of the most familiar cliches of films regarding manmade monsters is that the scientist has abrogated the prerogatives of God in the creation of human life. All such references, however bromidic, made the censors extremely edgy. They feared the charge of blasphemy from the church and the more pious moviegoers. So it was that *The Bride of Frankenstein*, at first blush a piece of cinematic carpentry that could give offense only to critics and purists, drew the censors' opprobrium for reasons of sex, violence, and blasphemy.

The producers had little devotion to aesthetics; this was not a Hemingway novel or a Tennessee Williams play. If they were too subservient to the censors, however, their monster film might lose its monstrosity. It was all very well for the Hays Office to decry brutality and gruesomeness, but that's what the filmmakers were selling.

Three years before, Universal had run into a fire storm of censorship—and a box office bonanza—with its original *Frankenstein* film. The movie's gruesomeness and irreverence were attacked by censorship boards in many states and all parts of the world. The profits of the original bred a sequel, but the censorship bred caution at the Hays Office. Breen needed no prophetic gifts to foresee serious problems with the state censor boards, and they materialized as expected.

Breen's efforts to immunize *The Bride of Frankenstein* to state and foreign censorship were no more successful than had been the efforts of his predecessor in the job in 1931. The Hays Office, on that occasion, had seen to it that one memorable episode ended on the cutting room floor. In that scene, the monster (Boris Karloff) comes upon a little girl who is throwing flowers in a lake. The monster joins her in this idyllic activity, but soon runs out of things to throw in the water. He glances at the little girl and moves toward her. The Hays Office cut the continuation of this scene during which the monster seizes the child and tosses her in the lake, registering perplexity when, unlike the flowers, she fails to float.

A mimeographed script was sent to Universal Pictures to the Hays Office on July 23, 1934. The sequel to the successful Frankenstein originally bore the title The Return of Frankenstein. *Joe Breen reviewed the script and dispatched the following letter:*

> We have read your script *The Return of Frankenstein*. . . .
> Throughout the script there are a number of references to Frankenstein . . . which compare him to God and which compare his creation of the monster to God's creation of Man. All such references should be deleted. . . .
>
> *Scene D-23:* This love scene between Hilda and Eric, which is watched by the monster, should be changed to avoid the obvious inference that the monster is watching a physical affair between the two people. We suggest a revision to make the scene an unsuggestive, unobjectionable, and harmless picture of the pure and innocent affection felt between simple folk. . . . This will eliminate Eric taking down Hilda's hair, any undressing . . . the kiss and the action of falling back on the bed. . . .
>
> *Scene F-26:* The monster's use of the word "mate" should be dropped in this scene. All material which suggests that he desires a sexual companion is objectionable. We suggest that you substitute the word "companion." . . .

On November 30, 1934, Universal Studios wrote to Joe Breen, sending him an updated copy of The Bride of Frankenstein *for his comments. On December 5th, Breen replied:*

There are . . . several items which should be modified. One of the principal elements which we believe needs further attention is the number of killings which this present script indicates. We counted ten separate scenes in which the monster either strangles or tramples people to death—this in addition to some other murders by subsidiary characters. In a picture as basically gruesome as this one, we believe that such a great amount of slaughter is unwise and recommend very earnestly that you do something about toning this down.

In a story of this particular flavor, care must also be taken to avoid any suggestion of irreverence, particularly with the use of the name of God. We suggest certain individual lines which we believe it will be advisable for you to delete in this connection.

Going through the script in detail, we call your attention to the following changes which we suggest you make:

Page 85: This dialog in which the three characters boast of their infidelity, immorality, and adultery should be modified. I call your attention specifically to the following lines: "We are all three infidels, scoffers at marriage ties . . ." ". . . have run away from his innocent spouse with innocent me but seventeen."

Page A-12: We suggest changing the word "entrails," as it will be offensive to mixed audiences.

Page A-16: We also suggest omitting this scene of the rat, as its portrayal has in the past proved offensive. . . .

Page B-7: We suggest omitting the line "It was like being God." This line in the past has proven somewhat blasphemous.

Page B-20: For the same reason, we suggest omitting the line ". . . as they say, 'in God's own image.'"

Page B-25: This scene of the miniature mermaid should be handled in such a way as to avoid any improper exposure.

Page B-26: You should omit the line "If you are fond of your fairy tales" as a derogatory reference to the Bible.

Page F-8: You should omit the figure of the statue of the Christ from this scene, substituting some other type of monument.

Your studio is, of course, too well aware of the difficulty which attended the release of the first *Frankenstein* picture. In a great many parts of the world, criticism at that time directed at the picture seemed to be based principally on the two elements of undue gruesomeness and an alleged irreverent attitude on the part of some of the characters, particularly wherever they suggested that their actions were paralleling those of the Creator. It is our belief that the ending of your present story should carry a sufficient moral lesson to obviate this latter criticism. . . .

With regard to the element of gruesomeness, it will depend

largely on the way the picture is actually shot. We again urge
you to use the utmost care and good taste, so that your picture
may meet with the widest possible favorable public reaction. . . .

*As a consequence of Breen's admonitory letter, James Whale,
director of* Bride of Frankenstein, *met with Geoffrey Shurlock
of the Hays Office. On December 7th, he wrote to Breen to inform him that, as a result of this meeting, he felt confident that
he could evade any possible trouble on the points the censor
had raised. He informed Breen how he intended to deal with
each of his caveats.*

1. The multiple killings: They would be minimized and most
would be lumped together in one brief montage, illustrating the
monster's reign of terror.

2. Infidelity: Instead of the lines about adultery in which
the man says "We are all three infidels who scoff at our marriage ties," the director suggested, "We are all three skeptics,
scoffers at all normal ties."

3. Entrails: He agreed to change the word "entrails" to "in-
sides."

4. The rat: He suggested substituting a bat or an owl for the
rat.

5. Blasphemy: Instead of "It was like being God," Whale
suggested the line, "It was like being the Creator himself." He
did not choose to kill the phrase "It seems like in God's own
image," but, in directing the scene, he assured Breen he would
eliminate the derision in the line. The mermaid, he promised,
would have very long hair that enveloped her body.

6. The Bible: Instead of "If you're fond of fairy tales," he
made the line "If you're fond of your Scriptures."

7. Statue: He agreed to change the figure of Christ to the
figure of Death.

In response to Breen's request that the film's conclusion point
a moral lesson, Whale observed that the entire picture was a
moral lesson. He declared that Mary Shelley, creator of the original novel, had insisted her book taught a moral lesson: the
punishment that befell a mortal man who dared to emulate God.
Miss Shelley conceded that her publishers, like the Hays Office,
did not see it that way.

In response to Breen's admonition about shooting the film with utmost care and good taste, Whale vowed that this was his intention.

Director Whale was bending over backwards to be agreeable to the censors.

By March 23, 1935, principal photography had been completed on The Bride of Frankenstein. Joe Breen screened the film and dispatched a letter to Universal Studios:

As you know, we have given much serious thought to your production of The Bride of Frankenstein, and, as I have indicated to you, we are gravely concerned about it. This picture seems to us definitely to be a violation of our Production Code because of its excessive brutality and gruesomeness. The shots early in the picture, in which the breasts of the character of Mrs. Shelley are exposed and accentuated, constitute a code violation.

However, we have the thought that careful and intelligent editing of the picture may remove the difficulties suggested by the version we saw on Thursday. To the end that this may be done, I respectfully suggest that you suggest to Mr. Laemmle [Universal Studio head] his consideration of the following recommendations:

[Each of the following comments is preceded by a bold red check, indicating concurrence on the part of Universal, or a cross, indicating their unwillingness to make the suggested change. The film was now complete and changes would be costly—but code approval was mandatory.]

[check] 1. Delete all the "breast shots" in Reel 1.

[check] 2. Delete the shots of the monster in the pool actually drowning Hans.

[cross] 3. Delete shot of the monster actually pushing Hans's wife into the cistern.

[cross] 4. Delete the shots of the little girls coming out of church in their white dresses and discovering the body of the little child lying on the ground.

[check] 5. Delete the shot of mother carrying the child's dead body in her arms.

[cross] 6. Delete the shot of the bloody hands of the monster in the hermit's hut.

[check] 7. Delete entirely the sequence of the idiot nephew strangling his uncle.

[cross] 8. Delete the close-up of the monster as he falls, crashing the lid of a car, and later seems to fondle the head of the corpse.

[cross] 9. Delete the footage showing the entrance of Dr. Praetoria into the vault, accompanied by the two men, and all their talk about the young girl, to cover the action of opening the casket.

[3 checks] 10. Cut the entire sequence of the deserted street and the murder of the woman by the half-wit.

[check] 11. Cut the shot of the heart being taken from the jar with the forceps.

[cross] 12. Cut the shot of the monster throwing the man over the roof.

You will note from these suggestions that we are seeking to lessen those phases of the picture which suggest excessive brutality. . . . We recognize that, in a story of this kind, it is necessary that a certain amount of . . . gruesomeness is necessary to the proper telling of the story, but the picture as we saw it the other day is likely to be quite offensive. It is our thought that the recommendations made herein above accomplish much . . . and that your story will suffer little, if any, as a result. Indeed it is our considered unanimous judgment that these eliminations will very materially help your picture from the general standpoint of entertainment.

It will be noted that there was no limit to the Hays Office's hypocrisy. Not only did they eliminate material parts of the film; they went so far as to suggest that they were creating a more entertaining horror film by removing the horror.

On March 25th, Breen sent a memo to the files of the Hays Office detailing the results of his conference at Universal with Whale and Laemmle. Breen's objections were reviewed. He acknowledged grudgingly that some of his suggestions had been acted upon, but that others were protested. It was agreed, wrote Breen, that the changes on which the studio concurred—the ones marked by a "check" in his previous memo—would be made in the film and that the results would be shown to Breen to see if this was adequate.

On April 15th, Breen wrote to Universal to say that he had screened the film with the agreed-upon deletions made and that Frankenstein's bride was ready for her coming out. The coveted censorship seal would now be issued, but Breen was whistling in the graveyard. He foresaw serious problems. In his April 15th letter, while formally declaring that the film was acceptable, he hoisted a red flag:

. . . As I have informed you verbally, however, it is more than likely that this picture will meet with considerable difficulty at the hands of [state and local] censor boards both in this country and abroad. The nature of the production is such as to invite very critical examination on the part of these censor boards, and you may well expect difficulty with it wherever the picture is shown.

This is an unfamiliar perspective from which to view the Hays Office—warning moviemakers of the dangers of censorship.

The Other Censors

Breen's warnings were prophetic:

Trinidad rejected the film. Its reason: "Because it is a horror picture."

Palestine rejected the film.

Hungary rejected the film. Its reason: "The picture portrays crimes and acts of a monster called into being through scientific experiments."

China made certain deletions, eliminating the scenes of the monster murdering Hans and his wife, the monster attacking the peasant girl, and Dr. Praetoria ordering his henchman to seize the woman.

Sweden eliminated two solid pages of dialogue and shots from the film, including the scene of the weeping woman in the cemetery, the scene of Frankenstein stealing the coffin, the scene of the hangman, the father with child in his arms, the monster drowning Hans and killing his wife, the scene of the monster throwing rocks down on his pursuers, the scene of the monster tied to a tree and being stoned, the monster breaking open a coffin. The deletions of the Swedish censors were so numerous that the film seemed destined to be released as a short subject.

Singapore eliminated the following elements: scenes where the man is thrown into well, the lynching of the monster, the scene where the coffin is opened, the kidnapping and murdering of the woman.

Japan had a lengthy list of deletions, including the scenes where the monster tries to choke the professor, where the mother finds her daughter dead, where the monster breaks up the grave, and where the corpse is visible in the coffin.

Quebec approved the film with only one deletion: the phrase "in God's own image."

British Columbia granted an adult permit.

Pennsylvania approved the film, deleting only the phrase "in God's own image."

Kansas approved the film without change.

New York State approved it without change.

Massachusetts approved it without change.

Ohio demanded a substantial list of deletions.

The Bride of Frankenstein had run into the very problems around the world and in the U.S. that Breen had predicted. The Ohio censors were particularly troublesome, and Universal Studios asked the Hays Office to help them with the Ohio problem. Breen wrote to his boss, Will Hays, and asked him to read Ohio's comprehensive list of eliminations, but Breen offered Universal little more than tea and sympathy. He pointed out to Hays that, when he had first viewed The Bride of Frankenstein, he had warned Whale and Laemmle that state censors would gut the film. "All of the Universal executives waved aside [my warnings]," said Breen, suppressing the wholly justified urge to add, "I told you so."

Chapter 7————————————
ROMANCES

ECSTASY

Louis B. Mayer met a Czech girl named Hedi Keisler when a notorious film she made called *Ecstasy* was playing to capacity houses in London. In it the eighteen-year-old Hedi appeared nude in a pastoral setting. Mayer signed her to a Hollywood contract and changed her name to Hedy Lamarr. However, knowing the limits of American censorship and the repressed tastes of American audiences, who had been conditioned by Hays Office prudery, Mayer considered Hedy too blatantly sexual for American movies. He never had the courage to permit her to live up to the voluptuous beauty she had displayed in *Ecstasy*.

Hollywood imported many foreign-born actresses during the Hays era—Ingrid Bergman, Marlene Dietrich—to augment the wholesome, apple-pie American beauties. None was as ripe as Hedy Lamarr. Her dappled nakedness in *Ecstasy* stimulated audiences around the world, but American filmmakers dampened her steamy appeal.

When its producer sought approval to show it in the United States, the Hays Office reaction to *Ecstasy* seemed to confirm Louis B. Mayer's assessment of the repressive tendencies of our censors and our audiences.

Hedy Lamarr, like others of her calling, took out an insurance policy on the years when her beauty might fade. She married an Austrian munitions maker who seemingly had the soul of a censor. He set out to buy up every existing print of *Ecstasy* and burn it. Fortunately for a prurient posterity, he failed: appreciative film lab technicians had copied the negative to keep it alive.

The most famous of the film's censorable scenes showed the

teenage Hedy skinny-dipping in a forest pond; but the censors grew irate at the most candid love scene ever committed to celluloid, which contained an extreme close-up of Hedy's face at the instant of sexual climax. This is the sort of shot that rarely appeared in episodes of the Hardy Family saga.

Ecstasy had been produced in 1932 and won its young star a worldwide notoriety. In 1936 a print was sent by the American distributor to the Hays Office for examination. Their wish—a triumph of hope over experience—was that the Hollywood censors would permit the film's exhibition in America. In a memo for the files, Charles Metzger of the Hays Office filed a summary of the film in question:

> This is the story, told somewhat symbolically with a minimum of dialog and a musical background, about a warm-blooded girl who married an impotent man who failed to consummate their marriage. . . . There was a divorce action filed . . . and she returned to the home of her father, a horse breeder, where her sexual urges continued to obsess her. She became acquainted with a young engineer near her father's home, and, when her sexual urge became especially powerful, went to him and spent the night, realizing the "ecstasy" of such a relationship. She and her lover met in a neighboring town with the thought of going away together, but her ex-husband appeared and committed suicide, and she left her lover asleep at the railroad station and departed for an unknown destination. . . .

A week later, his antennae vibrating, Joseph Breen dashed off a brief, overheated note to Will Hays, to alert him to the danger on the horizon:

> Two representatives of this office have seen the picture *Ecstasy*.
>   Attached hereto is a report prepared by Mr. Metzger. . . . As can be seen from the attached report, [the film] is highly—even dangerously—indecent.

During the following ten months, the U.S. distributor of Ecstasy perservered in his campaign to secure code approval for his film, which was winning worldwide acclaim. Breen was adamant. In a letter to Jewel Productions in Los Angeles on May 28, 1937, Breen wrote:

I regret to have to advise you that we cannot approve your production *Ecstasy* that you submitted for our examination yesterday for the reason that it is our considered unanimous judgment that the picture is definitely and specifically in violation of the Production Code.

This violation is suggested by the basic story . . . in that it is a [story] of illicit love and frustrated sex, treated in detail without sufficient compensating moral values. . . .

The Other Censors

The film had a limited run in American art houses without the Hays Office seal, but ran into stiff local censorship. Massachusetts ruled that the film could not be shown on Sundays.

Pennsylvania rejected the film in its entirety.

New York first rejected the film, then approved it.

Maryland made numerous eliminations, including the view of the nude girl gamboling in the woods. A list of the deletions made by the Maryland censor reflect the objections of the Hays Office and illustrate the reasons for the thorny reception they accorded the film:

Reel 1: Eliminate views of bridegroom handling boxes of condoms. . . . Eliminate shots of boxes of condoms on table beside bed, with camera panning from bed where bride reposes, to table where condoms are lying.

Eliminate all views of bride reposing full length on bed and camera panning her body from head to foot, and the following scene of camera panning to bridegroom sliding forward.

Reel 2: Eliminate scene of husband taking aphrodisiac.

Reel 3: Eliminate view of nude girl advancing to pool. Eliminate scene where nude girl turns over in water exposing bare breasts. Eliminate view of nude girl chasing horse.

Reel 4: Eliminate close-up of nude girl showing shame, covering herself with her hand, and bowing her head as man approaches.

Reel 5: Eliminate scene of preparing to breed mare. . . . Eliminate scene of iris—suggestive of dripping flower. . . .

NOW, VOYAGER

Olive Higgins Prouty's three-handkerchief novel seems the soul of propriety. It is the story of a twenty-eight-year-old woman (Bette Davis) who, because of her mother's domination, has a nervous breakdown and is being treated by a psychiatrist (Claude Rains). On a South American cruise she meets a married man (Paul Henreid) who, with his sympathy and understanding, helps her overcome her neurosis and become a contented, self-reliant woman. Fade-out. It is an innocent excursion into pop psychiatry, whose chief distinction, in retrospect, is a scene in which the hero lights a pair of cigarettes, one for himself and one for his companion, planting the twin seeds of love and lung cancer.

To the Hays Office it offered twin dangers. First, these voyagers were clearly not limiting their joint activities to viewing Mayan ruins. An adulterous affair was apparent to anyone above the age of twelve. The second bone in the censors' throat was the deprecation of Latinos, which the Hays Office had found so offensive in *Treasure of the Sierra Madre*. On an offshoot from their romantic cruise, Bette and Paul engage a colorful hack to drive them to an inland city. The censors feared that the ramshackle cab, the cretinous cabby, and the rutted road—all invented for the sake of comedy and romance—were offensive to their South American market. A limousine service on a six-lane highway would be more prudent, but would offer less romantic appeal.

The film was actually immaculate in its morals. A neurotic girl meets a married man on a South American trip. She realizes that her love cannot be returned. She returns to New York to help cure the man's neurotic daughter. What could be less objectionable?

The final script by Casey Robinson, based on Mrs. Prouty's novel, reached the Hays Office in the closing days of March 1942. Joe Breen wasted no time in reading it, and on April 2nd, wrote to Jack L. Warner, who was looking forward to shooting this excellent vehicle for Bette Davis. Breen wrote:

We have received and read the final script dated March 15, 1942 . . . for your proposed production titled *Now, Voyager* and regret to advise that the present version contains one element that seems to be in violation of the provisions of the Production Code and which could not be approved in the finished picture.

This unacceptable element is an indication of an adulterous affair between the leads Charlotte [Bette Davis] and Jerry [Paul Henreid]. . . .

Page 14: Please handle with care this "almost shockingly passionate" kiss.

Page 71: . . . We could not approve these scenes, which definitely suggest an affair between Charlotte and Jerry, where they are shown sleeping under the shelter.

Page 73: Jerry's line, "I had a dream when I woke up this morning, and I found that it was reality" seems to be suggestive. . . .

Addison Durland, the Hays Office's Latin American expert, had other fish to fry. His preoccupation was the tender sensibilities of Latin audiences. On April 6th he wrote to Jack L. Warner:

We have read the final script . . . for your proposed production titled *Now, Voyager*, bearing in mind the possible reaction of Latin American audiences.

We are concerned about the sequences . . . in the trip made by Jerry and Charlotte to Petropolis from Rio. . . . In our opinion the ramshackle car in which your characters make the trip should be eliminated. Rio is justly proud of its modern system of transportation; we would naturally expect to see a modern taxicab.

Its driver should not be this very ignorant, dim-witted, hysterically comic person [who is] unable even to cope with his machine. I feel sure that he will be considered a grotesque travesty. Besides, like all taxi drivers in all great cities of the world, he should know enough English to understand his passengers. . . .

WUTHERING HEIGHTS

It seems reasonable to suggest that Laurence Olivier has seldom considered motion pictures to have the importance of the stage. His work as star and director of *Hamlet* and *Richard III* seem somewhat inconsequential when compared to his lofty theatrical activities. One of the reasons why he failed to regard film as of primary significance was the strident structure of censorship that bound his work in that medium.

When Olivier accepted Sam Goldwyn's invitation to come to

America to play Heathcliff in *Wuthering Heights* in 1939, he must have blanched at the petty deletions and eliminations that were plaguing producer Goldwyn and director William Wyler on the Ben Hecht/Charles MacArthur adaptation of the classic Emily Brontë tale of tortured romance.

In December of 1938, Goldwyn sent the first draft screenplay of the strong, somber, sinister film to the Hays Office. Joe Breen read it and responded with a letter on December 3rd:

> We have received and read the script for your proposed picture *Wuthering Heights*. . . . Going through your script in detail, we call your attention to the following . . . :
> *Page 37:* Care will be needed in the scene of Heathcliff fighting off the dog to avoid any suggestion of cruelty to animals. . . .
> *Page 56:* We suggest making this action of Heathcliff slapping Cathy to avoid possible deletion by [state] censor boards. . . .
> *Page 116:* Some censor boards will delete the line "With no wear and tear on the kidneys."

THE LETTER

Bette Davis owes much of her success to the censorship code. The repressive proclivities of the Hays Office and the Legion of Decency inevitably turned sexual passion to unwholesome neurosis; and who better to portray the cold-blooded, moneyed, grasping female leads in such chilly films than Bette Davis, the bitch heroine with the pulsing eyes and the hysterical manner?

After the legendary sex goddesses of the thirties—the Mae Wests, the Jean Harlows, the Hedy Lamarrs—it seems in retrospect that, given the strictures of the censorship code, the pendulum would inevitably swing to the sexless, neurotic heroines of Bette Davis.

Whatever the sexual components of her films—and many like *The Letter* and *Of Human Bondage* drew the ire of the censors—Bette Davis's performances tended to put their sensuality under a cold shower.

In April 1938, Jack L. Warner sent Joseph Breen the Somerset Maugham screenplay of The Letter. *Breen's response carried a chill:*

We have read with great care the playscript of *The Letter*, by W. Somerset Maugham. . . .

As we read it, this is the story of a wife who murders her lover, but who, by lying, deceit, perjury, and the purchase of an incriminating letter, defeats justice and gets off "scot-free."

In the development of this story we have the murder of the lover; all the sordid details of the illicit sex relationship between the married woman and her lover; and very pointed and numerous references to the second mistress of the murdered man, who is characterized as a China woman. . . .

Because of all this, we could not . . . approve a motion picture based upon this story.

In this connection, you may be interested in knowing that, when this picture was produced by Paramount, at its Long Island Studios in 1929, it caused very considerable nationwide protest. In addition, it was rejected, in toto, in England, in Canada, and in Australia, and the company had much difficulty in securing permission to exhibit it in a number of other foreign countries. The British objection seems to hinge upon the characterization of the several British people engaged in an illicit sex relationship, and, more importantly, in the suggestion that Hammond, the murdered man, maintained a China woman as his mistress.

We have no reason to believe that the official attitude throughout the British Empire will be any different now than it was in 1929 and 1930.

In the Warner Brothers version, the Chinese mistress was changed to a Eurasian wife.

Chapter 8

EPICS

THE TEN COMMANDMENTS

With the exception of Busby Berkeley, who end-ran the censors by relying on leggy chorus girls, the most successful evader of the Hays Office was Cecil B. De Mille. He did this through the inspired expedient of telling biblical stories. The most pious audience of censors, women's clubs, congressmen, clergymen, or editorial writers were disarmed by sin and sensation, if they bore the imprimatur of the Good Book. Normally, a scene of orgy, rape, depravity, and perversion would send the reformers out shouting for scalps; but, when the tale was ostensibly lifted from the Bible, the censors said "Amen." An audience of churchgoers could enjoy having their libidos stimulated, so long as the sinners were punished in the final reel by an avenging God.

De Mille discovered this basic truth of censorship evasion as early as 1932 when, in his biblical epic, *Sign of the Cross*, he was able to film Claudette Colbert in a bath of asses' milk, her breasts bobbing on the frothy surface like two scoops of vanilla ice cream. The censors offered no objection, nor did they carp at the later scene, in which a naked Elissa Landis is chained to a stake in the arena, about to be raped by a gorilla. De Mille's biblical extravaganzas never failed to titillate and inspire, and he never disappointed at the box office. Sin and sanctimony were an unbeatable combination. A story made the rounds at the Paramount commissary, during the filming of De Mille's biblical classic, *The Ten Commandments*. It was said that the picture was going far over budget and prompted mogul Adolph Zukor to ask De Mille, "Why don't we just do *The Five Com-*
80

mandments and see if there's a market for it?'' There was always a market for De Mille's salacious epics.

The Ten Commandments offered the most pungent example of the law of compensating values that Joe Breen's letters referred to with such frequency. When De Mille plunged into production, he would demonstrate for a legion of epic-makers—from Joseph E. Levine to Dino de Laurentiis—how to turn sin into cash, while remaining absolutely moral. De Mille would, improbably, become Mr. Class and Mr. Crass.

He reached the zenith of fashionable debauchery in *The Ten Commandments's* climactic scene. Moses is on the mountain, calling on God for guidance while, in the valley below, Edward G. Robinson is exhorting the Israelites to idolize the golden calf. So persuasive is Robinson that he triggers the sort of graphic orgy the censors would normally leave on the cutting-room floor. In a trice, there are Hebrews engaged in all manner of depravity. The wine flows and the scene grows wild. Moses returns with the commandments in easy-to-take tablet form, but not before the audience has been treated to what mountain folk like to call "hein', shein', wein', and mein'." Every conformity of multiple sex flashes across the screen, with De Mille himself providing the voiceover catalogue of sins. Once Moses returns, to the dismayed sighs of the audience, the sinners are punished by a generation of penance in the wilderness. The law of compensating values has prevailed. Sin and ye shall be punished; but, in the process, De Mille had evaded the censors. The pious public has had the most fun outside of a mud-wrestling arena. Their joy has been virtuous, vicarious, and free of guilt.

In August 1954, a script for De Mille's forthcoming epic The Ten Commandments reached the Hays Office. This was to be the De Millenium, a graphic tale of the Jews, their long and bitter bondage to the Egyptians, and the man who led them out of slavery—Charlton Heston, of course. The mildness of the Hays Office caveats is a measurement of De Mille's success in seducing the censors. On August 26th, Breen wrote to Paramount:

. . . There are certain elements in the story which require some comment from the standpoint of the code. . . .

Pages A-2 and A-3: Care will be needed in the showing of Adam and Eve . . . with regard to nudity.

There are a number of scenes throughout the script that will require particular care with regard to costumes, especially of the women. There are particularly the diaphanous garments. . . .

The orgy scenes on Pages G-9, G-13, and G-15, will also merit careful attention. [They did not receive it.]

Page C-16: This cry of "Fire!" should be omitted. . . .

SPARTACUS

Spartacus is a testament to freedom by men who knew its value. Dalton Trumbo, whose civil liberties were brutalized by Senator Joe McCarthy, wrote the screenplay, and, after much agonizing thought, Universal decided to risk putting his name on the movie. Trumbo had been blacklisted in the era of the Hollywood witch-hunts. Universal at first feared boycott of their costly film, but finally decided to put Trumbo's name on the screen—a victory of freedom.

Spartacus is the story of a fight for freedom. It tells of a Roman gladiator who led a rebellion of gladiators and a large part of the slave population of pagan Rome; and, because Spartacus is the story of man's unending struggle for freedom and dignity, the film is a metaphor for the struggle for freedom of American filmmakers in the era of movie censorship.

There is a wry irony in this spectacular tale of men struggling against impossible odds for freedom when seen in the context of censorship, which suppressed so many ingredients of free expression in the film and which nearly caused the omission of the writer's name from the screen credits.

The elements of *Spartacus* that were most troublesome to the censors were the homosexuality of a Roman commander (played by Laurence Olivier), and the violence of the gladiators in subjugation and in battle. Even after the exercise of censors' prerogatives, the film remains a riveting, epochal adventure, created with vigor and intelligence.

Violence was as much a problem as sex to the Hays Office and the Legion of Decency. Stanley Kubrick exercised great care in filming the exhilarating battle scenes, as Spartacus's slave army meets the Roman troops. Several of the battle scenes drew the spears of the Legion of Decency, which found them too gruesome by half. The Legion was especially perturbed about one shot in which a gladiator is dismembered. Kubrick used dwarfs and armless men with breakaway limbs for a chilling authenticity. These scenes were eliminated, as was a moving scene in which Varinia (Jean Simmons) watches as Spartacus (Kirk Douglas) writhes in pain during the agony of crucifixion. Her dialogue, "Oh, please die, my darling," was eliminated, and the scene was edited to give the unmistakable impression that Spartacus was dead.

On August 14, 1958, Geoffrey Shurlock, the new administrator of the censorship code, received a copy of Dalton Trumbo's first draft screenplay for Spartacus, based on Howard Fast's widely read novel. He wrote to Kathryn McTagert at Universal Studios:

> We have read the . . . screenplay for your forthcoming production of Spartacus. . . . This present version contains several important unacceptable elements. . . .
>
> There seems to be a mild suggestion that Crassus [Laurence Olivier] is probably a sex pervert. . . .
>
> Page 24: The loincloth costumes [of the gladiators] must prove adequate.
>
> Page 27: The following line seems unduly bold: "It's a waste of money training eunuchs."
>
> Page 85: The dialog on this page clearly suggests that Crassus is sexually attracted to women and men. This flavor should be completely removed. Any suggestion that Crassus finds a sexual attraction in Antonius [Tony Curtis] will have to be avoided.
>
> Page 86: The subject of sex perversion seems to be touched on in this scene. Specifically note Crassus putting his hand on the boy and his reaction to the gesture.
>
> Page 87: The reason for Antonius's frantic escape should be something other than the fact that he is repelled by Crassus's suggestive approach to him.

The Other Censors

The British reduced to a minimum the scene in which Marcellus [a guard] is killed in a soup cooker. Spartacus holds the guard's head under the boiling soup till he drowns. This scene survives in the finished film; the sexual preferences of Laurence Olivier's character did not.

Chapter 9————————————
THRILLERS

REBECCA

One would suppose that Alfred Hitchcock would have little trouble with the censors. After all, his theory of filmmaking is pointedly antiviolent. His thesis is that one need not see violent and horrific acts. Real suspense, in the Hitchcock credo, comes from the audience's fear for their heroes. Not for Hitchcock were the monsters, werewolves, gargantuan gorillas, and cat people. The censors could seldom tax him with violence and brutal crimes. Why then was director Hitchcock hounded so by the the moral guardians? It will be observed in *Rebecca*—as well as the other films in the Hitchcock oeuvre—that, if he had no need for violence, he was devoted to sex, and generally an aberrant form of sex, at that. One of Hitchcock's biographers noted: "His people make love like they're committing murder, and they commit murder like they're making love." With such a confusion of homicide and passion, it is small wonder that the master of suspense should be dogged by the censors—more often for salacity than for horror.

In *Rebecca*, Robert E. Sherwood's screen adaptation of Daphne du Maurier's haunting novel, the censor landed hard on the Hitchcock version. The novel tells a suspenseful tale of a young woman (Joan Fontaine) who marries a distinguished Englishman (Laurence Olivier), but is cowed by consciousness of his first wife's perfections. Gradually, she learns that Rebecca was actually a fiend whom her husband had murdered. Altogether it is a neat film with a menacing mood, full of hidden meanings; but that was the very element that the censors tried to destroy.

84

No murderer could go free in a Hollywood movie, whatever the provocations of his fiendish wife. Indeed, the loathsome perversions of the first wife were also forbidden. A clear case of double casino and Catch-22.

To their credit, Hitchcock—and producer David O. Selznick, who had brought the director to America—managed to maintain the malignant mortmain theme of the original, even with the crime of the husband removed and the repugnance of Rebecca somewhat sanitized. Thanks to Hitchcock's flair for evoking tension, this saturnine tale of tortured love became a viable entry in the *Wuthering Heights* school of dour, somber, ultra-British melodramas.

Doubleday had published Miss du Maurier's mystery romance in 1938, and Selznick, the master of marrying the right directors and stars to best-selling fiction, lost no time in optioning Rebecca *for the screen. By the following summer, he had sent a temporary script to the censors, and on August 24, 1939, Joe Breen wrote Selznick to give him the bad news:*

We are in receipt of the script . . . for your production entitled *Rebecca,* and I regret to be compelled to advise you that the material, in our judgment, is definitely and specifically in violation of the Production Code. . . .

The specific objections to this material is threefold:

1. As now written, it is the story of a murderer who is permitted to go off scot-free.

2. The quite inescapable inferences of sex perversion.

3. The repeated references in the dialog to the alleged illicit relationship—between Flavell and the first Mrs. de Winter [Rebecca]. . . .

Before this story can be approved by us, it will be necessary either that you establish . . . that the first Mrs. de Winter died as a result of an accident . . . or that the murderer, de Winter [Laurence Olivier], be punished for his crime. It will also be necessary that you remove entirely from the script the suggestion of sex perversion. . . .

Going through the script page by page, we respectfully direct your attention to the following . . . :

Scenes 293 et seq.: Here are the scenes in which we get the quite definite suggestion that the first Mrs. de Winter was a sex pervert. Note please Maxim's [Olivier] speech beginning with the line ". . . You'd have been more frightened if you had known the whole truth. . . . I wanted to kill her then. It was four days after we were married. . . . She was incapable of love. . . . She wasn't even normal!"

Also note in Scene 394, Maxim's line, "She . . . told me things I could never repeat to a living soul . . . "

NOTORIOUS

The Hollywood censors, with the arrogance of a monarchal decree, had arbitrarily set thirty seconds as the maximum length of a screen kiss. When the stopwatch touched thirty, you passed from the romantic to the obscene. With his customary ingenuity, Hitchcock stymied the censors with a marathon kiss in *Notorious* that went well beyond the thirty-second limit. As Cary Grant takes a phone call from his FBI chief, Ingrid Bergman is nibbling away nonstop at her lover. The osculation goes on for nearly three minutes, as Hitch mocks the limits of the code and Bergman grazes on Grant.

Indeed, Hitchcock managed to inject a healthy dose of sex into a genre where it seldom found a home—the counterspy adventure. There is little brutality in the film—the usual source of audience terror in the spy genre. There is instead a pervading atmosphere of menace, as Ingrid Bergman uses her sex appeal to invade a den of Nazis in Rio.

The Madonna-faced Bergman seems an odd choice for a tramp; but then, the saintly Jennifer Jones seems an odd choice for a half-breed sexpot in *Duel in the Sun*. Even though Bergman seems miscast as a call girl in *Notorious*'s opening scenes, the Hays Office saw to it that virtually nothing of the call-girl characterization remained in the Ben Hecht screenplay. Hecht had created what the censors called "a grossly immoral woman," for good cause, but the character was scrubbed clean before the script passed muster. She was turned from a prostitute into a gold digger; from a woman who lived by her body to one who lived by her wits.

In addition to his marathon kiss, Hitchcock managed one other bit of moral flummery at the censors' expense. The code declares that love outside of marriage, which it righteously calls "impure love," cannot be presented as worthy of emulation. Yet any mature members of the audience know, without seeing rumpled bed sheets, that Grant and Bergman have passed the hand-holding stage. Breen and Hays had dictated that promiscuity had to produce guilt and remorse, followed by death. In *Notorious*, Bergman's impure love was followed by a suggestion of endless love with Cary Grant, hardly a tortuous punishment.

On May 9, 1945, producer David O. Selznick sent Joe Breen a copy of Ben Hecht's screenplay for Notorious, *based on a story concocted by Hecht and Hitchcock. On May 25th, Breen replied with evident disapproval:*

We have read with considerable care the temporary script . . . for your proposed production titled *Notorious* and I regret to be compelled to advise you the material in its present form seems to us to be definitely unacceptable. . . .

This unacceptability is suggested principally by the characterization of your lead, Alicia [Ingrid Bergman], as a grossly immoral woman, whose immorality is accepted "in stride" in the development of the story, and who eventually is portrayed as dying a glorious heroine. [In the final film she does not die, but is carried off to a fate somewhat better than death, by Cary Grant.]

There is, too, in contrast with her immoral characterization, an almost complete absence of what might be called "compensating moral values."

In addition, the frequent references throughout the story to Alicia's gross immorality, even when the references are intended to point up and emphasize her attempted regeneration, add . . . considerably to the unacceptability of this story.

It is our thought that it might be possible to tell the story if you were to establish early that Alicia is possibly a lady who lives by her wits—a gold digger possibly, but not a prostitute.

It might be indicated that motivation for this character is prompted by her total loss of faith in her father [who has been convicted of treason], which leads her to sour on society in general, and, instead of becoming a kept woman of loose morals, such souring process might be evidenced by her determination to get what she can of life, without paying any personal price for it.

In addition, you will have in mind . . . the need for taking some counsel about this story with representatives of the FBI, the Navy Department, [and] the Brazilian Government [the Nazis were ensconced in Rio]. I think you know the industry has had a kind of "gentlemen's agreement" with Mr. J. Edgar Hoover, wherein we have practically obligated ourselves to submit to him for his consideration and approval stories which importantly involve the activities of the Federal Bureau of Investigation. [It is interesting to speculate on the incentives that brought the motion picture industry to reach a "gentlemen's agreement" with J. Edgar Hoover, whereby his approval was required every time an FBI man appeared on the screen. Could it be that movie moguls—like America's recent presidents—feared the possible existence of an FBI file on their clandestine affairs which might be made public if the bureau was slighted?]

Under the provisions of the code, we have the responsibility to "represent fairly" the history, institutions, and citizenry of friendly foreign nations. Because of this, we suggest you consult with some responsible representative of the Brazilian government—possibly the Ambassador in Washington. [Everyone knows that there were no former Nazis living in quiet splendor in South America!]

In a memo to the files, Mr. Geoffrey Shurlock, then a junior official at the Hays Office, wrote:

Messrs. Shurlock and Lynch met with Messrs. Hitchcock and Hecht . . . re *Notorious*. In general it was agreed that the characterization of the female lead would be changed in such a way to avoid any direct inference that she was a woman of loose sexual morals. . . . Mr. Hecht indicated that they now expect to have the girl not die at the end, but live and marry the hero. It was made clear that in that case it would be absolutely necessary to avoid any suggestion of sexual promiscuity or looseness on her part. . . .

On July 25th, Breen wrote to William Golden of RKO-Radio, the releasing company for this Selznick production. His goal was to proceed from the general to the specific in whitewashing the Bergman character:

This goes to you in confirmation of our conference yesterday with regard to your script *Notorious*. [It has been agreed that] the characterization of the girl as a woman of loose morals is unacceptable. . . .

The following suggestions were discussed with a view toward correcting this objection:

Page 8: In this drunken party [where Grant meets Bergman for the first time] we suggest, first of all, not overdoing the drinking and drunkenness. Second, we suggest that the *whole party* is going to Havana, and not just Alicia and the old man.

Page 11: . . . We suggest rewriting the following dialog: "What this party needs is a little gland treatment."

Page 12: We suggest omitting the line "Once aboard the lugger, the gal is mine!"

Page 28: We suggest the advisability of having Alicia definitely deny Devlin's [Cary Grant] insinuations—even though he will not believe her.

We also suggest cutting down the frequent use of the word "tramp" as applied to Alicia. . . .

Page 157: We suggest the possibility at this point of a definite statement from Devlin that he has misjudged Alicia. It might be possible to rewrite the last line of his speech to read: "I'm going to follow you around on my hands and knees begging your pardon for what I thought of you."

By September 18th, Ben Hecht had revised the screenplay in accordance with Breen's demands, and on September 21st, the chief censor wrote to the studio:

We have read the script dated September 18th for the motion picture *Notorious*. . . . It might be possible to save a lot of rewriting if at some point your heroine were to definitely deny all these imputations [of promiscuity]; but, inasmuch as, in the present version she doesn't do this, the flavor remains that she is an immoral woman.

Page 4 et seq: We get the inescapable flavor that she and Ernest are living together.

Pages 16–17: Please change the line "Who . . . undressed me?" and the further line, "I rubbed you down—you were soaked." . . .

Page 41: We suggest rewriting this sequence to get away from the present flavor that these officials [Louis Calhern, Grant, etc.] know they are hiring a promiscuous woman. It might be possible to rewrite to to indicate that they decide to hire her because they know that Sebastian [Claude Raines] was once very much in love with her, omitting all innuendo as to her immoral character. [This was done.] Please omit the underline words in the line, "Miss Huberman [Bergman], morals aside, was chosen because . . ."

The Other Censors

Ireland banned the film for "ignoring the moral law by the casual treatment of marriage. . . . Ingrid Bergman marries a man in order to obtain from him military secrets and, at the same time, is carrying on an amorous intrigue with her lover."

STRANGERS ON A TRAIN

It has become a truism to assert that Alfred Hitchcock taught us to share the terror of the world that he admittedly suffered from himself. The tension in Hitchcock films springs from the confrontation between sanity and insanity, of the middle-class victim and the demented villain. *Strangers on a Train*, one of the director's most riveting films, presents this juxtaposition. It is intriguing that the architects of the censorship code, in forbidding nearly every social and sexual aberration—from drug addiction to perversion—failed to prohibit a depiction of madness. This oversight opened a rich vein for Hitchcock. The director's victims are almost invariable unbalanced, as in *Psycho* or *Vertigo*, and the melodrama flows from their dementia. In *Strangers on a Train*, the charming madman, Robert Walker, traps the boring tennis player, Farley Granger, and sucks us into his manic world.

The Hays Office had no objection to the distorted vision of Robert Walker. Many would find the sociopathic playboy obscene in his plan and perspective, but the censors were more concerned with the manifestations of his madness, not its roots. Hence, their niggling complaints were leveled at the scene where he demonstrates the art of murder at a cocktail party to the amusement of a wealthy matron. They bridled at the idea that he might be spending the weekend with a woman. They carped over the hero's wish to divorce his trampish wife; marriage was a sacrament, even when one's wife was carrying a lover's child. So, while the censors occupied themselves with relative trivialities, Hitchcock palmed the ace.

Like many of his other thrillers, *Strangers* is an imaginative suspense drama in which the palms grow moist. Raymond Chandler, the prolific creator of Philip Marlowe, combined with the director to write this tale of a neurotic playboy, Bruno Anthony, who wants to kill his father. On a train he meets a young man, Guy Cunningham, who is saddled with a promiscuous wife. He proposes trading murders so that neither will have an ostensible motive. The madman commits his half of the weird bar-

gain, then tries to force his innocent partner to deliver his share
of the deal by threatening to frame him.

In *Strangers on a Train*, more than in most of Hitchcock's
films, we see the director as a brilliant deviser of thumbscrews,
who delights in demonstrating for us our infinite capacity for
inflicting pain. It is ironic that the movie censors, whose job it
was to filter out scenes of sadism, brutality, and torture, should
have made so little effort and had so little success in eliminating these psychological agonies from Hitchcock's film.

*On October 9, 1950, Joe Breen wrote Jack L. Warner to tell
him of his misgivings on the Raymond Chandler/Alfred Hitchcock screenplay he had just received:*

We have read the script . . . for your proposed production
Strangers on a Train. . . . We feel there is an important element
in the story that does not meet the code requirements. . . . This
unacceptable element is the treatment of Guy's [Farley Granger]
marriage to Miriam [his trampish wife]. As presently written, we
feel this is an unacceptably light treatment of marriage. . . .

We feel also that the element of Miriam's extra-marital pregnancy should be eliminated. [It was not.] Such a delicate situation would require the most extreme care in its treatment on the
screen if it were to be acceptable. . . . We believe the story motivation is this plot would be sufficiently strong without the element of the illegitimate pregnancy.

Going through the script page by page, we call your attention
to [the following]:

Page 27: Please rewrite Mrs. Anthony's [Bruno's mother] speech.
. . . She seems to suspect that her son is going away for the
weekend with a girl.

Page 57: Please eliminate Anne's [Ruth Roman] speech:
"Even if you had done it, I'd have stuck by you. If you'd had
anything to do with it, I would have gone into hiding with
you anywhere." This speech has about it a condonation of
wrongdoing. . . .

Page 93: Please eliminate the reference to arsenic. We would
like to suggest that you substitute the word poison. . . .

Page 181A et seq: This fight scene must be handled with care
to avoid unacceptable brutality. Specifically, there should be no
kicking or kneeing. . . .

*By November 7th, Chandler and Hitchcock had made revisions
in their script, and Breen forwarded his complaints:*

Page 39: We assume that Professor Collins will not be offensively drunk. . . .

Page 89–90: Care will be needed with this scene in which Bruno demonstrates how he could strangle Mrs. Cunningham. Specifically, the close-up scene . . . should not be such as to show any questionable detail of the strangling. It should be handled largely by suggestion. [Of course, suggestion rather than explication was Hitchcock's forte.]

The Other Censors

Maryland censors eliminated the scene of Bruno strangling Miriam, as revealed in a reflector. They also deleted a line spoken by Barbara [Anne's kid sister] to her family and Guy: "I think it would be wonderful to have a man love you so much he'd kill for you"; and in the discussion of murder, by Bruno to Mrs. Cunningham, Maryland removed Bruno's speech: "Poison could take anywhere from ten to twelve weeks, if poor Mr. Cunningham is going to die from natural causes. I could take him out on the common, and when we get to a lonely spot, knock him on the head with a hammer, pour gasoline over him and over the car, and set the whole thing ablaze." [The Maryland censors were apparently afraid that, given these explicit instructions, Baltimore would be aglow with fiery cars.]

Maryland also eliminated the scene of Bruno strangling Mrs. Cunningham, including all close-ups of his thumb and fingers as he pressed them against her throat, causing her to gasp.

REAR WINDOW

The Hays Office was hypersensitive to displays of voyeurism. In films from *Gold Diggers of 1933* to *Baby Doll*, they have chastised filmmakers over the scenes of leering sexual curiosity. Yet to a remarkable degree, Alfred Hitchcock's work has dealt with voyeurism and suffered minimal restraint. Indeed the director has turned his audiences into a pack of voyeurs in the dark, shyly inspecting the lives of others. Nowhere is this practice more evident than in *Rear Window*; and yet, with all the complaints leveled at the script, never do the censors protest the fundamental voyeurism of the film.

Rear Window is like a metaphor of all Hitchcock's thrillers.

To some it is a slice of life; to others a slice of murder. Hitch's camera roams a courtyard in Greenwich Village. In his apartment, a magazine photographer [James Stewart] sits and examines his neighbors. Immobilized by a broken leg, he has nothing but his binoculars and his voyeuristic impulses to occupy him. He observes Miss Lonelyhearts, a man-hungry woman, an energetic ballet dancer, a honeymoon couple, and a murder in the making—a coarse jewelry salesman and his invalid wife. Tension grows as the photographer sees the salesman make several excursions with a suitcase, wrap a saw, and kill a dog who has been digging in the courtyard garden. The dog's curiosity is as lethal as the photographer's. Hitchcock joyfully shows us the violent, psychotic side of life, challenges us to peek in at it, and then traps us amidst the terror—as he traps the curious cameraman.

Hitchcock gave the censors plenty to protest about in the revealed lives of Miss Lonelyhearts, the ballet dancer, and the honeymooners. He also raised some hackles with the intimacies of photographer Stewart and his girlfriend, Grace Kelly. Nor did the censors appreciate the calculated coarseness of Stewart's housekeeper (Thelma Ritter). Indeed, they protested everything but the voyeuristic curiosity of the hero—and the audience that joined him at his binoculars. In a larger sense, *Rear Window* is an exemplary comment on the voyeurism of going to the movies.

On October 20, 1953, Paramount Pictures sent Joe Breen a copy of Rear Window, *the John Michael Hayes script based on a short story by Cornell Woolrich. Breen responded on November 1st with a letter to Paramount's Luigi Luraschi:*

We have read the script . . . for your proposed production *Rear Window*. . . .

Page 2: The picturization of the young girl who is described as wearing only black panties is unacceptable. It is apparent that she is nude above the waist. . . . We feel that this gives the entire section the flavor of a peep show, which is unacceptable. Moreover, I am sure you know we cannot approve scenes of girls clad only in panties and bra. They should be wearing at least a full slip.

Page 16: Stella's [Thelma Ritter] line: ". . . When General Motors has to go to the bathroom ten times a day, the whole country's ready to let go," should be rewritten to get away from its present impression of being toilet humor.

Page 21: Stella's line ". . . until you can't tell a petting party from an army physical. . . ."

Page 23 et seq: The entire element of the newly married couple, as seen through the window of their apartment, from time to time, is unacceptable as a play on the sexual aspects of a honeymoon.

Page 34: The action described as ". . . which shows off her figure to great advantage, especially when she leans toward three assorted men," would seem to indicate an unacceptable exposure of this girl's breasts.

Page 51: The undressing scene at this point seems to be unacceptably suggestive. . . . Specifically, we should not see the girl beginning to remove her brassiere.

Page 62: Lisa's [Grace Kelly] line, "Homework. It's more interesting," is unacceptably sex suggestive. . . .

Page 74: The laundry that the young girl is hanging out should not include any intimate feminine garments. . . .

Page 99 et seq: We think too much emphasis is given to the fact that Lisa is moving into Jeff's apartment . . . and the display of her pajamas, underwear, and other paraphernalia [should be] eliminated.

Page 115: The action of a man attempting to seduce Miss Lonelyhearts appears to become excessively sex suggestive. . . .

The Other Censors

India deleted a scene in which Grace Kelly is sitting on the thigh of James Stewart, "in which they are cuddling and kissing." They deleted one foot of film, and also the close embrace of Kelly and Stewart, another two feet.

THE BIRDS

Hitchcock's horror usually has a psychological flavor. He flaunts the conventional wisdom of Hollywood that violence and brutality lift an audience from its seat. He creates his effects by making the audience fearful for the screen character with whom they empathize. There are no bamboo shoots under the fingernails. Hitchcock rarely departs from this formula for terror through anticipation. An exception that proved the rule—and brought down on him the wrath of the censors—was *The Birds*. Here the director was very direct—he showed a gull swooping down to carve a chunk out of Tippi Hedrin's scalp. In another scene, we cringe at the gruesome details, as a flock of crows go gouging their way through a group of fleeing children. This was a more brutal, bloody presentation than Hitchcock fans, in or out of the Hays Office, were accustomed to seeing.

Censors rarely had to warn Hitchcock about undue gruesomeness. Not for him were giant apes devouring extras. True, in *Strangers on a Train* Robert Walker stomps on Farley Granger's knuckles, and in *Psycho* there was the memorable shower scene; but, generally, Hitchcock was less physical in his terror. With Hitchcock there was always a pattern of cumulative menace rising to an unbearable crescendo. In *The Birds* the threat was more palpable. The monsters were more diminutive than King Kong, but just as threatening, as when a flock of finches come flooding into a living room through the fireplace.

In his startling biography of Hitchcock, *The Dark Side of Genius*, Donald Spoto writes of how the director drove Tippi Hedrin to the brink of breakdown by exposing her to the attack of birds in the horrific attic scene, tying the hysterical birds to her supine body. The Hays Office frequently commanded filmmakers to seek the cooperation of the ASPCA to prevent the torture of animals. Under the circumstances, they might have summoned some other ASPCA—the American Society for the Prevention of Cruelty to Actresses.

In *The Birds*, Hitchcock created a genuine monster film, a tale of horror and a dramatic tour de force. His source was Daphne du Maurier's novella about a flock of birds who adopt the hunt-and-peck system with their mass attack on a village's horrified inhabitants. He created an unusual problem for the censors, who were unaccustomed to a marriage of Hitchcock and brutality. In *The Birds* they cried fowl.

In November 1961 Hitchcock sent the Hays Office a screenplay by Evan Hunter based on the du Maurier novella. Censor chief Geoffrey Shurlock replied with a letter to Peggy Robertson of Hitchcock's company:

We have read the script dated November 14, 1961, for your proposed production *The Birds*. . . .

We are seriously concerned . . . with one aspect of this unusual story—the gruesome details of the several attacks by the
birds on the human beings.

As we envision this action, we feel it could be presented in
such a shocking, brutal, and bloody way as to be unacceptable
motion picture fare. We must urge you most carefully to consider
this particular aspect as you plan and eventually execute the
staging of this action.

Page 65: It is unacceptable to show Melanie [Tippi Hedrin]
only in a bra and a skirt. . . .

As you know, the use of the words "hell" and "damn" when
restricted to one or two absolutely essential expressions is acceptable. [The code had recently been amended to this effect]
But the indiscriminate and repeated casual use of such expressions becomes offensive. We would like to suggest that you reex-
amine the script with the idea of eliminating all but one or two
of which you feel are indispensable.

*In January 1962 a shooting script reached the Hays Office and
Geoffrey Shurlock responded with this letter to Hitchcock:*

We have received the final script dated January 26, 1962, for your
proposed production *The Birds*. . . . In accordance with code
requirements, please consult with Mr. James Jack of the American Humane Association as to all scenes in which animals are
used. . . .

[Sadly, Hitchcock and the Hays Office showed more solicitude
for the birds than for the leading lady, who suffered grievously
under avian attack.]

Page 103: We again stress the importance of avoiding scenes
of excessive gruesomeness. . . .

Page 168: It would be important to avoid any offensive exploitation of the girl's nudity.

Chapter 10

COMEDIES

NINOTCHKA

The primary problem of filmmakers was the Hays Office and the state censorship boards that dotted the American landscape, but there was the occasional film which, due to its innocuous subject matter, was totally acceptable to American censors, but which surprisingly infuriated the foreign censors. One of these was *Ninotchka*, an airy comedy that offended the censors of most countries with Communist regimes. When *Ninotchka*, which had originally been released by MGM in 1939, was rereleased in 1946, the Communists were striving to assume power in Italy. Since the film mocked the repressive bureaucracy and humorless mien of the Soviets, Italy's anti-Communists used the film as a political weapon, exhibiting it all over the Italian boot. The movie was displayed everywhere, in movie houses, meeting halls, storefronts, and garages. Ultimately, the Italian censors banned the film, as "offensive to Communists." Estonia and Lithuania likewise rejected the film. Said the Lithuanian censor, in a prudent display of obsequiousness toward the power to their east: "The film reflects unfavorably on the feelings of a friendly neighbor." Despite this respect for Soviet sensibilities, the Lithuanian sparrow was gobbled up by the Russian bear.

When *Ninotchka* was released, Hollywood wags reflected that Joe Stalin might recall his emissary from MGM. It was, after all, an impudent and malicious show, which burlesqued the Bolsheviks unmercifully, and, at that stage in the Russian Revolution, such hardliners as Molotov were not famous for their sense of humor or their ability to laugh at their own foibles.

The film tells the story of a solemn Soviet commissar, played

97

with surprising comic élan by Greta Garbo, who is sent to Paris to sell the jewels of a Grand Duchess. There she meets an American capitalist [Melvyn Douglas] and learns of love, sex, and other irrelevancies to collectivism. In 1955, Cole Porter and Abe Burrows adapted *Ninotchka* to the Broadway musical stage under the title *Silk Stockings*. Cole Porter's bawdy lyrics were predictably absent when *Silk Stockings* became a Fred Astaire musical, with Cyd Charisse as Ninotchka. Missing were such censorable Porter lines as:

> But she knows that they will travel miles
> She can always lay 'em in the aisles
> If she's wearing silk and satin
> She can flatten Lord Mountbatten . . .

The Garbo comedy managed to stay clear of censorship trouble in America, despite the fact that the film—written by Billy Wilder and Charles Brackett—was in essence a bedroom comedy, whose fundamental ingredients were sex, sin, and temptation. In directing the frothy concoction, Ernst Lubitsch was his usual nimble self in keeping the lovers chaste and vertical. Lubitsch was a master of sanitized sex, and his footwork kept him free of the American puritanism, but he failed to reckon with the censorship of politics when *Ninotchka* crossed the Atlantic.

In the spring of 1939, as Hitler was indulging his appetite in Western Europe, Louis B. Mayer sent the screenplay of Ninotchka to the Hays Office. On May 24th, Joe Breen replied:

We have read the temporary script for your proposed production *Ninotchka*. . . .
    . . . We respectfully direct your attention to the following . . . . :
    Page 40: Ninotchka's [Greta Garbo] use of the word "biological" . . . as well as the line "I acknowledge the existence of a natural impulse," and Leon's [Melvyn Douglas] reply: "What could I possibly do to encourage such an impulse?" are questionable. . . .
    [Sixteen years later, undeterred by censors, Cole Porter would translate that offensive biological reference into a risqué song for the Broadway musical version. It was called "It's a Chemical Reaction, That's All" and included the lines:

> When the electromagnetic of the he-male
> Meets the electromagnetic of the female

If right away she should say come and be male
It's a chemical reaction, that's all."]

Page 72: We presume there will be no suggestion of a sexual affair between Leon and Ninotchka. . . .

Page 107: We ask that you rephrase Swana's speech, "I assure you, no visas will be necessary for my chateau."

Page 113: . . . Please make certain that the piece of lingerie that Ninotchka gives to Anna is not a pair of panties.

The Other Censors

Italy banned the film as offensive to Communists.

France banned the film, but approved it on appeal.

Mexico's censor passed the film, but it was vigorously opposed by the Mexican labor unions, which contained a strong Communist element.

Yugoslavia deleted footage showing a parade in Moscow.

Estonia rejected the film.

Lithuania rejected the film.

Bulgaria rejected the film because it showed:

1. Submarine warfare
2. Satires on Communist Russia.

MR. SMITH GOES TO WASHINGTON

When all the rival studios of Hollywood, with unaccustomed solidarity, agreed to set up a self-censoring machinery called the Hays Office, it was primarily over fear that the U.S. Congress, in its wisdom, might pass federal legislation mandating government censorship of the movie industry. Any who feel that such fears might have been paranoid are invited to examine the results triggered by Frank Capra's classic comedy, *Mr. Smith Goes to Washington*. Congress is a powerful body that can severely punish an industry that affronts it.

The film deals with an upstanding young man who is appointed to fill in the unexpired term of a deceased U.S. senator and who discovers a conspiracy on the part of certain senators to secure a large appropriation of federal funds for the damming of a creek in his home state. He stages a filibuster on the Senate floor that succeeds in exposing the fraud. An innocent, inspiring story, was it not? It was not, said the gentlemen of Capitol Hill. The U.S. Senate felt itself cruelly maligned by the motion picture industry and struck back. They wounded the movie moguls where they would be pained the most—in the wallet. They promptly passed Senate Bill No. 280, which made compulsory block booking of films illegal. The law demolished the vast and hugely profitable distribution system of the movie industry.

Director Frank Capra and Columbia Pictures president Harry Cohn did not foresee the volcanic effect of their film. Perhaps they failed to correctly assess the vanity of U.S. legislators. They held the world premiere of *Mr. Smith Goes to Washington* in the nation's capital. They invited every senator and congressman in Washington to the event. The National Press Club sponsored the affair and four thousand VIPs attended the screening in Constitution Hall. There were national radio broadcasts, reporters, and photographers by the score. Columbia's publicity department was congratulating itself on a breathtaking coup, but as the first reel spun along, it was not long before the distinguished senators were squirming in their seats. After all, Mr. Smith's appointment comes from a crooked governor who is dominated by a machine politician. Scenes on the Senate floor depict the Senate as smugly acquiescent in the perpetuation of fraud. Senators snooze as the voters are deceived. Congressional resentment rose sharply.

Believing itself ridiculed by *Mr. Smith,* the members of the most august body showed Hollywood the danger of maligning the mighty with the passage of the Neely Anti-Blockbooking Bill. It was a brutal reminder (if any had been needed) of the wisdom in creating the Production Code to forestall the interference and ire of the U.S. Congress. Hollywood had kept Washington neutral by keeping the screen relatively free of sex and sensationalism. What Hollywood failed to assess was that the U.S. Senate was far more sensitive to insult than to smut.

The initial interest in Mr. Smith Goes to Washington *(its source was a novel called* The Gentleman from Montana*) came from Paramount Pictures. A copy of the book was sent to the Hays Office in January 1938. Joe Breen, in his wisdom, saw trouble:*

> We have received with great interest the novel *The Gentleman from Montana,* which you submitted for our consideration. . . . This novel seems to us to present *enormous* problems. . . .

. Briefly, it is the story of a young scoutmaster [James Stewart] appointed to fill out the unexpired term of a U.S. senator, caused by the death of the senator from Montana. In Washington, he finds himself confronted by a network of crooked politicians, centering around a "pork barrel" rider, attached to an important administration bill sponsored by his companion senator from Montana [Claude Rains], at the behest of the Montana public utilities. He finally succeeds in getting this rider eliminated by means of a filibuster, and puts across his own bill for the establishment of a Boy Scout national park.

The difficulties that we sense in this story fall under the following general headings:

The United States Senate is a body of politicians who, if not deliberately crooked, are completely controlled by lobbyists. . . .

The unflattering portrayal of several senators from various specific states create the indication that a large number of senators are willing to barter their votes for tickets to the World Series.

The generally unflattering portrayal of our system of government, which might well lead to the picture being considered, both here and particularly abroad, as a covert attack on the democratic form of government.

For the above reason, we most earnestly ask that you take serious counsel before embarking on a production of any motion picture based on this story. . . . It looks to us like it might be loaded with dynamite . . . for the motion picture industry. . . .

Unfortunately for the motion picture industry, Breen's warnings fell on deaf ears. Even his prescience did not enable him to see the form the Senate vengeance would take. His words unheeded, the film business suffered a crushing blow.

Louis B. Mayer of MGM had also expressed interest in The Gentleman from Montana, and Breen sent the same letter, with its apocalyptic warnings, to Mayer. The flames of interest at Paramount and Metro had been damped, but Harry Cohn of Columbia Pictures had discovered The Gentleman from Montana. Geoffrey Shurlock wrote a memo to the files on the appealing but dangerous novel:

G.S. had lunch with Mr. [Rouben] Mamoulian who has indicated his interest in this story for Columbia. He has not yet read our correspondence [with Paramount and MGM] on it. I explained the difficulties presented by the original story and he was quite in accord with our attitude. However, he feels the story can be rewritten so as to remove all the questionable elements. [Famous last words.] He is to read our correspondence on the subject and will attempt a new treatment.

By January 1939, Sidney Buchman had completed a first draft screenplay based on The Gentleman from Montana. *Harry Cohn sent it to the Hays Office, and on January 30th Joe Breen wrote to Harry Cohn:*

We have read the first draft . . . for your proposed production titled *The Gentleman from Montana.* . . . We respectfully direct your attention to the following . . . :

Page 83: We suggest you eliminate from Saunders's [Jean Arthur] speech, "I was fed up with dirty politics—couldn't stand another minute of it—sick to death—those monkeys on a string. . . ."

Page 115: We suggest you eliminate or rewrite Saunders's line "Congressmen have done antics for the newspapers before."

Page 214: We suggest that you omit . . . Saunders's speech beginning with the line: "Me? How could I be decent? How could I have a shred of decency left. . . ."

On April 17th, Breen amplified his comments to Cohn with a further letter pinpointing dialogue that might offend Washington legislators:

Page 124: You might wish to consider the following dialog [directed to Mr. Smith]: "This isn't any place for you. You're halfway decent. You don't know it, but you're up to your knees in slime."

Page 175: We also suggest that you give further consideration to the advisability of the line ". . . and can buy the men to come here and get dams legislated."

By March 8, 1939, Joe Breen had consulted with his boss, Will Hays, about any possible problems accruing to the movie business from Mr. Smith. Incredibly, for a man whose life had centered about Washington as a member of President Harding's cabinet, Hays did not see the latent dangers in the film. Cynics may reflect that, as a member of the most corrupt administration of the century, Hays was conditioned to the aroma of pol-

itics and did not perceive that honest public servants might be outraged at implied attacks. Breen wrote to Cohn:

> In connection with your proposed picture titled *Mr. Smith Goes to Washington* and the general question of industry policy that is suggested by this story, I am pleased to advise you that Mr. Hays is of the opinion that the material is likely to be acceptable, *if* you exercise the greatest possible care in indicating that the indictment of members of the Congress is not a wholesale indictment, but rather an indictment of Senator Fletcher and the three congressmen who engage in a conspiracy. [In true bureaucratic style, Breen had passed the buck to Hays, and, when Hays failed to see the yawning maw of the dragon, Breen gave Columbia the all-clear.]
>
> It is advisable for you to emphasize that [most] Senators and Congressmen are sturdy men of integrity and are motivated by the highest possible ideals, and that it is only these few . . . who are guilty of any unethical and dishonest practices. . . .

MR. DEEDS GOES TO TOWN

There is something so wholesome, so decent, so thoroughly American in his taciturn and gangly manner, that is hard to see how the censors could fault a film in which he appeared. Yet they carped at the sleeping bag he shared with Ingrid Bergman in *For Whom the Bell Tolls,* and they disapproved of his Quaker wife wielding a pistol in *High Noon.* Gary Cooper's image would seem to have been immune to censorship. When his artless manner was combined with the special warmth of director Frank Capra, it would seem likely to disarm the self-proclaimed moralists. Of course, this same Frank Capra stirred a storm of injured virtue on the Potomac with *Mr. Smith Goes to Washington,* and the censors did not appreciate the joke Capra played at their expense in *It Happened One Night.* In his famous Walls of Jericho scene, in deference to the censors' sensibilities, Clark Gable hangs a blanket across the motel room he shares with Claudette Colbert.

Admittedly, the Hays Office found little to complain about in *Mr. Deeds Goes to Town.* Released in the midst of the Depression, this sentimental comedy had a spontaneity and joy that American audiences embraced. Cooper played Longfellow Deeds, a simple man leading an uneventful life in Mandrake Falls, writing greeting cards and playing the tuba in the town band. He inherits his late uncle's estate of twenty million dollars. From then on, all is chaos for Mr. Deeds. He is hounded by people bent on defrauding him, and the only person he trusts, the inevitable sob sister (Jean Arthur), betrays him. When he learns of her perfidy, he decides to give away his millions. To the Hollywood set, this constituted true obscenity, but it did not violate the code.

When *Mr. Deeds* premiered in New York on April 16, 1936, Hitler was on the march and America's sympathies were clearly with his victims. This was reason enough for German censors to reject the film, and indeed they did. Yet, according to Robert Kaufman, the Hollywood screenwriter and producer, when Russian troops smashed into Hitler's bunker at Berchtesgarten, they found three American films of which the führer was inordinately fond. They were *It Happened One Night*, *Top Hat*, and *Mr. Deeds Goes to Town*.

In the summer of 1935, Columbia's Harry Cohn assigned screenwriter Robert Riskin to write a scenario based on a short story called "Opera Hat" by Clarence Budington Kelland. The script was sent to the Hays Office, and on August 29th, Breen sent a letter of modest concern to Cohn:

> We have read the first draft of your script *The Opera Hat.* . . .
>
>   Page 33: A substitution should be made for the word "Nuts!" ["Nuts" was one of the forbidden exclamations listed in the censorship code, doubtless because of its genital implications. In an early Bette Davis epic, when the censors protested the ejaculation "Nuts!", the screenwriter changed the word to "Almonds!"]
>
>   Page 37: The word "lousy" is liable to be censored. . . .
>
>   Pages 73–74: The dialog concerning the procuring of women for Longfellow [Gary Cooper] is plainly suggestive and offensive. . . .
>
>   Page 77: Censors delete the word "snatch." . . .
>
>   Page 102 et seq: The episode of the chiseling girl being planted in Longfellow's bedroom, is objectionable to us as now written. . . . It is certainly objectionable for her to step out of bed in undies. . . .

On December 13th, Breen had examined more of the Mr. Deeds *script and wrote to Harry Cohn:*

Page 50: The underlined words in the bodyguard's speech ". . . stick to your tail" and Longfellow's reply, "I don't want anybody sticking to my tail" should be deleted.

The Other Censors

Germany rejected the film without stated reason.
Ohio censors deleted the scene where a character is talking to Mr. Deeds about producing women for his entertainment.

TOPPER

Cosmo Topper was a metaphor for the movie censor of the thirties. The creation of adman-turned-author Thorne Smith, Topper was fortyish, respectably suburban, dead to romance and adventure, and sexually repressed beyond all hope of redemption. In the movie *Topper*, which was optioned for the screen by the Hal Roach Studios, Topper is shocked and repelled by the blatant, bawdy sex that his friends, the Kerbys, try to bring into his life. Like the Hollywood censors, Cosmo Topper badly needs some loosening up. He is appalled to find himself involved with a most intimate item of female lingerie, too much liquor, and a delicious roommate. Unlike the censors, however, Cosmo Topper gives in to the high spirits of his friends, George and Marion Kerby, whose mortal existence ends in a car crash, at which point they are transformed into a pair of rowdy and lascivious ghosts. Joe Breen and Will Hays resisted the temptation to sink to the sinful and sensational level of some of Hollywood's rowdy screenwriters.

The vogue of madcap sex comedies that swamped Hollywood during the Depression led to the inevitable discovery of the prankish, sensual novels of Thorne Smith. The key ingredients of his books—and the key ingredients of *Topper*—were fantasy and sex. Smith's books seem rather tame today, just as the sins that Joe Breen protested in the thirties seem tame and almost charming in their innocence.

In the farcical film, Cosmo Topper (Roland Young) is a repressed bank president who encounters playboy George Kerby (Cary Grant) and his uninhibited wife Marion (Constance Bennett). When their car overturns on an icy road, the Kerbys are transformed into ghosts. They repent their useless lives as humans and resolve to perform one worthwhile deed. That the deed was to brighten the humdrum life of Cosmo Topper with a constant round of debauchery, drink, and diabolical sexuality, was not what the impeccable Hays Office considered "worthwhile."

On March 18, 1937, Joseph Breen wrote to Nat O'Brien of the Hal Roach Studios to tell him his mordant reactions to the screenplay for Topper. *Wrote Breen:*

We have received and read the final script for your proposed picture *Topper* and regret to inform you that this story is a violation of the principles of the Production Code. A picture made from this present script would result in one which we would be forced to reject. The violations in this script which cause the above decision are:

    1. All the business to do with the embroidered panties.

    2. The sexual implication and flavor which came into the script through Marion Kerby's efforts to advance the rejuvenation of Topper, their trip to the Sea Breeze Hotel, causing him great embarrassment, and most of the details and dialog around the hotel . . . are decidedly unacceptable.

    Page 51, Scene 106: The underlined portion of Topper's line, "Oh, but I can remember you, <u>every alluring curve of you,</u>" must be eliminated.

    Page 137, Scene 289: George's dialog ". . . I'm going down there and kick her in the pants!"

When the filming of Topper *was complete and the representatives of the Hays Office screened a rough cut of the film, they agreed to issue their seal of approval, but only on the condition that certain objectionable elements of the film were removed. Breen wrote to Hal Roach:*

We had the pleasure this afternoon of witnessing a projection room showing of your feature production titled *Topper.* . . . Enclosed here is the association's formal Certificate of Approval . . . with the understanding the following cuts will be made:

    1. The line where Cary Grant says, "Tell him to go and C-O-P somewhere else."

    2. Two lines: "Who was she, a striptease girl?" and Roland Young's line, "Certainly, she was a striptease artist."

    3. The reaction of the fat lady after she is hit on the poste-

rior, and her subsequent line, "I'm not accustomed to be slapped in the lobby . . ."

The Other Censors

Belgium eliminated the words "fallen woman," so that the film might be shown to children.

The Dutch East Indians eliminated the line, "No one but a fallen woman would do a thing like this." They also eliminated the line "Oh, confound it, madam, if he wants the pants let him have them."

Japan deleted all kissing scenes and eliminated the scene of the cop taking a milk bottle from Marion and throwing it into the trash can. It also deleted all references to butt-biting, scanty clothing, dressing, beds, and living on top of a volcano. It eliminated the line "None that I like as well as you."

Ohio and Massachusetts passed the film without eliminations.

HERE COMES MR. JORDAN

Late show and video addicts who have seen the 1941 comedy *Here Comes Mr. Jordan* or the eighties version, *Heaven Can Wait,* concocted by Warren Beatty and Buck Henry, will doubtless find the films delightful examples of fantasy and farce. They will hardly see the story from the perspective of the censors who first encountered the Columbia film. To the Hays Office the movie invaded territory seldom, if ever, explored for humorous purposes. The censors feared that moviegoers of deep religious conviction would find it difficult to see humor in a pictorial presentation of life after death. They viewed this as a bold undertaking and had deep reservations about the story. The Hays Office was not ready in the winter of 1940 to abandon their serious convictions about what became of people when they died or to trust that the general public would be emotionally equipped to lay aside their own beliefs on the subject long enough to enjoy the comedy.

Here Comes Mr. Jordan tells the story of a boxer whose spirit is grabbed prematurely by supernatural agents. The ethereal creatures (Claude Rains and Edward Everett Horton in the original, James Mason and Buck Henry in the remake) agree to let the boxer live out his allotted span, but, since our hero has been cremated, they agree to return his spirit to a satisfactory substitute.

The Catholic Legion of Decency was such a driving force in the enforcement of the censorship code that the religious aspects of Hollywood films preoccupied the censors very nearly as much as the sexual ones. Hence, Breen was sensitive to giving offense to legions of churchgoers with this amusing mixture of fiction and fantasy. Whatever Joe Breen's personal views on afterlife and predestination, he did not relish boycotts by pious folk who felt themselves affronted by a mockery of their most deeply held beliefs.

In December 1940, Harry Cohn of Columbia Studios sent a treatment (an explicit narration) of the story Heaven Can Wait *to the Hays Office. On December 15th, Joe Breen responded:*

I have just received the play treatment for your production *Heaven Can Wait* and advise you that, as now written, it seems in violation of Production Code.

We consider the use of some religious concepts as a springboard for this comedy-fantasy might give offense to the mass of churchgoers. For example, the angel impersonating characters of Mr. Jordan [Claude Rains] and the various messengers, the references to the Recording Angel, especially "the Chief," will be taken as a derogatory satire on the religious beliefs of large numbers of people.

Secondly, certain religious groups will resent any expressed opinion on the controversial topic of predestination.

However, according to an agreement reached at the conference with [executives] of your studio . . . it was agreed that a screenplay be attempted. . . .

Going through your planned treatment in detail, we call your attention to the following points . . . :

1. . . . This script should be written with no drinking in it whatsoever. . . .

2. It is understood that all profanity will be omitted.

3. Please handle the proposed relationship between Penny and Mr. Farnsworth with care.

4. Finally, we recommend that any conversation [about] future life, recording angels, etc. . . . be either omitted entirely or worded very carefully. . . .

BEDTIME FOR BONZO

Because of Ronald Reagan's ideological views on the subject of sex in films and his attorney general's continued attacks on pornography, it is interesting to note how this innocuous film, in which Reagan costarred with a chimpanzee, was greeted by the censors.

It is further interesting to perceive Ronald Reagan's personal taste for sexual humor. For a public figure who deplores the sexual content of films and magazines (he expressed regret that his son Ron was writing for *Playboy*), Reagan has displayed a surprising taste for humor that is either sexual or scatological. He once cracked that "gays could find a home in the Department of Parks," and coming out of anesthesia after surgery, doctors reported that he told "a dirty joke." Many Reagan jokes have had about them the aroma of the barnyard.

That the Hays Office would find cause for objection in *Bedtime for Bonzo* is surprising. The contrived story is as titillating as a sister's kiss. It is the story of a psychology professor [Ronald Reagan] who, with the use of a chimpanzee, seeks to prove that environment is more important than heredity, in order to win the love of the Dean's daughter. Very racy ingredients to be sure.

Just as Reagan has traveled far since this 1950 film, so has its director, Fred De Cordova. De Cordova is the genial, witty executive producer of "The Tonight Show," where Johnny Carson regularly lampoons De Cordova's former star. Reagan's humor is often as salacious as Carson's, but the innocent delivery of both removes any possible stigma.

The screenplay for the best known and most ridiculed film of Ronald Reagan was sent to Joe Breen in June 1950 by William Gordon of Universal Studios. On July 7th, Breen responded:

We have read the second draft continuity . . . for your proposed production *Bedtime for Bonzo*. . . .

Going through the script in detail we wish to call your attention to the following . . . :

At the outset we direct your particular attention to the need for the greatest possible care in the selection of . . . dresses of your women. The Production Code makes it mandatory that the intimate parts of the body, specifically the breasts of women, be fully covered at all times. . . .

Valery's line, "Is there any law that says we have to raise a family?" seems unduly pointed. . . .

The humor surrounding bottles of milk and the dialog referring thereto, have an offensive connotation. . . .

Along this line we ask that you alter the following dialog: "After one week on your Grade A alone, I feel like a new man . . ."

Page 112: "Razzberry" is on the Association's list of unacceptable words and expressions and could not be approved.

Chapter 11

THE MARX BROTHERS

MONKEY BUSINESS

When Groucho Marx appeared as the star of a long-running TV game show called "You Bet Your Life," he worked out an accommodation with the television censors. Each week he would tape an hour's worth of the show. Then his producers would cut out all Groucho's bawdy, naughty lines. This would leave thirty minutes, which just happened to be the length of the show.

Back in the thirties, when premier satirist S.J. Perelman wrote a movie called *Monkey Business* for the Marx Brothers, knowing Groucho's taste for blue humor, he included numerous censorable jokes in the script, and they were all predictably excised by the Hays Office. Some of Perelman's best lines were scissored out, and the humorist's fury at the gutting of his gems must have been equal to Groucho's.

The marriage of Groucho Marx and Sid Perelman was made in heaven, and *Monkey Business* sparkles with risqué humor that delighted Marx Brothers fans as much as it irked the censors.

Groucho's preoccupation with sexual matters was a problem for the censors, but it could be argued that his raunchy comedy was more a sign of impotence than virility. There is a sexual frustration in his constant ogling. He is incessantly talking about women, but, when one appears and seems willing, he invariably throttles his sexual urge. Given a sexual opportunity, the seemingly lecherous Groucho promptly backs off. In *Monkey Business* he emerges from a woman's closet to find that she is quite accessible and requires no seduction. Groucho can't handle this and retreats, hiding behind a wisecrack. Ripe young women seemed to frighten Groucho away. His lechery and debauchery were all talk. He was, in effect, a closet celibate. That may be why Margaret Dumont is ever present. She offers no real sexual threat; Groucho's innuendos fall on deaf ears and sexual culmination seems as remote as Miss Dumont's sense of humor. With the ubiquitous Dumont, Groucho's bawdy jibes are just so much innocent childish prattle. Unfortunately for Marx Brothers fans, the Hays Office found nothing innocent about Groucho's gaggery and proceeded to root it out.

On April 20, 1931, Jason S. Joy of the Hays Office wrote to B. P. Schulberg, president of Paramount Pictures:

We have read the first white script of *Monkey Business* and in our opinion some further consideration from the standpoint of the code should be given to the following . . . :

Page 85: The underscored lines of the following dialog are likely to cause offense . . . :

GROUCHO: "You bet I'm shy. I'm a shyster lawyer. And who are you, he countered roguishly, <u>his beautiful white body aching to be held.</u>"

GROUCHO: "I know, you're a misunderstood woman who's been getting nothing but dirty breaks. Well, we can clean and tighten your brakes, <u>polish your frame and oil your joints,</u> but you have to stay in the garage all night."

GROUCHO: "Now madam, <u>Lie right down</u> and tell me your troubles. You needn't be afraid to talk to me—I used to be a <u>floorwalker in a ladies washroom.</u>"

Page C-1: The action which shows Harpo standing in front of the women's lavatory and hiding the letters 'WO," so that several men mistakenly enter and are thrown out, is likely to offend by reason of its vulgarity. . . . [This sight gag, one of the funniest in the Marx Brothers repertoire, happily survived.] The same is true of the scene on this same page that shows Harpo entering a bathroom, where a girl is sitting in a tub, and reappearing a few minutes later with his clothes dripping wet. [This scene perished.]

Page J-2: The stage direction indicates that following a shriek within the house, Harpo and Chico reappear wearing bathing suits of "Miss Clean Living" and "Miss Virtue," [and] carrying the banners of other bathing beauties. We believe that this action is likely to cause offense by reason of its suggestiveness. . . .

Page N-10: The following dialog is likely to cause some offense by reason of its vulgarity . . . : [Harpo is using his inimitable sign language to convey a message.]

    GROUCHO: I've got it. It's something about a woman.

      CHICO: A corset.

    GROUCHO: No, but you're getting closer.

      CHICO: I wish I was. . . . What was her name? If we can get that, the rest is easy.

    GROUCHO: Easy! You don't know the woman.

Page M-13: Care should be exercised in the scene in which Harpo wrestles with the dowager, in order to keep it free of any vulgarity.

Five years later, the Hays Office had teeth, Joe Breen was in charge, and a strict Production Code was in effect. On September 26, 1936, John Hammell of Paramount wrote to the censorship board requesting a Seal of Approval, so that Monkey Business might be rereleased. Breen's reply reflected the toughened attitude of the censorship body:

In reply to your letter . . . regarding the desire of your New York offices to secure a code certificate for a reissue of the Marx Brothers picture titled *Monkey Business*, please let me say that, if this approval is given, it will require that you make the following eliminations:

  Reel 2: Eliminate use of Harpo standing by the sign "MEN," man entering the door, exits catapulted through door, camera panning as Harpo moves away from entire sign revealing the word "WOMEN." [Once again, the famous scene dodged the bullet.]

  In this reel, also eliminate scene of Gibson sticking Harpo with pin on the posterior. [The bit remained.]

  Reel 6: Eliminate the following line by Groucho: "You won't even have to take a physical examination, unless you insist upon it." [The line was lost.]

  Eliminate the following portion of the underlined speech by Groucho: "I've known and admired your husband for years and <u>what's good enough for him is good enough for me.</u>" [The line remained.]

  Also eliminate accompanying line of Groucho pulling other man's wife down on his lap. Eliminate the dialog:

    WOMAN: You have me at a disadvantage.

    GROUCHO: Not yet. [The line remained.]

The Other Censors

Ohio eliminated the line, "What's good enough for him is good enough for me." Pennsylvania eliminated the view of Gibson sticking Harpo with a pin in the posterior.

Alberta eliminated "You have me at a disadvantage," and the answer "Not yet."

Kansas and New York approved the film without change.

A NIGHT AT THE OPERA

Censorship is thought to be a tool of totalitarian states, where it is able to impose a mind set on audiences, fostering allegiance to the regime in power. The ultimate threat that censorship fights is anarchy, and the Marx Brothers were nothing if not proponents of anarchy. Interestingly, they roused the censors not with their anarchistic attitude, but with their innocuous sexual jokes.

The brothers were probably the first demonstration of comedic protest against the orderly state. Groucho was the original madman hero, and his madness was neither noble nor heroic. Their manic eruptions against all rules of order—whether in an opera house or a sanitarium—were a self-destructive liberty that left chaos in its wake. Their humor was manic and anti-social, but it was also hilarious. The hilarity was all that the censors—and their audiences—saw. Their attack on society, which, in a totalitarian state would never have been tolerated, went unnoticed in America.

Groucho is the most human of the mad trio. He is the conduit between the audience and the brothers. Groucho has recognizable emotions. He is stimulated by women and by money. The censors accepted his avarice, feeling that audiences would not be offended by his money-grubbing ways, but they drew the line at Groucho's lechery, sensing that American audiences would be offended by such naked lust. Hence, the Hays Office zeroed in on any lines or business that articulated Groucho's instincts of the flesh. Groucho announces his lust openly, probably because he is essentially impotent in the films. His risqué lines are just schoolboy jests. But his anarchy is sincere, his mockery of every basic institution—medicine, law, business, government, sports, and the military—is genuine. Rarely did the censors delete any of these mocking lines. Sex was the only enemy that engaged them.

The Marx Brothers seem to have been immune to charges of ethnic humor. The same censors who made Walt Disney change the feigned Jewish accent of the Wolf in *Three Little Pigs*, raised no objection to Chico's improbable Italian accent, his absurd, tight-fitting jacket and pointed hat.

Whatever the Hays Office caveats on madness, or human malady, there was no objection to Harpo, the maniacal mute, who talked in whistles and beeps of his auto horn. Despite the censors' sensibilities, *A Night at the Opera* retains one of the most joyous Marx Brothers scenes extant, which is not without its sexual implications—the Cabin Scene. Groucho and his two brothers find themselves in a tiny stateroom. Two chambermaids enter and start making the bed in which Harpo is sleeping. An engineer arrives to turn off the heat. A manicurist comes in his wake. The engineer's assistant is next, then an ingenue seeking a missing aunt, then a cleaning woman, a steward, and lastly Margaret Dumont. Both the situation and the dialogue are borderline suggestive, but, providentially, they escaped the censors' scissors and have came down to us in all their splendid lunacy.

On June 12, 1935, Joe Breen wrote to Louis B. Mayer of MGM. He had received a copy of the screenplay for A Night at the Opera, *written by George S. Kaufman and Morrie Ryskind, to be produced by Irving Thalberg and directed by Sam Wood. Wrote Breen:*

Yesterday, we received a read a copy of your script for *A Night at the Opera*. . . . We call your attention to the following . . . :

Scene 13: Care should be taken to avoid offense in this scene of Harpo masquerading as a woman. He should not be finally revealed in running pants. . . . The girl who escapes from the closet should not be in underwear. . . .

Page 18: The expression "Lichee nuts to you," should be changed. . . .

Page 44: This entire gag of Groucho inviting Mrs. Claypool [Margaret Dumont] into his cabin is open to grave question. . . . We specifically suggest that the underlined portions of the following lines be deleted: "You come to my room and I'll guarantee there'll be a situation. If not, I'm not the man I used to be."

[And then moments later:] "<u>And if I come in here again, Mrs. Claypool, there will be no beating around the bush.</u>" [The lines were cut.]

Page 48: The underlined portion of the following line should be dropped: ". . . Take those pajamas off that sleeping beauty. <u>I've got other plans for those pajamas.</u>" [The line was deleted.]

Page 59: The business of the girl under the shower being discovered by Harpo should be deleted. . . . [It was.]

Page 124: When Groucho is burned, it should not be his posterior. [It wasn't.]

The Other Censors

Italy made cuts to remove any inference that the characters were Italian.

Japan elminated scenes of Harpo sleeping in the stateroom, hanging onto the chambermaid as if to embrace her. Also eliminated were the close-up of the girl whirling, which showed her legs above the knees, and the shot of Harpo sticking his head through a dancing girl's legs.

Australia made some changes in the stateroom scene too. After the engineer says "We've come to turn off the heat," they eliminated Groucho's reply, as he gestured to Harpo embracing the chambermaid, "You'd better start on him."

Latvia eliminated scenes of Laspare, the pompous tenor, thrashing Harpo with a cane. Also cut was the scene of Harpo at the table making a sandwich of Groucho's cigar and Chico's necktie. Also killed was Groucho's dialogue in the exchange with the opera impresario (Sig Rumann). Informed that it will cost $1,000 a night to employ Rumann's client, Groucho replies, "A thousand dollars a night! You can get a record of Minnie the Moocher for seventy-five cents. For a buck and a quarter you can get Minnie."

New York State eliminated the following Groucho line: "How do you like that? Every time I get romantic with you, you want to talk business. I don't know, there's something about me that brings out the business in every woman." Also cut were Groucho's lines as he and Margaret Dumont ascend the gangplank to the luxury liner.

DUMONT: "Are you sure you have everything, Otis?"
GROUCHO: "*I haven't had any complaints yet.*"

In another scene, the mute Harpo drinks glass after glass of water in an effort to stall making a speech. Cut was Groucho's line, "They may have to build a dam in back of him."

Kansas deleted the line after Margaret Dumont's demand that Groucho talk business: ". . . there's something about me that brings out the business in every woman."

Ohio objected to the line about a buck and a quarter for Minnie, and so did Maryland. Ohio further objected to the following exchange:

> MRS. CLAYPOOL: Will you please get off the bed. What will people say?
> GROUCHO: They'll probably say you're a very lucky woman.

Virginia objected to the line about Minnie: "I haven't had any complaints yet," and ". . . you're a very lucky woman," Virginia also objected to one line in the famous stateroom scene that is spoken as attractive young women come pouring through the door. Says Groucho: "Come on in, girls, and leave all hope behind."

Virginia also objected to a Groucho line in the scene in which he is being summarily fired. The director of the opera company declares that Mrs. Claypool has decided to dispense with Groucho's services. Snaps Groucho: "Why, she hasn't even had them yet."

A DAY AT THE RACES

When Frank Capra made *Mr. Smith Goes to Washington*, congressmen were up in arms; when Chaplin began shooting *The Great Dictator*, the British government protested that Hitler might be offended; when W.C. Fields made *The Dentist*, the American Dental Association was in a lather; but when the Marx Brothers made *A Day at the Races*, none of the people it caricatured took umbrage. The film tells the story of a rundown sanitarium with a ludicrous staff; yet no doctors were irked. Harpo plays a demented jockey; yet no steeplechasers registered complaints. Chico plays a hustler who sells racing guides from an ice cream cart; yet neither book publishers nor ice cream makers took offense.

It was the Hays Office's job to see that the product of American film studios did not affront any large or influential groups.

"There is nothing as cowardly as a million dollars," Henry Morgan once observed, and there were many millions involved in Hollywood's output; but the Marx Brothers seemed constitutionally unable to give offense—except to those with an aversion to farce. Their stories were so implausible, their characters so improbable, their behavior so eccentric, that it was difficult to identify with their plights.

When their slapstick humor began to wane and Paramount Pictures declined to renew their contract, MGM's Irving Thalberg saw the problem: They lacked reality. So in *A Day at the Races* he made the brothers less frenzied and more sympathetic. He made them victims. He even cut away from them long enough to show a scene of appealing lovers and venal villains. Wonder of wonders! Thalberg inserted a plot! He built sets on the massive MGM sound stages and included some love songs.

Thalberg had another brilliant idea. He sent the Marx Brothers out on the road to perform the movie's comic scenes before live theater audiences. This enabled the Marxes to develop their timing and the screenwriters to see which lines didn't play. Thalberg's innovations made *A Day at the Races* and *A Night at the Opera* the Marx Brothers' most inspired romps.

If it failed to give offense to jockeys and doctors, however, there was one group that remained to be satisfied—the censors.

On November 5, 1936, Louis B. Mayer sent a copy of the George S. Kaufman/Morrie Ryskind script for A Day at the Races *to the Hays Office. On November 6th, Joe Breen responded:*

Yesterday we received and read the script for your proposed picture entitled *A Day at the Races*. . . . We call your attention to the following . . . :

Page 3, Scene 60: Underlined portion of the following line must be deleted or changed: ". . . It's the old story—the old story <u>of the night watchman and his wife</u>."

Page 9, Scene 70: Underlined portion of the following dialog must be deleted or changed: "I'd like a suite of rooms, <u>two nurses,</u> and don't call me for three months."

Page 10, Scene 7: The underscored line of the following exchange must be deleted or changed in order to avoid any play on a "pansy" gag: [Groucho, as Dr. Hackenbush, has arrived at the sanitarium. He gazes at a portrait on the wall and addresses the present owner, Maureen O'Sullivan.]

GROUCHO: I knew your mother well. I proposed to her.
MAUREEN: That's my father.
GROUCHO: <u>No wonder he turned me down.</u>
[The line remained.].
Page 12, Scene 7: The underscored line of the following exchange must be deleted or changed:
GROUCHO: I took four years at Vassar.
MAUREEN: But Vassar's a girls' school.
GROUCHO: I found that out the third year. . . . I'd have been there yet, <u>but I tried to make the swimming team.</u>
[The line remained.]
Page 28, Scene 20: Groucho's use of the word "tramp" should be dropped. [The word was dropped.]
Page 33, Scene 20: [Chico runs an ice cream ring at a racetrack. He spies Groucho placing a bet. He intercedes and sells him a tip on a horse. When Groucho fails to understand the tip, Chico produces a code book from the ice cream wagon and sells it to him. When Groucho fails to understand the code book, Chico sells him a master code book. By the time the transaction ends, Groucho finds himself with a library of code books that fill his arms and are gripped between his legs.] The following line should be deleted or changed: "Say, am I dripping books down there?" [The line was cut.]
Page 64, Scene 74: The underlined portion of the following dialog should be dropped: ". . . I've been so lonely for you— <u>night after night</u> in my little room at the sanitarium, Room 412."

On December 4th, Joe Breen wrote once again to Louis B. Mayer. He had received revised pages for A Day at the Races *and they had raised further objections:*

Page 35, Scene 32: The underlined portion of the following dialog must be dropped: "*If she said anything about a hayride, it's a lie!*"
Scene 73, Scene 115: Care should be taken in the showing of the men in underwear. . . .
Page 81, Scene 135: Care should be taken with the business in which Harpo attempts to tell Chico about Flo, in order to avoid the use of suggestive [gestures]. [The mute Harpo is trying to tell Chico, a la charades, that a vamp is out to seduce Groucho. The gesticulations the censors feared were the ones meant to indicate a woman. The business remained.]
Page 84: Any suggestive inference in the following line will not be acceptable: "Oh no, not for me—three men on a horse."

[The three brothers were all seated in the vamp's lap. The scene remained, with no discernible suggestive inference.]

Page 86, Scene 136: To escape deletion by [state] censor boards, the camera should not emphasize the business of Groucho locking the door. [The action was cut.]

Page 90, Scene 136: The underlined portion of the following line should be deleted or changed: "Shall we sit down and bat it around?" [The line was cut.]

Anything suggestive in the reading of the following lines will not be acceptable: "You're either nearsighted or near-seated." [The line remained.]

The Other Censors

Spain approved the film, but deleted all the humorous dance scenes.

Latvia rejected the entire film. The reason was expressed by their censors in the single word: "Worthless." Latvians evidently do not raise their children to take the world lightly.

Japan deleted the scene in which policemen are falling from the rear of a water wagon. [In Japan, respect for the law is a sacrament.]

Austria approved the film after elminating the scene of Groucho, Harpo, and Flo embracing. Austria also deleted the scene of black couples dancing in jazz rhythm. [In 1936, theories of racial purity were taking root in neighboring Germany. One wonders why Austria did not censor the entire film, which starred three Jewish brothers.]

England approved the film in its entirety, with the sole deletion of a shot of a horse falling during the big race. Massachusetts approved the film without deletion.

Both Maryland and Ohio approved the film with one deletion—Groucho's reply to Margaret Dumont in the following exchange:

MARGARET DUMONT: Oh no, no, Doctor, please don't go. I'll take care of your salary.

GROUCHO: Oh yeah? The last job I had, I had to take it out in trade, and this is no butcher shop. Not yet, anyhow.

Chapter 12

CHAPLIN

MODERN TIMES

When reformers zeroed in on Hollywood, it was not only the things the stars did on the screen that provoked them. It was also the things the stars did *off* the screen in their private lives. America was stunned by the graphic details of scandals that involved some of Hollywood's most famous stars. One of these was Charles Chaplin. As much as American audiences adored his creation of the Little Tramp and roared at his brilliant comic inventions as a director of comedy, they disapproved of his taste for teenage girls and his love affairs with his leading ladies. Chaplin cut capers with his young discoveries that stretched the fame of his performances from the screen to the bedroom. His most widely publicized scandal involved his escapades with sixteen-year-old Lita Grey. Another of his lovers, on and off the screen, was Paulette Goddard, the gamin in his film, *Modern Times*.

Chaplin was more secretive about his creative life than his romantic flings. He had been working in secret on the story for *Modern Times* for nearly a year, and only his closest confidants were privy to his plans. During this time, his studio's sound stages were being readied for the moment when Charlie would launch his new vehicle. Carpenters added a bathroom to the dressing room that his costar and lover, Paulette Goddard, would use. Chaplin was even surreptitious about the movie's title. In November 1933 he sent a sealed envelope to the Hays Office via registered mail. The envelope informed the censors that the title of his forthcoming film would be *Modern Times*, but Hays was

121

admonished to leave the envelope unopened until Chaplin himself announced the production.

Modern Times was to be Chaplin's most ambitious undertaking to that point. It would be two solid hours of continuous hilarity. Chaplin was not married to a plot line. The film was divided into five main sequences and six minor ones. The episodes lacked cohesion, but the audience rode on gales of laughter. The longest and most carefully developed sequence was the opening one, in which the hapless Charlie is employed in a vast dynamo factory—a pathetic cog in a relentless wheel. Laughter aside, the production line is a mass obscenity, a violation of natural law. The Hays Office saw nothing obscene in this degradation of the human spirit. Instead, they complained of profane language, a gurgling stomach, and the udders of a cow!

On January 6, 1936, Joe Breen wrote to Alfred E. Reeves of the Charles Chaplin Film Corporation, to tell him his reactions to the landmark film, written, produced, directed by, and starring Mr. Chaplin, Wrote Breen:

> As you know, we had the very great pleasure this afternoon of witnessing a showing of your production of *Charlie Chaplin in Modern Times.* . . . In accordance with our verbal recommendations, we respectfully urge upon you the following eliminations:
>   1. The first part of the "pansy" gag.
>   2. The word "dope" in the printed title.
>   3. Most of the business of the stomach rumbling on the part of the minister's wife and Charlie.
>   4. The entire brassiere gag in the department store.
>   5. The close-up shot of the udders of the cow.

All five of the recommendations made by Breen were carried out in full.

The Other Censors

Japan eliminated the scene in which constables and the mob formed as strikers fight, and it eliminated the dialogue that reads "Determined to go back to jail. . . ." Also eliminated was the scene in which Chaplin hits the constable on the head with a bat, as well as the scene in which a constable is hit with a piece of brick, and the dialogue: "We ain't burglars—we're hungry."

On April 6th, the chief Italian censor wrote to the Breen Office to say that he had just been advised that the police throughout Italy had received instructions to withdraw *Modern Times*. He wrote that, although he had not been notified officially of the banning of the film, police commissioners all over Italy had received orders to stop the showing of the film. Two years later, when Chaplin mocked Benito Mussolini in *The Great Dictator*, he achieved some measure of revenge for the Italian banning of *Modern Times*.

THE GREAT DICTATOR

When Charles Chaplin set out to make his thinly veiled attack on Nazism in 1938, the chief censor that stood in his path was the British Film Censor Board. In the overheated state of European politics, and given Chamberlain's policy of appeasement of the German Führer, this was to be expected. The secret cables from the German consul and the British Film Censor Board to the Hays Office provide an intriguing look behind the scenes and reveal the power that motion pictures had accrued to prick the pompous and move the masses.

It would take more than Teutonic rage and British timidity to keep *The Great Dictator* off the sound stages, and, in 1938, as Hitler was brutalizing Jews in Berlin and annexing Czechoslovakia, it was released around the world.

When the band strikes up "Send in the Clowns," one's mind goes at once to the censors of Chicago, who held the dubious distinction of being the buffoons of local American censorship. They were quick to ban *The Great Dictator*, fearing that this savage satire of Hitler might offend Chicago's large German population. Justice Clark of the U.S. Supreme Court provided some unintentional comic relief when, in supporting Chicago's cretinous ban, he cited the unusual standard used by a police sergeant, who was Chicago's chief censor (and who possessed no known credentials for the position beyond his experience in booking burglars). Said the sergeant in a burst of incoherence: "Children should be allowed to see any movie that plays in Chicago. If a picture (like *The Great Dictator*) is objectionable for a child, it is objectionable, period."

Chaplin's original concept for *The Great Dictator* might have

troubled the Hays office. He conceived the idea of two rival dic-
tators, one of whose wife was intended as a role for Fanny Brice,
the farcical comedienne. The relationship between the Jewish
wife and the Nazi tyrant would have drawn blasts from the censors—and perhaps the Anti-Defamation League—while offering
little opportunity for real satire. Here is a scene that Chaplin
wrote and later discarded:

Scene: Mrs. Hinkle [Fanny Brice] alone—boredom and sex
starvation with Freudian fruit symbols. Enter [Dictator] Hinkle
from speech. She's mad at him, orders him about. He's preoccupied with matters of State.

FANNY: I'm a woman. I need affection, and all you think about
is the State. *The State!* What kind of state do you think
I'm in?

HINKLE: You've made me come to myself. I'm not getting any
younger. Sometimes I wonder.

FANNY: Life is so short and these moments are so rare. . . . Remember, Hinkle, I did everything for you. I even had an
operation on my nose. If you don't pay more attention
to me, I'll tell the whole world I'm Jewish!

HINKLE: Shhh!

FANNY: And I'm not so sure you aren't Jewish, too. We're having gefilte fish for dinner.

HINKLE: Quiet! Quiet!

FANNY: Last night I dreamt about blimps.

HINKLE: Blimps?

FANNY: Yes, I dreamt we captured Paris in a big blimp and we
went right through the Arc de Triomphe. . . . [She
presses grapes in his mouth as she plays with a banana.]

Providentially, Chaplin discarded this farcical approach for a
more truly satiric idea. The Hays Office had only modest con-
cerns about the film. Indeed, by the time the movie was released, the earlier British wariness had vanished. *The Great
Dictator* premiered in London in December 1940 in the midst
of the Blitz. Adolf Hitler was a lethal foe and Britons, from
Churchill on down, relished the Chaplin ridicule. They were,
in fact, more taken by Chaplin's mockery of the Führer than
were American audiences—the United States was not yet at war
with Germany, though they would be within a year. Britons loved

Chaplin's basic joke: the resemblance of Hitler to the world's greatest clown, Chaplin himself. The bold contrast between the ghetto Jews and the fascist chancellor made for audacious fun.

The final speech of the movie retains its controversy to this day. Some censors said it smacked of sentimentality or Communism, but it was widely quoted. In this final speech, Chaplin summarizes the hopes for a better world, offered in a time of terrible agony. Chaplin wrote and orated:

> The way of life can be free and beautiful, but we have lost the way. Greed has poisoned men's souls—has barricaded the world with hate—has goose-stepped us into misery and bloodshed. . . . Machinery that gives abundance has left us in want. Our knowledge has made us cynical; our cleverness, hard and unkind. We think too much and feel too little. More than machinery, we need humanity. More than cleverness, we need kindness and gentleness. Without these qualities, life will be violent and all will be lost.

On October 31, 1938, a letter from Dr. George Gyssling, the German Chief Consul, reached Joseph Breen at the Hays Office. It said he had noted a newspaper article headlined "Charlie Chaplin to Burlesque Hitler." The story reported that, in a forthcoming film, Chaplin would play a defenseless little Jew who is mistaken for a powerful dictator, while, in the other role, one would see Chaplin as the dictator himself. The article went on the state that, though Hitler would not be mentioned, it would not take a Sherlock Holmes to see it was the Führer that Chaplin was burlesquing. If this were true, seethed the German Consul, it would lead to "serious troubles and complications." Hitler was presently altering the map of Europe, but peace still reigned between Germany and the arsenal of democracy. Breen responded to Herr Gyssling on November 2, 1938:

> I have your note of October 31st, which had reference to a newspaper article which purports to set forth certain plans which Mr. Chaplin has for making a picture which "will burlesque Hitler." We in this office have no knowledge of any such film, but I am sending a copy of your letter to Mr. Chaplin's manager today.

Breen did so, writing to Alfred Reeves of the Charles Chaplin Film Corporation, requesting information of Chaplin's plans.

Reeves responded promptly, telling Breen that he was sending the copy of the German's letter to Chaplin's home "for his consideration." Chaplin, a man of robust social conscience, might be excused for greeting Herr Gyssling's protest with a mixture of whimsy and contempt. His reply is not a matter of record, but the Consul's complaint did not alter Chaplin's intentions for *The Great Dictator*.

The British were as wary of their potential foes across the Channel as were the Americans. Brook Wilkinson, the head of the British Film Censors Board, dispatched a cable to Joe Breen at the Hays Office. Chamberlain sat at 10 Downing Street as Hitler roamed the continent. The British censor did not want to rock the boat. His cable to Hays declared that he had heard Chaplin was planning a film titled *The Dictator*. Would it be possible for Wilkinson to acquire an outline of the story? Having regard to the "delicate situation that might arise" in England, if personal attacks were made on Hitler, Wilkinson wanted, in the centuries-old parlance of diplomats, not to give offense. After all, the Führer's prickly temper was world-famous. The British censor concluded by observing the delicacy of the situation and asking Joe Breen to cable whatever information he could assemble, with the greatest expedition.

It is intriguing to view this correspondence within the context of the times. The communications from the German consul and the British censor were dispatched in October and November of 1938. A month before, Prime Minister Neville Chamberlain had returned from Munich after meeting with Hitler, boasting of "peace in our time." In October, Hitler had ordered the liquidation of Czechoslovakia. In November, as Breen wrote to Chaplin to learn if he was planning a film that might irritate the Führer, synagogues were being burned, the homes and shops of Jews were being destroyed and looted, and a night of horror was gripping Germany. That same month, Czechoslovakia ceded Germany 11,000 square miles of its territory, while England stood by in silent acquiescence. A few weeks later, to please Hitler, the Czech cabinet suspended all Jewish school teachers.

America was not without its self-appointed censors in attacking Chaplin for his planned satire of Hitler. On February 27, 1939, a letter was sent from Walter McKenna to U.S. Senator Robert Reynolds. The burden of citizen McKenna's message was that no resident alien such as Chaplin should be permitted to use the U.S. film industry to air his "private grievance" against a foreign power. There was no doubt, observed McKenna, that this thinly disguised film would create international repercussions. The U.S. government should look into Chaplin's motives, before the film had a chance to "antagonize certain . . . governments." Chaplin's purpose, charged McKenna, was clearly "to stir up further strife between Germany and the U.S."

McKenna's letter, which Senator Reynolds, a member of the U.S. Senate Committee on Foreign Relations, had sent to Breen, was forwarded by the chief censor to Charles Chaplin. Whether Chaplin's film effectively entangled America in a war with Nazi Germany is a matter that must be left to more profound consideration.

The Other Censors

Peru rejected The Great Dictator.

Spain rejected it.

Paraguay first rejected the film, then approved it.

Argentina passed the film, but it was banned by the mayor of Buenos Aires.

Japan predictably rejected it, declaring: "All anti-Nazi pictures are banned in Japan." Three years later, the attack on Pearl Harbor supported these sentiments.

MONSIEUR VERDOUX

While the Hays Office chased down obscenities, double entendres, and pats on the posterior, Charlie Chaplin had a somewhat different set of moral values. He saw obscenity in the waste of human life produced by the great war that had ended the year before. In Monsieur Verdoux he presents a Bluebeard whose mass murders are trivial compared to the glorified slaughter of war. The comparison shocked the Hays Office, which pointed out sententiously that murder has always been abhorred in civilized society and that war as always been ennobling—at least for the country whose army is being discussed.

The American Legion, as representative of war veterans, found the movie blasphemous and waged a vitriolic campaign to drive the antimilitary film from the theaters. They were extremely successful in their vigorous efforts, and Chaplin's mordant film disappointed him in its box-office receipts. The American Legion was shocked at the profane thesis of Chaplin's film; in its posters and mailers, the Legion left no turn unstoned in labeling the movie—and Chaplin—heinous and un-American.

Chaplin was as bitter about the film's censorship as the censors were about the film's theme. Chaplin was not accustomed to making such substantial alterations in a script at the behest of censors; his changes were usually of the creative kind. One speech in particular drew the fire of the Hays Office. *Monsieur Verdoux* is the story of a man who is murdering widows. When he goes on trial, his speech to the court was not deemed acceptable to the sensibilities of postwar America, and the Hays Office demanded numerous cuts. In the speech to the court, Verdoux defends his homicides as mere caprice: "As for being a mass murderer," says the defendant, "does not the world encourage it? Is it not building weapons of destruction for the sole purpose of mass killing? Has it not blown unsuspecting women and children to pieces? . . . As a mass killer, I am an amateur by comparison."

Chaplin had always found respect and deference at the Hays Office. This time he encountered irritation and reproach. He devoted twelve pages of his memoirs to his relations with Joe Breen over *Verdoux*. The correspondence between himself and Breen, and a marked copy of his screenplay, reside in Chaplin's archives. They gave him little pleasure. After first disapproving the story as a whole, the Hays Office retreated to attacking those elements that appeared to be antisocial—the basic theme of the film. Chaplin's goal was to indict the military and judicial system, and, if that were deleted, the film would have lost its reason for being.

Breen repudiated Verdoux's thesis about private murder, as opposed to public slaughter. Amid all the bloodletting, Breen objected to a scene that suggested Verdoux had slept with one of the wives he had murdered. He protested that a girl Verdoux picks up appears to be a streetwalker and is repelled that the lady goes on to become affluent, as the mistress of a munitions maker.

At one point in their acrimonious dialogue, Breen invited Chaplin to the Hays Office to discuss the script. Chaplin recalled in his memoirs that the chief censor seemed amiable, but that one of his aides greeted Chaplin by saying: "What have you against the Catholic Church?"

Monsieur Verdoux was Chaplin's first film in six years, and proved a bitter disappointment to his audiences. It is, after all, a comedy of murder; but, if the idea offered humorous possibilities, Chaplin chose not to pursue them. He seemed obsessed with the philosophic points to be scored. He wrote few amusing lines for his own delivery and told a story that violated Hollywood's conventional ideas of what movie audiences would accept. This was not surprising. The Hays Office had conditioned the American moviegoer with a generation of conventional and moralistic themes. Chaplin gave them neither. He supplied a grim, sordid story of murder, and a long series of cynical, indifferent murders. He didn't even supply a happy ending.

On February 20, 1946, Joseph Breen wrote to Charles Chaplin at the Chaplin Studios:

We have read with the greatest care and attention your script presently titled *A Comedy of Murders*, and regret to inform you that a screenplay prepared from this material would be unacceptable. . . .

The reasons for this unacceptability are several:

Principal among them is the fact that the story contains a false enunciation of moral values which seems to be in fundamental conflict with the theory of sound ethics as set forth in the industry's Production Code. . . . We pass over those elements which seem to be antisocial in their concept and significance. These are the sections in the story in which Verdoux indicts the court system and impugns the present-day social structure, since considerations of this sort might not be regarded as strictly within the literal province of the code. Rather we direct your attention to what is even more critical and properly a matter of adjudication under the code. This is Verdoux's *rationale* of his crimes in terms of their moral worth.

Specifically, it seems to us that the closing pages of this script present an evaluation of the moral heinousness, or lack of heinousness, of Verdoux's Bluebeard career. As we read the several final speeches of Verdoux to the court defending himself on the various charges of murder, citing that he was a piker in murder compared to killers like Hitler and Mussolini, and attempting to assay their meaning and intent, it seems to us that the burden of the argument comes inevitably down to this conclusion: that

Verdoux's "comedy of murders" is not such an outrageous transgression against moral order as the court would make it seem.

To substantiate this analysis, please note Verdoux's line of argument before the court and in his jail cell. The trial concluded and the judge ready to pronounce sentence, Verdoux is invited to express his mind on the proceedings. He rises before the assembly, essentially a man who has been "battered about by the system." Of course, no recognition is made of the fact that his second buffeting by the system is due to the position in which his criminal career has placed him. Nevertheless, Verdoux forthwith launches into a moral, but effective, castigation of the prosecuting attorney, the representative of orderly legal machinery, on the grounds that the prosecuting attorney has found Verdoux's mass murders "monstrous." He "spoofs" the horror manifested by the attorney, saying in effect that this is nothing more than sham exhibitionism; and, in pointing the finger at the vast loss in human lives incurred in war, seeks to minimize the heinousness of his crimes. His claim is, derivatively, that it is ridiculous to be shocked by the extent of his atrocities, that they are a mere "comedy of murders" in comparison with the legalized mass murders of war, which are embellished with gold braid by the "system." Without at all entering into any dialectics on the question of whether wars are mass murders or justifiable killings, since this would inescapably lead to interminable and fruitless discussions . . . we point out to you that the fact still remains that Verdoux, during the course of his speech, makes a serious attempt to evaluate the moral quality of his crimes and to *minimize* the evil of them. . . . This is the principal reason for the unacceptability of the story.

The second basic reason for the unacceptability of this story we can state more briefly. It lies in the fact that this is very largely the story of a type of confidence man who induces a number of women to turn over their finances to him by beguiling them into a series of mock marriages. This phase of the story has about it the distasteful flavor of illicit sex, which in our judgment is not good.

Thirdly, the characterization of "the girl" as clearly that of a prostitute, who, because of her life of prostitution, flourishes materially, is clearly unacceptable. . . .

Lastly, there is the question of Verdoux's attitude toward God in a few of his final lines in this script. As they are now written, they seem to us open to serious question as possibly blasphemous in flavor, if not in fact.

Because of the serious character of these basic objections, we will not attempt to get a report on the several details which present problems in this story. . . .

A stunned Chaplin responded with a letter to Breen in which he said that the moral interpretation that the Hays Office had ascribed to A Comedy of Murders, *and the supposition that it seemed to be in fundamental conflict with a theory of sound ethics, was very confusing to Chaplin. He had tried very hard, he said, to understand Breen's letter, but without success. Chaplin complained that Breen's expressions of "generalities, suppositions, and misnomers" left him perplexed, and declared that, if the censor chief would "elucidate and be more specific, I shall be more competent to discuss these imputations with you." On February 28th, Joe Breen responded to Chaplin:*

I regret that you found our letter . . . not quite clear. In response to your request that we state our points more specifically, please note that it is our considered judgment that a motion picture following along the lines of the script *A Comedy of Murders* would be unacceptable . . . for the following reasons:

1. The situation in the story, wherein it is shown your lead lives concurrently with more than one wife. This in our judgment is definitely immoral. . . .

2. The several speeches of your lead in the closing pages of the script have the effect of quite definitely clouding the issue between right and wrong. These speeches indicate what purports to be the inconsistency of applauding those who kill in war as great heroes, and, at the same time, condemning to death others who murder.

3. The characterization of the girl as a prostitute. . . .

4. Certain of the final lines of the script are open to the question of being possibly blasphemous. . . .

I think it is pretty well established that mankind has agreed, down through the centuries, that to *kill* under certain circumstances—for lawful war—is not a violation of the moral or the human law. On the other hand, to *murder*, to kill unlawfully, is universally agreed to be a crime against both the moral and the human law. . . .

Chaplin joined the ethical argument on March 5th. In a letter to Breen he asserted that the question was "a philosophical and a moral one." Chaplin doubted if anyone, including the devisers of the Production Code, could determine what is right or wrong. The dialogues of Plato, said Chaplin, had struggled with this theme. Chaplin observed dryly that he did not believe it to be the prerogative of the censors to demand from a writer that a character be definitely set in his philosophy. Such prerogative, said Chaplin, comes dangerously close to encroaching on one's constitutional rights of free speech. Chaplin questioned Breen's assertion of the nobility and lawfulness of war. "War has always been analogous with evil," snapped Chaplin.

In summing up the film, Chaplin concluded that the question of right and wrong is self-evident! His story ridiculed and de-glamorized a career of crime and clearly demonstrated that crime did not pay. Chaplin assured the censor that he did not arrive at his theme by "flippant thinking." He had lived with it, he declared, for over two years, and tried to construct a sincere and constructive comedy. In all his pictures, he solemnly concluded, he had been conscious of their moral aspect and "always tried to avoid the vulgar and salacious."

In his comedy, Charlie Chaplin was a man of his time. In his view that movie censors were dangerously encroaching on the writer's constitutional rights, he was decades ahead of his time. Eventually, the movie industry and judicial system that he mocked in *Monsieur Verdoux* caught up with Chaplin—when he was long in exile.

Chapter 13

W.C. FIELDS

THE BANK DICK

W.C. Fields's malign feelings toward children, dogs, women, and mankind in general must have held a special place for the censors. In one of his films, Fields sips a soda in an ice cream parlor, turns to peer bitterly at the camera, and says: "This scene was meant to be in a saloon, but the censors made us change it."

Drunks and drunkards reposed in a special purgatory at the Hays Office. "Liquor and drinking," stated the sanctimonious Production Code, were subjects that "must be treated with discretion and restraint." For a bibulous fellow like Bill Fields, such a proviso limited his art and was an insult to his life-style.

Fields's comedy, so reliant on malevolence and alcohol, raised hackles at the Hays Office. In a larger sense, it was strange that the censors, so skeptical and shrewd in other matters, should take Fields for a comedian. The wretchedness of his life, his sad, mottled face, the fear that led him to hide away his money in hundreds of bank accounts under names as bizarre as the ones he invented for his screen characters and screenwriting pseudonymns—all suggest a man sunk in despair and anxiety, not a clown or comedian.

Fields had less trouble with the censors in the early thirties, before the birth of the Legion of Decency. In his 1932 film *The Dentist*, a leggy patient wraps her thighs about Fields, who is attempting an extraction. The censors passed the copulative scene (though the American Dental Association filed a protest); but, by the time Fields wrote and starred in *The Bank Dick* in 1940, the censorship code had more teeth than the leggy patient.

The censors' chief complaint with *The Bank Dick* revolved

133

around Fields's alcoholic tastes and lecherous eye. There was also a drunken movie director, which the Hays Office feared would remind moviegoers of an ugly scandal that had occurred ten years before involving a famous Hollywood director. Off-screen scandal was as much the responsibility of the censors as on-screen sex.

Despite Breen's emendations, *The Bank Dick* was one of the best of Fields's films. His lampoon of a special bank officer was thoroughly Fieldsian, which is to say it was unvirtuous, vague, clowning, and completely delightful. The original screenplay is credited to Mahatma Kane Jeeves, one of Fields's eccentric noms de plume. Fields is full of bits of sly pantomime, even if his dialogue drolleries were well laundered by the censors.

In a story that may be apocryphal, a man came into Fields's bungalow on the Universal lot and offered to sell him, for $1,000, a three-word subject for a movie. Fields agreed and the stranger handed the actor a slip of paper on which appeared the words "The Bank Dick."

On July 2, 1940, Joe Breen had received the first seventy-five pages of The Bank Dick from Universal Studios, and had a long list of amendments to suggest:

We have read the incomplete script . . . for your proposed production *The Bank Dick.* . . .

In going through the script page by page, we respectfully direct your attention to the following . . . :

Scene 2: The reference to Mrs. Brunch regarding her living "with some nice man out of wedlock" will have to be changed.

Scenes 19 et seq: We ask that you do not name any of your characters "Filthy."

Page 20 et seq: We ask that you change the names of "Irving and Pincus Levine" in order to get away from too definitely identifying these persons with any particular race.

Page 65 et seq: All the play between Egbert Souse [Fields] and the girl's legs is very questionable.

Page 68: The wiggle of the girls' backside should not be offensive.

Scene 90: Please eliminate the expression "nuts to you" from Egbert's speech.

Page 108: It were better . . . if you did not suggest that Snoop is about to vomit.

Scene 110: Snoop's lines ". . . Take me to a culvert—I want to spew" should be eliminated.

Scene 144, Page 68: We . . . direct your attention to the by-play between Egbert and the stenographer because of her legs.

Scenes 144 et seq, Page 69: It will not be acceptable to use the expression "black pussy." It will, however, be acceptable to use the expression "black pussycat."

On August 26th, additional pages, new and revised, for The Bank Dick, had reached the Hays Office and produced these demands from Breen:

Scene 101: The action of Egbert giving the rear of the girl a good double-0 should not be offensively suggestive.

Scene 124: [State] censor boards are likely to delete the "nude picture of a girl" [on the calendar].

Page 157: Dr. Stall's "fairly feminine voice" should not have about it any possible suggestion of "pansy."

Scene 162: The doctor's lines about the castor oil "two nights running" . . . is questionable.

In responding to Breen's communiqués, Edward F. Cline of Universal Pictures, the film's director, indicated that Universal would accede to most of the censor's demands.

He agreed to change the name of the character "Filthy" to "McNasty."

He assured Breen there would be nothing offensive in the way Fields ogled the girl.

Regarding the picture of a nude photo of a girl on a calendar, Cline insisted that there would be nothing offensive in the way Egbert looked at the calendar, but respectfully requested that he be allowed to retain the photo. The director defended his use of the photo of the nude girl on the calendar and faithfully promised not to show the girl's posterior in the shot.

Regarding Egbert's glance at the girl's behind, there would, said the director, be nothing offensive in the way Fields eyed the girl.

The director further assured Breen that the doctor's "feminine voice" was never intended to connote homosexuality. The script should have read that his manner with the patient would merely be "solicitous."

Regarding the line about castor oil and "two nights running" with its scatological implication, the director heatedly denied that there was any reference to a bathroom joke. [There is some doubt that Breen swallowed the assurance along with the castor oil.]

By November 6th, photography on The Bank Dick *had been completed, and the film had been screened for the Hollywood censors. Now that they had seen the actual film, a number of new objections were raised. Wrote Breen:*

We had the pleasure this afternoon of witnessing your production *The Bank Dick* with W.C. Fields. . . .

Before we can approve this picture, however, it will be necessary that some changes be made:

1. The gag suggesting that the dog has wet Fields's legs will have to be eliminated.

2. Pronunciation of the word "Swissesse" (ass) will have to be entirely removed.

3. The underlined portion of the following lines spoken by Mr. Fields will have to be entirely eliminated: "Looks like the Mona Lisa only a little heavier."

We would like to ask if there is not some way in which we can cut down the several scenes showing the drunken motion picture director being walked up and down the street in order to sober him up. It is our judgment that there is too much of this, and it is likely to give offense to our patrons everywhere, and it is especially unfortunate that this kind of action should be linked with a motion picture director. [The scandal involving handsome and respected movie director William Desmond Taylor had involved murder and drugs. The public outcry against jazz-age Hollywood had helped spawn the Hays Office, and Breen had no desire to recall to the public mind the debauchery of some movie directors.]

You may advise us when the eliminations have been made which have been requested [and] we shall be glad to send you our formal Certificate of Approval.

On the file copy of Breen's letter of final eliminations, the censor scribbled an emphatic "okay" next to each demand, indicating the studio's acquiescence:

The dog urinating on Fields.

The reference to the word "ass."

The reference to the Mona Lisa.

NEVER GIVE A SUCKER AN EVEN BREAK

W.C. Fields contrived to die on Christmas Day, which was perhaps the greatest joke this malevolent prankster was to play on his critics in and out of the censors' offices. To examine a script written by Bill Fields was to splutter with laughter, fear, and dismay. In the spring of 1941 he sent a new script to the Hays Office for their perusal. It was then called *The Great Man*; it would later bear the somewhat longer and more Fieldsian title *Never Give a Sucker an Even Break*. The censors found the scenario totally unacceptable, principally because of the suggestive quality of its scenes and the outrageous behavior of its star. As Breen leafed through its pages, he found it awash with drink—fully sixty scenes were laid in cocktail lounges, bars, and assorted saloons. True, it would be surprising to find a Fields movie set in a health-food store. Still, sixty scenes!

The Great Man is somewhat autobiographical. Fields plays an actor who has written a story; but en route to a film studio for a conference, he finds his path beset with many woes. Predictably, the woes involve sex and drink. Arriving at the studio, Fields acts out the story for the movie producers. The script for *The Great Man*—as opposed to the script that Fields is bringing to the fictional studio—was reminiscent of a patchwork quilt. It was written under another of Fields's slapstick pseudonymns—Otis Cribblecarbus Incognito—and it provided its author with a chance to display his anxieties, clumsiness, and whimsy. Like most of Fields's films, it starts nowhere, passes through various cafés and feminine legs, turns the language upside down, and then culminates in a desperate chase. Nothing that happens in Fields's entire odyssey bears very much relation to anything else. Detractors called it silly, fans called it brilliant, and the Hays Office called it unacceptable.

On April 17, 1941, a six-page, tightly typed letter was dispatched by Joe Breen to Maurice Pivar, the censorship official at Universal Pictures. Wrote Breen:

We have read the script for your proposed picture *The Great Man* and regret to report that in its present form this script is not acceptable. . . .

The unacceptability . . . is due to the following:

    1. This script is filled with vulgar and suggestive scenes and dialog, which will be pointed out hereinafter.

    2. The script contains innumerable jocular references to drinking and liquor; sixty scenes . . . are laid in a cocktail lounge, in addition to numerous other scenes laid in bars and saloons, all of which will have to be deleted. . . .

We call your attention to the following . . . . :

Scene 2: The word "stinker" will be deleted by some [state] censor boards. Also the word "stinkeroos."

Scene 6: Here begin the numerous scenes in which Fields is seen looking at girls' legs or breasts and reacting thereto. . . .

Scene 21: The business of Fields scratching the match on the seat of the man's pants will have to be handled carefully. . . .

Scene 28: Here begin the unacceptable scenes and dialog dealing with drinking. . . .

Scene 29: If [Franklin] Pangborn plays his role in any way suggestive of a "pansy" we cannot approve. . . . It will be acceptable to play the Pangborn character as a fussbudget. . . . In Pangborn's speech, the name "Fuchawantz" is not acceptable. . . .

Page 22: Pangborn's reference to "tighter than Dick's hatband" is questionable. . . .

Scene 168: In Fields's speech, the word "physiology" should be deleted or changed.

Scene 276: The Indian's remark, "My name *Falling Water O'Toole*" is unacceptable. . . .

Scene 281 et seq: All of this business dealing with the "chamber pot gag" is completely unacceptable. . . .

Scene 367: . . . Fields's remark "Did you ever gondola?" and Mrs. Hemoglobin's answer are unacceptably suggestive. . . .

Scene 411 et seq: You will have in mind that we cannot approve scenes of comedy in connection with marriage ceremonies. . . . It is permissible to have some comedy *before* a marriage ceremony begins, but, once it begins, the ceremony must be played straight. . . .

Chapter 14————————
MAE WEST

I'M NO ANGEL

Hollywood historians have propounded the theory that the Legion of Decency was established primarily to remove Mae West from the screen. It was scarcely six months after the release of her salacious *She Done Him Wrong* that the most virulent form of censorship took hold in the movie colony. Undoubtedly, the clerical reformers had more to be disturbed about than the buxom Miss West, but the theory of cause and effect has much to commend it.

What so outraged the churchly moralists, the congressional critics, and the journalistic muckrakers was Mae West's habit of mocking the repressive sexual attitudes of the public and the censors. It is a moot point whether the well-padded temptress should be applauded or attacked for triggering the most restrictive form of censorship that Hollywood had ever encountered.

From the day in 1932 when Mae West brought her risqué comedy and bosomy body from Broadway to Hollywood, those who were charged with protecting the public morals were up in arms. What most affronted the censors was the fact that Mae West was asserting a radical thesis—that a woman's sexual appetite was as great as a man's. It was not until Dr. Alfred Kinsey published the fruits of his research in 1948 that Miss West's theory was given substantial support. In the meantime, her declaration of a woman's sexual needs seemed blasphemous.

Everything about Mae West agitated the censors—her languid, undulating walk; the vulgar poetry with which she could mount a staircase or come to rest on a piano bench. The censors were unaccustomed to such frank sensuality on the screen.

I'm No Angel was the high-water mark of Mae West's assaults on the moral establishment. It appeared in 1933—before the Legion of Decency gave teeth to the Hays Office. The Legion arrived too late to exercise any restraint on *I'm No Angel*. The film's comedic mixture of suggestive songs and banter passed through the Hays Office before Joe Breen had settled in with his strengthened Production Code and his mandatory Seal of Approval, but the Mae West movies that were still to come would lose their bawdy edge.

On June 23, 1933, James Wingate of the Production Code Administration wrote to A.M. Botsford about Mae West's forthcoming feature:

We have read the script of *I'm No Angel*. . . . As to theme, the story seems to present no difficulty, but, of course, it will depend very largely on the way in which many of the scenes are treated as to whether or not it will be satisfactory under the code. . . . Consequently, we wish to reserve our final opinion on the story till we have a chance to see it on the screen. There are a number of details which seem questionable and to which we believe some further consideration should be given.

Page A-5: . . . Portions of the barker's speech seem questionable and ought to be omitted. The lines:

"A dance of the mid-way"

". . . the old biological urge"

". . . the only girl who has satisfied more patrons than Chesterfields."

Page A-6: That portion of the barker's speech in which he says, ". . . and see her rollin' . . ." should be omitted.

Page A-25: The titles of Tira's [Mae West] various records seem to be in violation of the code because of their suggestive meaning. [Mae West wrote most of her own lines and they were often suggestive.]

The line in which the chump says "You bet your life, no one does it like that Dallas man" should be changed. . . .

Page A-35: . . . We feel that you should delete from this scene that portion of the line in which Tira says ". . . Will he or won't he?"

Page A-36: . . . The shot of a feminine arm handing the phone to Benny when he is in bed, is overly suggestive. . . .

Page A-59: . . . The barker's statement that ". . . she's safer in that cage than she is in bed." . . .

Page B-12: The line in which Tira says "I am—one man at a

time" in reply to the manicurist's statement of her being a one-man woman. . . .

It would be wise to eliminate the underscored word in Clayton's line, "In that case, how about coming up to my <u>bed</u> room?"

Some of the [state] censors may regard the scene in which Tira spits a stream of water that lands on Alicia's back as distasteful. . . .

You should omit that portion of the line in which Slick says, "I took her away from a Polack weightlifter and he got her from a ——."

Mae West's songs were often as risqué as her badinage. On July 5th, James Wingate of the Hays Office wrote to Paramount to cavil at some suggested lyrics:

We have read the six lyrics written for your production *I'm No Angel*. In the lyric "There's No One Like My Dallas Man," the following lines seem to us to be dangerous:

Fourth stanza: "With a special whip . . ."

Fifth stanza: "He can ride . . ."

In the song "They Call My Sister Honkytonk," [eliminate] the fourth stanza in its entirety.

In the song "I'm No Angel," it seems to us that the following lines will prove overly suggestive . . . :

Second stanza: "But baby, I can warm you with this love of mine."

Third stanza: "Love me, love me, love me, honey, love until I just don't care."

Fourth and fifth stanzas: In their entirety.

In "I've Found a New Way to Go to Town," it seems to us that the fourth line in the third stanza "It takes a good man to make me" is overly suggestive. . . .

The lyrics of Mae West exercised a special fascination on a generation of Americans. Horowitz and Collier write in their revisionist history of *The Kennedys* how teenager John F. Kennedy bribed a friend to strip naked and sing a Mae West ditty to old Joe Kennedy, for the pleasure of seeing his father grow apoplectic. Of course, these lyrics seem laughably innocuous when compared with the explicit sexuality of some of today's rock tunes, which have called to arms a covey of congressional wives. Doubtless today's rock lyrics will seem innocuous to some future generation of reformers.

On July 11, 1933, James Wingate wrote to Paramount with some additional objections to I'm No Angel:

> Page A-8: In this speech of the barker's, we believe that the line "She'd give the old biological urge to a Civil War veteran" should be modified. . . .
>
> Page A-11: We believe the underlined words "Make 'em wait for it" should be deleted. . . .
>
> Page A-12: We believe the following lines in this lyric should be modified . . . : "All you need's the price," "Come on and pay," and "If you buy, she'll sell."
>
> Page A-17: Care will be needed with this scene of Tira undressing. . . .
>
> Page A-24: It is possible that the line "Take a lot, and give as little as possible" will be censorable.
>
> Page C-21: We suggest care with Tira's line "You'll like what I've got in mind . . ."
>
> Page C-24: We believe the underlined words "I'm always wonderful at night" should be deleted. . . . [This line was part of a steamy seduction scene in which Mae West vamps a youthful Cary Grant.]
>
> Page C-25: We believe the underlined words "When I'm good I'm very good, but when I'm bad I'm better" should be deleted. . . . [This dialogue remained in the film and became one of the most famous lines in film history.]

The Other Censors

Denmark deleted scenes of suggestive dancing in Reel 1 and eliminated "distasteful love scenes" in Reel 2.

Norway marked the film "for adults only" and deleted the scene of Mae spitting at the woman and the steamy flirtation scene between Mae West and Cary Grant in the hotel room. It also deleted "bad and immoral content of dialog."

Singapore at first banned the film and later passed it.

Japan deleted "objectionable dialog." In Reel 2 it killed the line: "No, no, give me the pillows." It deleted kisses in Reels 2, 3, and 7, and the line in Reel 5: "I am—one man at a time."

England eliminated Mae West's dance in Reel 1.

Australia made numerous deletions including the line, "If I weren't a married man, I could go for you, lady." It also eliminated underlined portion of Tira's dialogue: "I'm tired from tossing my hips," and it eliminated Tira saying to the other girl,

"Take all you can get and give as little as possible," and the famous Mae West line, "When I'm good I'm very good . . ."

Australia also eliminated the dialogue between West and Grant on the piano bench:

GRANT: "Move over, honey. Don't stop."
WEST: "I never stop."

Quebec had numerous eliminations including Mae West's line, "If you're half the man I think you are, you'll do." Alberta eliminated various lines including, "With the right kind of encouragement, she'll throw discretion to the winds."

It also eliminated the line, "She's safer in that cage than she is in bed," and the reply, "I don't doubt it." Mae's famous line, "It isn't the men in your life, it's the life in your men," was also cut out.

Maryland, Virginia, Kansas, Ohio, New York, and Pennsylvania made substantial deletions.

KLONDIKE ANNIE

After the creation of the Legion of Decency and the power it gave the Hays Office, Mae West's films grew increasingly chaste. Nonetheless, Mae became the perennial target of William Randolph Hearst, the Rupert Murdoch of his time. The publishing magnate heaped all manner of abuse on the lush blonde. Despite the blandness of her current vehicle, Hearst banned the mention of her name in all his papers—just as he had banned Orson Welles's after *Citizen Kane*. (On that occasion, Hearst was rabid over the fictional presentation of his life and livid that the film began with the word "Rosebud," the name Hearst had given to his mistress's, Marian Davies's, genitalia.)

When the innocuous *Klondike Annie* appeared, Hearst himself wrote a shrieking jeremiad that appeared in bold type in his numerous papers. "Are we again to have placed before us . . . motion pictures that exalt disreputable living and glorify vice?" asked Hearst. The question arose, said the publisher, upon viewing Mae West's *Klondike Annie*. "It is an immoral and indecent film," declared Hearst. He asked what Will Hays and his censors were doing when this film crossed their desks. "Were they asleep?" The publisher reminded Hays and his minions that it was their duty to assure that films were wholesome and healthy. Hearst had little faith in the state censors as backstop. "Censors in some states," he said, "may cut a few of the worst scenes, but they cannot cleanse it." Hearst was intemperate in his attack. "The story, scenes, and dialog are basically libidinous and sensual." He observed that decent people were certain to protest the vulgarity and lust that spilled from the screen and howled that Mae portrayed "a white woman in the role . . . of consort to a Chinese vice lord." Hearst lobbied the churchmen of the nation to mount a boycott of *Klondike Annie* and concluded his diatribe by declaring that movie producers obviously have no fear of public indignation. Therefore, the public had no choice but to withhold its patronage from such films as this, which "pander to the lewd elements of the community."

The day after this attack appeared, Hearst struck again with another angry editorial aimed at *Annie*. This time Hearst focused on Mae West's history, with emphasis on the police blotter. The editorial pointed out that in 1927 Mae West wrote and produced a play called *Sex* in New York City. The play was raided as obscene by the New York police, and her producer and members of the cast were indicted. Mae was convicted and sentenced to ten days in the workhouse. With this record of police raids, conviction, and a term on Welfare Island in her past, said Hearst, Mae West had been approached by the movie industry as a fresh subject to "introduce into the wholesome homes of the country and present to people with clean moral families." The sweetness of the American home, as seen through the sanctimonious pages of the Hearst press, is enough to decay the teeth. Hearst observed that Mae West's movie scripts were largely responsible for the uprising of the Church against filth in film that resulted in the "temporary improvement" of the morals of the movies.

The sudden and savage Hearst campaign against Miss West was apparently inspired not by *Klondike Annie*, which was like a fifth carbon of Mae at her best, but by a slighting remark she had made about movie actress Marion Davies, Hearst's protégé and mistress.

This campaign of vilification did not put an end to Mae West's career. She continued undaunted, though her movies became more and more sanitized, and her film career continued until 1943. Despite Hearst's scorn, all Miss West ever showed of herself on the screen was a fair amount of cleavage and some bawdy humor from her own pen. It was unjust that Mae West should be so pilloried, by tainted publishers and puritanical censors, for mocking the repressive attitudes toward sex that characterized the times. With her ample bosom and insinuating speech, she laughed at the hypocrisies of Hollywood morals, and she left as her epitaph the exaggerated suggestiveness of her trademark line: "Come up and see me some time."

On June 29, 1935, John Hammell of Paramount Pictures wrote a letter to Will Hays outlining the story lines for Mae West's forthcoming picture, Klondike Annie. General Hays, as he preferred to be addressed in recognition of his former responsibilities as Postmaster General, replied on July 2nd. Wrote Hays:

I have just received and read carefully the outline . . . for your next Mae West picture. After careful consideration and discussion, we believe the outline contains one element which is very questionable. We judge from your letter that, during part of this picture, Miss West will be masquerading as an exponent of religion or a religious worker. . . . It is our belief that it would be imperative that you make clear throughout the script that Miss West is not masquerading as a preacher, revivalist, or any other character known and accepted as a minister of religion, ordained or otherwise. Rather, her assumed character should be that of a social service worker, rescuing unfortunate girls, along the lines of numerous rescue missions.

Second, there should be no feeling of burlesque of this social worker. There should be no tongue-in-cheek portrayal of any scenes or dialog in this connection, although Miss West will be seen as entering this work in order to escape the law. Her activity should be shown as genuine to the point where eventually she herself becomes a changed woman.

Your outline contained no indication that the matter of Miss West killing the Chinese gambler would be satisfactorily cleared up. This approach will be vitally necessary. We assume there will be no suspicion of a loose or illicit sexual relationship between Miss West and the Chinese gambler, or any of the other characters in the your story. Rather . . . it will be definitely indicated that the woman Miss West represents is basically good.

Two months later, the story line had blossomed into a screenplay, entirely written by Mae West, down to the last line of saucy dialogue. The scenario was messengered to the Hays Office and prompted the following letter from Joe Breen on September 3rd:

> We have read the incomplete script dated August 27, 1935, for your proposed production titled *The Frisco Doll*.
>
> The action in this play in which Doll [Mae West] masquerades as an exponent of religion . . . is in our judgment of sufficient importance to make the entire story unacceptable. . . .

The following day, Breen augmented his general criticism in a lengthy letter to Paramount:

> With further reference to the incomplete script for *Frisco Doll* . . . we respectfully submit for your consideration the following details:
>
> *Page C-10:* Doll's line, "Say, I can tell you what King Solomon knew but didn't tell!" should be entirely deleted.
>
> ". . . It's a terrible cold sheet that only one person sleeps under," may be deleted. . . .
>
> *Page D-1:* Please be careful not to characterize the "painted women" as prostitutes.
>
> *Page D-4:* . . . Doll's speech, "You can't save a man's soul unless you get close to him. It's the personal touch that counts," has a double meaning. . . .
>
> *Scene B-2 et seq:* We presume that the statue in the captain's cabin will not be a nude statue.
>
> *Scene B-8:* The underlined portion of the following line [will be deleted]: "No, he's just one of these guys that gets you in a corner and breathes in your face."
>
> *Scene C-12:* Doll's line, "Yes, men are at their best when women are at their worst" [will be deleted] . . .
>
> Under the general heading of good welfare, we would like to suggest the possibility of working into the script as part of the activity of the settlement worker, shots of Doll playing games with the rough miners, possibly teaching them Mother Goose rhymes.

Mae West's insinuating songs continued to raise the censors' eyebrows. Joe Breen wrote to Paramount about one of the songs in the film:

> We have the lyrics for "I Hear You Knocking" . . . and believe that three of the lines should be rewritten before the lyric could

be acceptable. . . . To this end, we suggest that you rewrite the expression "But I can't give in" in the sixth line of the chorus; "Does me so much good" in the first line of the second chorus; and the line "He does his lovin' like a daddy should" in the third line of the second chorus.

By early February of 1936, Klondike Annie was in the can and had been screened for the censors. On February 7th, Charles Metzger made a list of criticisms assembled from the observations of all the Hays Office censors who attended the screening. The points were reviewed with the film producers, and a series of checks and crosses indicated which points the studio was willing to alter:

Reel 3: Scene of Lou [Mae West] on couch wiggling her body and evidently deciding to inflame Bull [Victor McLaglen] so that he won't turn her over to police. [Check—agree to cut.]
Scene of Lou in Bull's arms. [Cross—unwilling to cut.]
Scene of Lou combing Bull's hair, and his shirt is open at the neck. [cross.]
Delete shot of Bull with his hand on Lou's knee. . . . [Check.]
Reel 4: Cut Lou's line, "Give a man a free hand and he puts it all over you." . . . [Check.]
Reel 8: Lustful look in Bull's eyes when Lou sits on the arm of his chair and he looks down at her breasts. [Cross.]
Lou's line that, "when she is caught between two evils, she likes to take the one she never tried before." [Check.]

Probably as a result of the fulminations of Hearst and the Catholic Church, Paramount subsequently notified the Hays Office that all the desired changes would be made. An edited film was shown to the censors with all the objectionable scenes and lines removed, but when the Hays Office issued its Seal of Approval and the film opened commercially, members of the Hays Office staff went to see the movie in a local theater—either distrusting Paramount or wishing to satisfy their appetite for the West charm. Whatever their motive, they found to their horror that the lines that had ostensibly been removed from the film were still on display. Outraged, Breen wrote to Paramount declaring that the seal was being revoked until the demanded changes had been made in all prints. The changes were made and the seal was reissued. Good try, Mae.

Chapter 15
COMEDIES FROM BROADWAY

BORN YESTERDAY

Garson Kanin has never made a secret of his contempt for the movie industry he served or the censors who made his task as writer and director more difficult than it needed to be. Kanin was the leader of Hollywood's witty elite, who were planning, like commandos behind enemy lines, to bring more sophisticated wit to the screen than the moguls or the censors thought the audience wanted. Perhaps his finest comedy of sexual friction was *Adam's Rib*, but it was *Born Yesterday*, his tale of a vacant blonde and a king of junk, that brought him the greatest conflict with the censors.

Kanin's work and wit as a writer were often at the mercy of the censors, almost as much as they were vulnerable to the insensitivity of the movie magnates who paid the bills—men like Sam Goldwyn and Harry Cohn. He took as much pleasure in slipping a line or scene or situation past the repressive censors as he did in slipping them past the studio heads.

Kanin's gifts go beyond those of a writer of witty plays, films, and books of movie nostalgia. He had a gift for casting that let him recognize the special talent of Judy Holliday, who starred in *Born Yesterday* on Broadway and in the 1950 film. Kanin wrote *Born Yesterday* with a wonderful combination of wit and indignation. Much of the indignation was directed at corrupt politicians, which put him on a collision course with the Hollywood censors, who well remembered how costly to the industry was another comedy about corrupt legislators—*Mr. Smith Goes to Washington*. That comedy at the expense of Washing-

148

ton venality had cost the industry dearly, when a testy Congress stripped Hollywood of its block-booking privileges. The censors saw little wrong with a tycoon buying all the junk in the world, but when the big goon started buying U.S. senators, they called a halt.

The censors were also uneasy about the sexual relationship between the unsavory war profiteer and his dumb blonde, turning her from a credible mistress into an improbable fiancée.

Like so many films that the censors found encrusted with immoral elements, *Born Yesterday* is a supremely moral story. In the hands of a crusading writer, the erstwhile chorus girl Billie Dawn learns to think in terms of moral values and democratic ideals. The landmarks and monuments of the nation's capital give her the spiritual assurance to challenge the belligerent junk dealer and put an end to his powers. With or without the occasional ripe remark, *Born Yesterday* was a thoroughly moral and ethical story.

In January 1949, Harry Cohn sent to the Hays Office a screen adaptation written by Julius and Philip Epstein based on Garson Kanin's smash Broadway comedy Born Yesterday. *Joe Breen's response was not encouraging:*

. . . Regarding your proposed production titled *Born Yesterday*, there are some details in this script . . . which need further study. To those we respectfully direct your attention.

As a general observation, we would like to suggest that you carefully examine the present script with a view to deleting from it all action and dialog having to do with drinking. . . .

We would also like to suggest . . . that in the scene in which Eddie and Brock [Broderick Crawford] are packing the suitcases for the trip to Washington, you insert an affirmative speech to Billie [Judy Holliday] indicating that the chief reason for his insisting that she go with him to the nation's capital is because of the necessity for her having to sign certain papers in connection with Brock's various enterprises. . . .

In going through the script page by page, we respectfully direct your attention to the following . . . :

Page 7: Here and elsewhere, the swing in Billie's walk should not be offensive.

Page 36: We suggest rewriting Billie's line, "I can't tell you exactly, but it didn't do the plumbing no good."

Page 36: The underthing which Eddie holds up should not be one of Billie's "intimate garments."

Page 65 *et seq:* Here and elsewhere, please eliminate the word "broad." . . .

Page 65: Please eliminate the expression "bolix."

Page 70 *et seq:* Please eliminate the words "louse" and "lousy." . . .

Page 79: Please rewrite Billie's line, "If you don't act friendly, I don't act friendly. If you know what I mean." [This dialogue remained in the film and became one of the most famous lines in comedy history.]

Page 139: Please rephrase Billie's line, "How come you haven't made a pass at me yet? I've been awful patient."

Page 170: Please eliminate the burp from Brock.

On March 22, 1949, Rita O'Connor, an aide to Harry Cohn at Columbia Pictures, sent Breen a revised copy of the screenplay. Breen responded on March 29th with a list of additional changes:

Page 17: Brock's reaction to the line "Treat him like a doll you're trying to romance" is unacceptable as containing an inference of sexual perversion.

Page 68: We feel that there has been injected into this present version a definite and unacceptable flavor that Billie is trying to seduce Paul [William Holden]. This unacceptable flavor begins on this page with Billie's dialog, "Are you one of these talkers, or would you be innarested in a little action?" [This too became one of the film's famous lines.]

Page 17: The following dialog is unacceptable on account of the vulgar connotation: "Let me give you some advice, sonny boy. Never shovel it with a shoveler. I can sling it with the best of them." [The line was softened.]

Page 58: The following dialog we believe should be rewritten as offensive: "You know what a Senator is to me? A guy who makes a hundred and fifty bucks a week." Also the line, "But who wants to see her in the daytime?". . . .

Page 68: This scene should be played in Billie's sitting room, not in her bedroom. Also there must be no flavor about it that she is making a direct proposition to Paul for a sexual affair.

Harry Cohn sent the final script for Born Yesterday to Joe Breen on April 25th and produced the following response:

Page 12: At the bottom of the page, Brock should be wearing a T-shirt in addition to his shorts.

Page 78: The expression "four-letter words" should be changed. . . . [The phrase was deleted.]

Page 103: Billie's dialog again on this page seems to refer to her attempts to [seduce] Paul. The specific lines that bring out this flavor are . . . "You dropped the ball." This should be rewritten to make it plain that she is referring to her attempts to get Paul to fall in love with her, not to seduce him. [The line was delivered "inoffensively."]

Page 152: Omit the underlined word in the line, "There's a shortcut from my <u>bedroom.</u>" [The line was killed.]

Breen's letter to Harry Cohn precipitated a meeting between the two strong-willed men on June 23rd. Geoffrey Shurlock reported on the meeting for the Hays Office files:

Messrs. Breen and Shurlock had a meeting with Harry Cohn with regard [to *Born Yesterday*]. Mr. Cohn insisted that he would make certain that there would be no offense in the relationship between Billie and Paul in the finished picture and that there would be no suggestion that Billie was trying to get Paul to sleep with her.

The specific suggestion was made that in the scene in Billie's bedroom . . . the action would point up that Billie was trying to get Paul to kiss her—not to get into bed with her. [If this is the message that the average filmgoer takes away from *Born Yesterday*, it tends to support P.T. Barnum's speculations on the birth rate of the gullible.]

The Other Censors

The following is a summary of lines removed by foreign censors, including those of Australia and British Columbia, and state censors in Maryland and Pennsylvania: Harry Brock's lines: "Tell her yourself. She ain't pregnant"; "A broad's a broad"; "Dumb broad"; "Crazy broad"; and his "Let me give you a piece of advice. Never bull a bull artist. I can sling it with the best of them." Also cut was Billie's line, "Oh, Harry didn't want me being in the show. He didn't want to share me with the public. Besides, it gives him nothing to do nights."

THE MAN WHO CAME TO DINNER

When Warner Brothers transferred this hit Broadway comedy to the screen, it was little wonder that it was not so outrageously funny on film as it was on stage. The Hays Office had pruned all the salacious humor from the George S. Kaufman/Moss Hart script. *The Man Who Came to Dinner* is the story of a man thrust by accident into the home of unwilling hosts in an Ohio town, and relates how he makes himself obnoxious to everyone in the household. Kaufman and Hart used as their model for the overbearing invalid an audacious and volcanically witty columnist named Alexander Woollcott, and to make him as insufferable as possible to his reluctant hosts, they had him visited by characters loosely modeled after the lecherous Groucho Marx and the homosexual Noël Coward. All these bawdy elements of the stage comedy were scrupulously eliminated by the censors, which meant that moviegoers were never exposed to the saucy gags concocted by the playwriting team.

George S. Kaufman had a great gift for blue humor, which accounted for the naughty lines he created for the Marx Brothers in such classics as *A Night at the Opera*. The Epstein Brothers were assigned to adapt the play to the screen, and so they doubtless felt no personal loss when some of Kaufman and Hart's most amusing lines fell to the censor's blue pencil.

Like so many other comedies that came to Hollywood from Broadway, *The Man Who Came to Dinner* was deemed too sophisticated for the mass of moviegoers. The Hays Office censors clung to the condescending theory that witty lines—whether in the lyrics of Cole Porter or the comedies of George S. Kaufman—that had failed to corrupt New York's tired businessmen would have a ruinous effect on the impressionable clods who lined up at the cinema box offices. There was something both false and patronizing about this attitude. Joe Breen and his associates at the Hays Office would have laughed at the notion that their characters were being blighted by exposure to the uncleansed scripts and films they daily examined. Yet they felt duty bound to protect the public from these obscenities. It suggests the wisdom of Oscar Wilde's observation, "A reformer is a man who wants to protect you from all the sins of which he has grown tired."

There is a tender irony in the story of *The Man Who Came to Dinner*. The chief character is a well-known lecturer who has come to a small Midwestern town to speak at the local women's club. He has been invited to dinner at the home of a stuffed-shirt family, has an accident at their doorstep, and is brought inside. He wreaks havoc, with his offensive remarks and his libidinous friends. It was the women's clubs of America who were the most vocal critics of the movie industry, which had led to the formation of the Hays Office, as well as to virulent state censorship boards in such midwestern states as Ohio and Kansas. The family that finds themselves being tyrannized by the vitriolic, housebound Whiteside is a microcosm of all the heartland women's clubs that reacted with such repugnance to the excesses of Hollywood.

Warner Brothers had optioned The Man Who Came to Dinner *for the screen, commissioned the famous Epstein brothers—authors of* Casablanca—*to write the film adaptation, and in November 1940 sent the script to the Hays Office. On November 27th, Joe Breen wrote to Jack Warner:*

We have read the screenplay adaptation of the very excellent stage play *The Man Who Came to Dinner.* . . . It will be necessary that you omit many of the lines which are spread throughout the present screen adaptation, which are suggestively offensive:

Page 1: The clerk's line, "When you get married, you both have to take a test" should be omitted.

Page 10: All the business showing the various angles of "waiter's behind" must be omitted, as well as Whiteside's [Monty Woolley] line: "Not from where I sit."

Page 16: Whiteside's line, "I may vomit" as well as his line on page 17 [to the nurse], "You have the touch of a sex-starved cobra."

Page 32: Whiteside's line "I assure you, he used the bathroom too" is questionable. . . .

Page 42: Whiteside's line ". . . You sex-ridden hag" will have to be eliminated.

Page 44: Whiteside's line " I would have given you my old truss" should be eliminated. . . .

Page 66: Lorraine's line referring to Cybil Cartright, "You could practically see the airport," should be eliminated. [This was a cleaned-up version of the line in the play, in which, speaking of an English girl's attire, a character says: "She was wearing one of those new cellophane dresses, and you could absolutely see Trafalgar Square."]

Page 73: Maggie's [Bette Davis] line referring to Lorraine [an arrogant film star] ". . . as snug as a bug in somebody's bed" should be eliminated.

Page 73: The reference to the brassiere by one of the men should be eliminated. [This was a memorable moment in the play, in which Banjo, a character modeled after Groucho Marx, bursts into Whiteside's room, whips a pink undergarment from a tissue-wrapped package, and announces, "This brassiere was once worn by Hedy Lamarr."]

Page 76: [Eliminate] Beverley's line: "A large, moist incestuous kiss." [Beverley was a caricature of Noël Coward.]

Page 77: It is necessary that you exercise the greatest possible care in order not to suggest that Beverley is a pansy. Note, for example, his reference to Whiteside as "Sherry, darling." . . .

Page 78: Beverley's line "She is poised only to change girdles and check her oil" must be eliminated.

It is amusing to note that Breen begins this letter by praising "the very excellent stage play" and then proceeds to dismember it.

LIFE WITH FATHER

When playwrights Howard Lindsay and Russell Crouse made a free adaptation of Clarence Day's stories about *Life with Father*, and when this comedy, with Mr. Lindsay himself playing Father Day, ran for seven and one-half years (or 3,224 performances) on Broadway to break every record and become a warm memory for millions of theatergoers, it had a generation of critics asking a puzzling question: Who would have guessed that this family comedy, neither sexy nor sophisticated, would flourish so famously? When Warner Brothers adapted this long-running hit to the movie screen, it raised another puzzling question along Sunset Boulevard: Who would have thought that this family comedy, neither sexy nor sophisticated, would raise such a storm among the Hollywood censors?

True, it was not the sex in *Life with Father* that agitated the Hays Office, since there was precious little sex in the story. What concerned the censors was the suggestion of blasphemy in a story about the efforts of a middle-aging woman who tries to persuade her overbearing husband to be baptized.

There was also the matter of the mild profanity that was sprinkled throughout the play, and one particular bit of blasphemy that was as famous in its way as another profane line that filmmaker and censor had battled over several years before: "Frankly, my dear, I don't give a damn." The offending line in

Life with Father read: "No, I'm going to be baptized, dammit."
Two damns, several years apart, equally essential, equally innocuous, triggered battles that shook the Hays Office to its foun-
dation.

In November of 1939, early in the run of the smash comedy
that would run for seven record-breaking seasons on the Great
White Way, Louis B. Mayer sent a copy of the Lindsay/Crouse
play to the Hays Office for their comments on its vulnerability
to the censorship code. On December 5th, in a letter to the MGM
mogul, Joe Breen responded:

[You have] been kind enough to send us a copy of the New York
stage play *Life with Father.* I am sending this to let you have our
reaction to it.
   While we continue to be of the opinion that the material in its
present form is not acceptable . . . we do feel that with some
important changes, the play might be made into an acceptable
screen production.
   As we read it there are three problems suggested by the stage
play . . . :
      1. The characterization of the minister as a comedy character.
      2. The profanity which is spread throughout the play.
      3. The comedy which is suggested by the efforts on the part
of the mother to persuade the father to be baptized.
   It seems to us that the first two of the above factors can be
handled very easily. The character of the minister can be played
straight; . . . the profanity can be eliminated entirely. . . .
   The conversation on the part of the wife to persuade her husband to be baptized is, of course, delicate material, but we feel it
can be satisfactorily handled without giving offense to patrons
who may be sensitive on any point having to do with religion.
   As we read the play, the comedy that has to do with discussions about baptism is acceptable, but it will be necessary . . .
in the preparation of this screenplay based upon the stage play
to exercise the greatest possible care in the development of the
situation arising out of this particular phase of the comedy. . . .

MGM did not pursue Life with Father and seven years passed—
in which the play continued to pile up thousands of performances on the New York stage. As Mayer's convictions foun-
dered, Jack L. Warner's flourished. In February 1946, Warner
commissioned screenwriter-playwright Donald Ogden Stewart

to write a film adaptation of Life with Father, *and sent it to the
Hays Office. Joe Breen responded to Jack Warner as follows:*

> Going through the script in detail, we call your attention to the
> following . . . :
> [Breen's letter reflected all the caveats of his earlier letter to
> Mayer seven years before. He urged Warner to omit anything that
> might offend "religious-minded people," and pressed him to root
> out the various "damns" and "damnations" that father shouted
> across the footlights]

*Theologians have speculated on how many angels could dance
on the head of a pin. This dilemma brings to mind another
question of how many censors could dance on the head of a
mild profanity. On May 18th, Joe Breen wrote to Eric Johnston,
the president of the Motion Picture Association of America and
father of the Production Code Administration. Warners was about
to put* Life with Father *into production, and, at the eleventh
hour, a decision was needed from the highest level on a crucial
matter. Wrote Breen to Johnston:*

> Please note our attached letter to [Warners] on the final script.
> Note specifically the one-line paragraph on Page 2 . . . with
> reference to . . . the exclamation "Dammit!"
> You will recall in the stage play, after many trials and tribula-
> tions, the father is persuaded to submit himself for baptism. . . .
> In the screenplay, in the next to the last scene of the picture, the
> father comes out of the family home in the early morning to take
> his place in the family carriage . . . in which are seated his wife
> and several of the children.
> As he comes down the steps, glaring at the family, a policeman
> approaches, tips his cap to the father, and says: " 'Morning, Mr.
> Day. Going to the office?"
> To which the father replies, "No, I'm going to be baptized,
> dammit!"
> In the stage play, this speech by the father is one of the high-
> lights of the entire story. Warner Brothers are anxious to retain
> it and have asked our approval. We have advised Mr. Warner
> that it is not within our authority to do this, in as much as the
> word "damn" is on our list of "forbidden words." . . .
> It is our considered judgment that the use of the word "damn"
> in *Life with Father* does not come within the scope of the special
> resolution which does allow for the use of the word "damn."

In several instances in the past, the Production Code Administration has withheld its approval of the use of the word "damn."

An appeal was taken to the president of the Board of Directors of the Motion Picture Association in New York.

Upon such appeal, the Board allowed the company to use the word, even though its use appeared to be in violation of the provisions of the code. Another notable case is that of *Gone With the Wind*, in which the Board permitted as a tag line Clark Gable's famous reply, "Frankly, my dear, I don't give a damn."

I am given to understand that Mr. Warner proposes to appeal to you in order to secure permission from our Board to use the word "damn."

It is our unanimous judgment that, if a way can be found to allow Warner Brothers to use this word, no serious harm will be done. . . .

On March 22nd, Eric Johnston responded to Breen with an airmail letter authorizing the word "dammit" in *Life with Father*. A carbon copy was sent to Jack Warner, who doubtless rejoiced at this small blessing. Reading this lengthy exchange of correspondence, in which three mature men of tremendous power and position pondered the question of whether, in 1946, an actor could say "dammit" on a movie screen, reminds one of just how gun-shy Hollywood was about the pious members of its audience, as well as how morality is such a matter of time and place.

The Other Censors

The film was banned in Turkey. Said the Turkish censor: "The theme deals with religion and is, therefore, unsuitable for distribution."

In Holland, the film was approved for exhibition only to those over eighteen and only after several significant cuts had been made. Said the disapproving Dutch censor: "The main character in this picture is a father who acts eccentrically and tyrannically in his family. This causes several silly situations. Everything is concentrated on the fact that at a certain moment, it turns out that the father has not been baptized. His wife tries to persuade him, but she does not succeed, until, during a serious illness of hers, he promises to be christened, which after renewed resistance of the man, and cunning intrigues of the woman, finally happens. . . . The sacrament of baptism is no theme for comedy."

The British censors made deep deletions in the film, cutting material that related to church and clerical matters.

Pennsylvania, unimpressed by the Breen/Johnston dispensation, eliminated the word "dammit," so that the climactic line in the film, as heard by moviegoers in Philadelphia, Pittsburgh, and Allentown, became, "No, I'm going to be baptized [pause]."

Kansas, Maryland, Massachusetts, New York, and Ohio approved the film without eliminations.

PYGMALION

George Bernard Shaw was infuriated by movie censorship on both sides of the Atlantic. The iconoclastic playwright was appalled at the sanctimony and implausible morality of the movies. He heard much about the danger to the public morals that the Hays Office was designed to thwart. Said Shaw: "The danger of the cinema is not the danger of immorality, but of morality. . . . People who, like myself, frequent the cinemas, testify to their devastating romantic morality. There is no comedy, no wit, no criticism of morals by ridicule or otherwise . . . nothing that could give a disagreeable shock to the stupid or shake the self-complacency of the smug."

Shaw had built an international reputation for wit by shocking the stupid and shaking the smug. With the leveling process of screen censorship, it was not surprising that the famous dramatist would find little to satisfy his tastes.

One screen comedy that undoubtedly pleased him was the adaptation of his classic comedy *Pygmalion*, which, inexplicably, Shaw granted permission to be filmed. (Shaw generally vetoed all attempts to purchase film rights to his plays. To Sam Goldwyn, Shaw said: "You and I are interested in two different things, Mr. Goldwyn. You care only about art and I care only about money.")

Shaw's famous comedy about the transformation of a Cockney flower girl into a lady by a phonetics expert was the first authorized screenplay written by the world's leading living dramatist at the time. Predictably, the censors found numerous elements that were not in accordance with the dreaded Production Code. Much of their objections centered about the pliable morality of Eliza's father, who seemed ready to sell his daughter to Professor Higgins for pocket change. The suggestion that Eliza was born out of wedlock, which had failed to corrupt a generation of theatergoers in London and New York, was considered too hot to handle by the Hollywood censors.

Despite the carping of the Hays Office crew, *Pygmalion* proved a mine of entertainment riches. (Lerner and Loewe found the same riches when they brought it to the musical stage as *My Fair Lady*.) *Pygmalion* brought lovers of fine art flocking to movie theaters everywhere, and, since Shaw meant to protect his coruscating dialogue from the Hollywood adapters, he wrote the screen version himself. Thus, the motion picture *Pygmalion* marked the debut of a most promising screenwriter indeed. Shaw added a jocular prologue to the film. Squinting through his bushy brows at the camera lens, the wry Mr. Shaw was probably thinking of the repressions of the censors and the frustrations of the moviegoers when he observed with a grin that, with *Pygmalion*, he intended to "teach America what a film should be like." Unfortunately, the Hays Office was simultaneously teaching Mr. Shaw the same thing.

As producer Gabriel Pascal prepared to film Pygmalion, *he wanted to assure himself that he would be free to exhibit the completed film in America. He thus sent Shaw's completed screenplay to the Hays Office. This produced a letter to Pascal from F.S. Harmon of the Production Code:*

We have read with pleasure the script for your forthcoming feature *Pygmalion*. . . .

We call your attention to the occasional bits of profanity which definitely violate one section of the code. . . .

Page 3, Scene 38: In view of the meaning which the word "baggage," as applied to a woman, has come to have in the U.S., we request a substitution of some other expression.

Page 107, Scene 326: . . . Please eliminate the expression "You *damned impudent slut."*

Page 47, Scene 58 et seq: We are confident that the scenes of Mrs. Pearce disrobing Eliza and giving her a bath will be handled within the careful limits of good taste. The code prohibits the exposure of sex organs, including the breasts of women.

Page 63, Scene 82: As to the exchange of pleasantries between

Eliza's father, Doolittle, who asks five pounds from Higgins; Colonel Pickering's statement that Professor Higgins's [Leslie Howard] intentions are entirely honorable; Doolittle's reply: "Of course they are, Governor. If I thought they wasn't, I'd ask fifty"; and Higgins's comment, "Do you mean to say, you callous rascal, that you would sell your daughter for fifty pounds?"; please change the following reply by Doolittle: "Not in a general way, I wouldn't . . . but to oblige a gentleman like you, I'd do a great deal, I assure you," so as to avoid leaving the impression that, in a final showdown, this father would have been willing to sell his daughter's virtue.

MGM wished to distribute the British-made Pygmalion *in the United States with the completion of the film, on September 9, 1938, Joe Breen wrote to MGM's Louis B. Mayer:*

This goes to you in confirmation of our review of the British picture titled *Pygmalion,* which you submitted to us for review; and we wish to report that in its present form it does not seem to be acceptable. . . .

In order to bring the picture within the provisions of the Production Code, the following changes would seem to be necessary:

All profanity must be deleted.

In the first scene with the father, delete certain pointed suggestions that he has gone there with the idea of "selling" his daughter. In the second scene in which the father appears, it will be necessary to remove the suggestion that his daughter is an illegitimate child and the further suggestion that he had been living with the girl's mother outside of marriage. This comedy treatment of illicit sex is . . . not acceptable.

Chapter 16

DRAMAS

THE BEST YEARS OF OUR LIVES

World War II profoundly affected American films. As American filmmakers returned from their exposure to war and foreign societies, they had imprinted on their collective consciousness the realities of the world that they had never, in their pre-war careers, been permitted to put up on the screen. The brutality and sex that they encountered bore little relation to the saccharine fairy tales that the Hollywood censors used to impose on them. The censorship myths—of twin beds and honeymoons and covered navels—made no sense at all. The returning screenwriters and directors found the Hays Office and its repressive rulings laughable.

Some of the most moderate filmmakers were taking the blasphemous step of questioning the very raison d'être of the Production Code. One of these was Samuel Goldwyn. Like Louis B. Mayer—who had said "our duty is to create beautiful pictures about beautiful people"—Goldwyn was devoted to decency and wholesomeness in his films. Yet, as the war ground to a close, Goldwyn said of the censorship code, "I think it is about time we all joined to do something about this awful millstone around the neck of the motion picture industry."

And so, in 1945, with the proclamation of this epic Goldwynism, the producer optioned a bestselling novel by MacKinlay Kantor titled *Glory For Me*, which told some mature stories about the real world of three returning servicemen. Audiences were ready for more realistic films. They had had enough of Betty Grable and her innocuous musicals, John Wayne and his celluloid heroics, Bette Davis and her neurotic romances. They were hungry for realism of a sort that seldom found its way through the Hays Office filter.

When *The Best Years of Our Lives* appeared, some of the inhibitions of the Hays Office were loosening, and the threats of the Legion of Decency were not enough to stem the tide. From this point on, a producer's boldness would be rewarded, but boldness was still required. Joe Breen had numerous complaints with *Lives*. There was too much drinking; Dana Andrews had not been celibate in the European theater; Fredric March actually slept with his wife on his first night home from the wars; Harold Russell's girl friend kissed him with passion on his return. But Goldwyn's film was the first indication that the war had changed Hollywood, and producers' attitudes toward sex and life would never be the same.

The Best Years of Our Lives was the postwar film that many, who had grown weary of irrelevant censorship, had long awaited. In retrospect, its drama seems somewhat tepid, but, in 1945, it provided audiences with emotional dynamite. The soda jerk who became an army officer, the bank official who came back a sergeant, and the seaman who returned minus both his hands, were unsparing in their truth. Though Joe Breen quibbled over the number of imbibing scenes, *Lives* was a monumental postwar film. The troops—both in the story and behind the camera—had come home for good.

On July 30, 1945, Samuel Goldwyn sent a copy of MacKinlay Kantor's Glory For Me to Joe Breen, declaring that he planned this as his next picture, and that Robert E. Sherwood, the distinguished playwright and presidential speech writer, was going to do the screenplay. Breen responded on August 1st:

> We have read with great care the MacKinlay Kantor story called *Glory For Me* that you have been kind enough to submit for our examination, and I regret to be compelled to advise you that, as now written, the story contains many unacceptable incidents, lines of dialog, and characterizations which, under the provisions of the industry Production Code, could not be approved. . . .
>
> Regarding the story of the sergeant [Fredric March], it is our thought that . . . the incident where the sergeant and his wife sleep together on the night of his return . . . seems to be unduly intimate in its details.
>
> With regard to the story of the lieutenant [Dana Andrews], we

feel that it will be necessary . . . in dealing with his story to change the characterization of the lieutenant in such a way as to keep it free from any suggestion of his frequent sex sins while he was overseas. . . .

The scene in which the lieutenant finds his wife in company with another man has to be very carefully handled. . . . It will be likewise necessary to eliminate from the screenplay the many offensive or questionable sex lines that run throughout the book. . . .

Eight months later, Goldwyn sent Breen the Robert E. Sherwood script for the film that bore the title The Best Years of Our Lives. *Again Breen was prompt, yet thorough, in his response. His objections were numerous and filled a tightly typed eight-page letter. On April 1st he wrote:*

We have read with considerable care the script for your production *The Best Years of Our Lives*, and, on Saturday last, had an opportunity to discuss the story with Messrs. Sherwood and William Wyler at Mr. Wyler's home. . . .

You will have in mind the need for the exercise of the greatest possible care in the shooting of all scenes of kissing. These should not be prolonged, or lustful, and there should be no *open-mouthed kissing*.

The several scenes in your picture having to do with the breakup of the marriage between Fred [Dana Andrews] and Marie [Virginia Mayo] should be reexamined and possibly rewritten in order to get away from any suggestion of the condonation of this tragedy. This is important.

In going through the script page by page, we respectfully direct your attention to the following:

Page 24: Please note the reference to Wilma kissing Homer [Harold Russell] "passionately."

Page 46: The quote "plenty of girls" suggested at the top of the page should not be suggestive of prostitutes.

Page 51: The "Italian expletive" should not be vulgar or offensive.

Page 54: Please rewrite Al's line "And we'll all reenlist in a pig's ———."

Page 67: We suggest the elimination from Fred's speech in Scene 80 the line, "Come here, Peggy, and give me a great big kiss," and Peggy's [Teresa Wright] reply, "I'm not *that* Peggy."

Page 77: . . . In passing we would like to suggest that there be twin beds.

Page 108: The British Board of Film Censors always eliminated the expression "bum."

Page 122: We presume that in the scene of the "old-fashioned bathroom," there will be shown no toilet.

Page 132: Please eliminate the underlined portion of the following line by Homer: "A <u>hot</u> blonde baby."

Scene 139: We would like to ask that you eliminate entirely scenes of drinking, specifically all the business of the young seventeen-year-old daughter preparing and shaking the cocktails. . . . These are specifically the kind of scenes which offend our patrons. . . .

Page 167: The dresses of both Marie and Peggy should not expose their breasts, and the action of Marie moving the vase of flowers so that it does not mask her breasts should be entirely eliminated.

Page 169: Al should not belch. . . .

Page 184: We suggest the elimination of the expression "Jew-lovers." . . .

We can see the results of these Hays Office demands in notations made in the margins of the file copy of Breen's letter. Director Wyler and screenwriter Sherwood bowed to the threat of action by the British censors and removed the word "bum," which, to the British, connotes the posterior. No toilet would be shown, they assured. They agreed to kill the line "a hot blonde baby." They wished to retain the action of the seventeen-year-old girl mixing cocktails. They removed the shot of the girl moving the vase to reveal her breasts. The belch was stifled. The term "Jew-lovers" was removed.

SUNSET BOULEVARD

The rule of compensatory punishment established by the Hays Office dictated that if one sins, one pays the piper. Though the rule has seldom applied to the careers of Hollywood producers, it was strictly enforced in the movies they created. *Sunset Boulevard* provides a useful example. Told against the background of the film colony, it unreeled a tale of a faded queen of silent movies who clings to her delusions of past grandeur. Billy Wilder and Charles Brackett concocted a story in which a penniless, cynical screenwriter is snared in the former star's web of illusions and lured to her quilted bed.

The Hays Office felt that William Holden, who played the down-on-his-luck writer, should pay for his sins of ambition, and so the film had to be oddly distorted: Holden tells his story as a voiceover narrator, as the audience gapes at his dead body floating in the star's decaying swimming pool. Before the main titles, he has been shot dead by the star—rivetingly played by Gloria Swanson—for having had the temerity to trash her delusions.

There is an irony of sorts in the code's insistence that unbridled ambition and sexual depravity must be punished by death. If such compensation were typical of Movieland, you would hear nothing but gunfire all day long, and the streets of Hollywood would be choked with funeral processions.

The original writ of the Hays Office was to improve the image of the movie industry. The American public had read of a series of ugly scandals involving drugs, adultery, and murder, and been repelled by this Sodom with modern plumbing. For this reason, the censors disliked films like *Sunset Boulevard*, which spread the decadent side of Hollywood life across the screen. This caustic drama, after all, described a scandalous situation involving the ambitions and frustrations of a cardboard city. The censors were uneasy about such a civic portrait and the chance that it might reawaken the unwholesome image they had been taking such pains to bury.

In April 1949, Paramount sent a copy of the Billy Wilder/ Charles Brackett script for Sunset Boulevard to the Hays Office. On April 21st, Joe Breen responded:

We have read the pages . . . for your proposed production Sunset Boulevard. . . .

Page 12: Please eliminate Gillis's [William Holden] line: "I'm up that creek and I need a job."

Page 49: Please eliminate the reference to Miss Desmond [Gloria Swanson] having been married three times.

In a follow-up letter to Paramount on May 24th, Breen wrote:

We have read a considerable number of changed pages for your proposed production Sunset Boulevard. . . .

The most recent of this material seems to indicate the introduction of a sex affair between Gillis and Norma Desmond, which was not present in the earlier material. Whether or not this overall story will [sustain] a sex affair, we cannot say. However, it seems to us at this point that there is no indication of a voice for morality by which this will be condemned; nor does there appear to be a compensating moral value of the sin. We are quite aware that the story is told in flashback and the leading man is shown to be dead when the story opens. . . .

It is interesting to note that the public acted as "censor" to leave one of Billy Wilder's favorite scenes on the cutting room floor. As the film was originally shot, the movie opens with the body of William Holden being rolled into the city morgue, where it joins numerous other corpses. Some of these bodies, in voice-over, tell the deceased screenwriter how they died in the Hollywood jungle. When Paramount previewed the film, these talking corpses produced inappropriate laughter in the audience. Wilder reluctantly cut the morgue scene from the film, a victim of the censorship of the marketplace—which many contend should be the only censorship.

The Other Censors

Ohio eliminated a sequence between the faded star and the screenwriter. He has returned after having been called home and finds Norma lying in bed with her wrist bandaged. He sits on her bed, takes her bandaged hand, and says, "Happy New Year, Norma." She replies, "Happy New Year, darling." Ohio eliminated the shot of her reaching up, clutching his coat collar, and drawing him down to her—fade-out.

A PLACE IN THE SUN

An illicit love affair, an unwelcome pregnancy, a young woman seeking an abortion, a young man unwilling to marry the girl he has impregnated—these were some of the taboos that George Stevens confronted when he sought to contemporize and transfer to the screen Theodore Dreiser's ponderous, powerful novel, *An American Tragedy*.

Ten years before, Stevens would have been unable to deal with any one of these ticklish subjects, but by 1949 he was able at least to suggest most of them. Still, the Hays Office kept each of these proscribed situations—love affair, pregnancy, abortion—from being presented explicitly and forthrightly. The boy could not be shown leaving the girl's room the morning after their night of love. The visit to the doctor was kept free of any clear reference to the wanted abortion. The affair between the tainted hero and his factory girl friend demanded a disapproving voice of morality. The relationship between the boy and his society girl had to be kept scrupulously free of sex. The kisses had to be as dispassionate and as brief as possible. These caveats aside, George Stevens was able to convey, by suggestion and indirection, far more than any moviemaker had dared to propose before.

Stevens called his movie *A Place in the Sun*. It told the story of George Eastman (Montgomery Clift), an ambitious young nephew of a wealthy manufacturer, who goes to work for his uncle and has an affair with a girl at the factory (Shelley Winters), who becomes pregnant. George falls in love with a wealthy girl in the town (Elizabeth Taylor) and is convicted of murder when the pregnant girl is drowned in an accident resulting from his plans for a murder and his failure to save her from the accident. George is innocent of murder, of course, and, as he goes to the electric chair, the clear implication is that society is being indicted. That was Dreiser's American tragedy—a tragedy of avarice and ambition, two sins not specifically forbidden under the Production Code.

In September 1949, Paramount sent the Hays Office the lean screenplay that George Stevens had had adapted from Dreiser's cumbersome novel. Joe Breen handled the hot potato deftly, replying on September 30th:

We have read the script for your proposed picture *Modern Story*. . . . We call your attention to the following . . . :
Page 12: There must be nothing questionable about this sun suit. . . .
Page 41: As written, this scene is unacceptably suggestive and must not be played with the camera on the radio and the voices coming from offscreen. [Montgomery Clift and Shelley Winters are dancing in the room as a preface to love.] The camera must be focused on the principals so we see that they are dancing.
Page 42: We believe that Scene 63 is unacceptably suggestive. We submit that the point of illicit sex has been sufficiently estab-

lished without showing George leaving Alice's room next morning.

Page 57: Please rewrite the following speech by Alice as overly pointed [about her pregnancy]: "The first night you told me, you remember? The first night you came here, remember? You said I wouldn't have to worry. You said nothing would happen—remember?"

Also please omit the underlined words in Alice's line: "<u>It's happened</u>."

Page 59: Please omit the following dialog—the last line being definitely suggestive of abortion: "Oh, no change at all? Just the same?. . . . No, I haven't thought of anything yet."

Page 66: The two lines at the bottom of the page are unacceptable, as a discussion of abortion: "There must be someone, some place you can go. . . ." "That's what you've been saying week after week. . . ."

Page 96: Please, also, omit the line "We can spend the night there—in the lodge."

Page 106: We feel this story needs a voice of morality between George and Alice. We think that one of them, preferably Alice, should take some cognizance of the moral wrong of their predicament. . . .

Page 128: It will be most important to avoid any possible inference of a sex affair between Angela [Elizabeth Taylor] and George. For this reason, we believe some change will be necessary in connection with this slow dissolve. . . . [A slow dissolve on an embrace implies to a mature audience impending intercourse.]

Two months later, on November 1st, Breen wrote to Paramount concerning the script:

We have read [additional] pages for your production of *A Place in the Sun:*

Page 29 et seq: The kissing here and elsewhere throughout the story should not be unduly passionate, or long, or open-mouthed.

Page 41: As presently described, we feel the scene in Alice's apartment is unacceptable as to detail. We . . . request that you do not indicate that George spends the night there.

On November 14th, Breen again wrote to Paramount:

We have read [revisions] . . . for your proposed production *A Place in the Sun. . . .*

The scene between Alice and Dr. Wyeland as presently written is unacceptable because of the suggestion that Alice is seeking an abortion.

The present scene of Alice and George going to a motel is unacceptable. We feel this merely overemphasizes the illicit relationship between the two. . . .

Page 90: George's line, ". . . Just the sort of place for a honeymoon. There's a lodge on it and we could spend the night there and tomorrow we can . . ." is unacceptable.

The Other Censors

Ohio said: "In the sequence between George and Alice in her room, in scene where they dance offscreen, eliminate the second time she whispers 'George . . .' and eliminate light changing to dawn and sound of rooster crowing."

THE MAN WITH THE GOLDEN ARM

Otto Preminger is often praised for his courage in making the film *The Man With the Golden Arm* from Nelson Algren's unsparing novel of dope and addiction. The Hollywood censorship code was unyielding in its prohibition of any film dealing with drug addiction, and, in making *Golden Arm*, Preminger was clearly flouting the Hays Office injunction. Yet an examination of the film, which starred Frank Sinatra as Frankie Machine, the man with the monkey on his back, reveals that Preminger's courage was more in producing the movie than in the movie itself.

In the lacerating novel, Frankie Machine, the luckless hero, is powerless to shake the drug habit, but in Preminger's film, Sinatra rids himself of his dependency and ends up in the arms of Kim Novak—just as he would a few years later in *Pal Joey*. Perhaps it would be the conquest of hope over experience to expect Preminger to deny the audience a happy ending in addition to challenging the powerful Production Code.

United Artists distributed the film, and they showed their mettle and their disgust with the obsolescent censorship code by resigning from the Motion Picture Association of America, the Hays Office's parent body. Seeing their organization begin to unravel, the MPAA promptly called a meeting of studio presidents to weigh the need for present alternatives in the code to reflect "changing community standards." It was suddenly discovered that drug addiction and narcotics traffic were national problems that cried out for public attention. Like most bullies, the rule of life of the censors was "push or be pushed," and with United Artists jumping ship, the Production Code was being pushed.

With *The Man With the Golden Arm* playing to big box office around the country, the studio chiefs decided on some cautious amendments to the censorship code. A revised document appeared: The forbidden topic of narcotics was no longer forbidden. Other subjects that had been taboo for two decades suddenly shed their prohibitions. With the stroke of a pen, filmmakers were free to deal with prostitution and abortion, and, wonder of wonders, such prosaic epithets as "hell" and "damn" were admitted to the movie lexicon.

There is one final story in the history of *The Man With the Golden Arm*. In the past, the Legion of Decency had always been much stricter than the Hays Office in their moral sensibilities, but, in this case, while the Hollywood censors declined to place their seal on Preminger's film, the Legion failed to officially condemn it. The Legion acquiescence reflected the recognition by the Catholic Church that the moral climate was changing.

On January 12, 1950, R.P. Roberts, of Roberts Productions, sent a screenplay of The Man With the Golden Arm *to the Hays Office. After careful scrutiny, on March 7th Joe Breen responded:*

> We have read the script . . . regarding your proposed production of *The Man With the Golden Arm* and regret to report that this basic story is unacceptable . . . and a motion picture based upon [it] cannot be approved.
>
> The unacceptability of this story stems from the fact that it violates the following provision of the Production Code:
>
> "The illegal drug traffic must not be portrayed in such a way as to stimulate curiosity concerning the use of or traffic in such drugs; nor show scenes . . . which show the use of such drugs or their effects and details."
>
> In view of the fact that this dope addiction problem is basic to

this story, we suggest that you give careful consideration to this material. . . .

Breen's letter seemed adequate to dampen Roberts's interest, but the following month, Pandro Berman, a senior producer at MGM, took an interest in the property and discussed it with a representative of the Hays Office. In a memo to the files, E.G. Dougherty of the Hays Office, wrote:

> Mr. Pandro Berman of MGM discussed the novel The Man With the Golden Arm with Mr. Dougherty today.
> He stated his interest in trying to develop a story line based on this novel on the subject of a man breaking himself of the habit of dope addiction.
> I told Mr. Berman we can see no possibility . . . of handling this subject of dope addiction. . . .

Not entirely dissuaded by Breen's admonitions, R.P. Roberts developed a screenplay based on Golden Arm and sent it to the Hays Office. On June 21st, Breen replied with the crash of a hammer on an anvil:

> I have read with extreme care the revised script for your proposed production The Man With the Golden Arm and it is our considered and unanimous opinion that this story is totally in violation of the Production Code. . . .

Fade-out, fade-in. Breen out, Shurlock in. Five years later, in the spring of 1955, Otto Preminger sent the Hays Office a new screen adaptation of Golden Arm. The director-producer declared that he considered the way this controversial theme was handled to be most important. Preminger believed, he said, that a film done with integrity could perform a public service and he would appreciate Shurlock reading the new screenplay with care. Two weeks later, on July 3rd, Shurlock replied:

> I . . . regret to have to report your script for The Man With the Golden Arm is fundamentally in violation of the code clause which prohibits our approving pictures dealing with drug addiction.

Shurlock, a man of erudition and sensitivity, discussed the script with Preminger on the phone, and, a few days later, he wrote to the director again:

As discussed over the telephone, this letter is written as an ad-junct to our previous letter of July 6th, to list some . . . items in your script. . . .

Page 39: With regard to the action in this Café Safari, please be advised we cannot approve any stripteasing or bumps and grinds. . . .

Page 65: In this scene where Molly [Kim Novak] is undressing, we suggest that at no time should she be shot in anything less than a slip.

Page 142: The action on this page which suggests that Zosh deliberately commits suicide to avoid capture . . . is in violation of the code.

Without the approval of the Hays Office, and in the face of their opposition, Otto Preminger and United Artists proceeded to film The Man With the Golden Arm. *In December, Shurlock screened the film and wrote to Preminger:*

. . . We have today reviewed your picture *The Man With the Golden Arm.*

As we advised you, the picture is basically in violation of . . . the Production Code. . . . For this reason, it will not be possible for us to issue an Association Certificate of Approval.

Also, for the record, even if the basic story were acceptable, we feel that there would be two minor items in the picture which would need correction. The first of these is the scene of the prep-aration of the hypodermic needle when the leading man is given his first injection by the narcotics peddler. The second of these unacceptable elements consists of certain shots of the stripteas-ers. . . .

The events described above—the withdrawal of United Artists from the MPAA and the amendment of the censorship code to permit the treatment of the subject of narcotics—transpired on the heels of this correspondence.

It might be said that Otto Preminger was a man bent on sen-sationalism and that *The Man With the Golden Arm* was an unrelieved depressant; but so indeed were the plays of Tennes-see Williams, Eugene O'Neill, and the Greek tragedies. Premin-ger's defiance of the censors had not thrown open the gates to filmmaking freedom, but it had at least left them ajar.

THE BICYCLE THIEF

One remarkable movie established an international reputation a few years after the close of World War II. It was called *The Bicycle Thief* and was directed by Vittorio De Sica. Robert E. Sherwood called it "a heartrending work of art"; Arthur Miller said it was unique, "one of those conquests of art which heretofore movies have not been able to manage"; Helen Hayes called it "a perfect work of art"; S.J. Perelman called it "magnificent"; Elia Kazan called it "a wonderful picture"; but the opinion of these artists notwithstanding, the Hays Office would not approve *The Bicycle Thief* for exhibition in the United States. There were two troublesome scenes—a shot of a boy urinating against a wall, and a scene where a boy pursues a thief into a Roman bordello. The code authorities demanded the excision of these two shots if the alien film was to be allowed into America.

The year was 1950 and, considering the problems of the moviemaking business at the time—from plummeting business in the face of television to cries for national censorship in the U.S. Senate—the Hays Office position on *The Bicycle Thief* indicated the kind of antediluvian thinking that was sadly out of tune with the times. It was puzzling that the Hollywood censors could stonewall the demands for liberalization in their own repressive code at such a time. They seemed to be imperiling the very industry they were created to preserve.

The Hays Office painted the problem as a matter of morals; yet, to those who had seen the film, it was hardly that. The American censors had described the offensive scenes in lurid terms, but, as a matter of fact, they were neither offensive nor indecent, and hardly an affront to good taste. Indeed, in the context of this magnificent film, the scenes were perfectly right and perfectly moral.

The first fleeting episode—of the boy relieving himself—was poignant and amusing, and no reasonable person would be offended by it. The second episode of controversy, involving pursuit of a suspect into what appears to be a bordello, is even more innocuous. There is nothing the least bit appealing about the drab little apartment, nothing seductive about the depressed-looking women having their breakfast.

Much of the American media joined the film's producers in speculating that the Hays Office was opposing the film out of resentment toward foreign filmmakers—that *The Bicycle Thief* was banned as part of an attempt to sabotage foreign films in the United States. Joe Breen heatedly denied the charge, citing the hundreds of "toilet gags" and prostitute scenes which he had kept off the screen during his watch. Whether his motive was genuine or parochial, the Hollywood censors were closing the doors to one of the greatest films of the postwar era.

There was one additional irony to the Hays Office's demands. At the same time that Breen was brandishing his scissors, the Hays Office's parent body was fighting a battle in the courts against state censorship. Yet curiously enough, *The Bicycle Thief* had been approved without cuts by the censors of New York, Ohio, and Pennsylvania. The observer was forced to ask: Was the Hays Office trying to be more censorious than the state censors it was attacking?

On January 31, 1950, Joe Breen screened The Bicycle Thief *and was quick to communicate his dismay to Art Mayer and Joseph Burstyn, the movie's U.S. distributors:*

. . . We had the pleasure of viewing your Italian picture carrying the title *The Bicycle Thief.*

It is [our] considered unanimous judgment . . . that in its present form this picture is *not* acceptable under the provisions of the Production Code.

We feel, however, that it can be made acceptable if the following eliminations are made in all prints put into general circulation:

1. The shot of the little boy about to make his toilet against the wall.

2. All the interior shots in the bordello into which the boy chases the thief.

If these eliminations are made in the picture and you give us your assurance that the version of the picture which may be approved by us will be the only version exhibited in this country, we shall be glad to send you our formal Certificate of Approval. . . .

Director De Sica was irate and sent a cable to his American distributors. He declared he was astounded at the requested cuts. He pointed out, with justice, that his film had circulated successfully all over the world, including in England, which, at times could be prudish and repressive, without meeting such demands. As to the bordello scene, De Sica stressed the delicate way in which it had been conducted. He observed that there was more sex in the average American film than in his. As to the scene of the boy urinating against the wall, he remarked that, in its spirit and execution, it was simply candid. De Sica referred to the religious town of Brussels, Belgium, whose emblem is a boy in similar circumstances; a representative statue stands in a town square. All things considered, concluded De Sica, he preferred to protect the integrity of his film and to await a decision "before the tribunal of public opinion."

Upon receiving Breen's letter and De Sica's cable, and after being exposed to the avalanche of praise from America's critical community, distributor Burstyn advised the censor that De Sica had instructed him to make no eliminations in the film. He expressed his personal reaction, predictably agreeing with De Sica. He declared that, by no stretch of the imagination, could the two scenes that offended Breen be considered immoral. He observed that the film had been chosen as the best film of the year by the National Board of Review, that it had won the New York Film Critics Award as the Best Foreign Language Film of 1949, that it had won all the awards at every film festival in Europe, and that it had been acclaimed as a great moral and artistic document by artists, writers, and civic-minded public officials.

He then hinted darkly that there might be motives in Breen's refusal to issue a Seal of Approval to his artistic masterpiece that had nothing to do with immorality. The implication was clearly that Breen feared that this foreign film would make serious inroads in the American audiences, thus hurting the American movie industry, which paid Breen's salary and whose welfare he was determined to protect. This was, indeed, a time when Hollywood moviemakers feared the invasion of the foreign imports. *The Bicycle Thief* was the Toyota of the movie industry. Burstyn implied that Breen feared the competition of De Sica's film and other candid foreign movies and wanted to keep it from American screens, or at least to launder it so that it did not offer elements that the U.S. moviegoer could not get in sanitized American films.

The Hays Office responded like a gored bull. They promptly issued a publicity release brimming over with righteous indignation. In the release, Breen asserted that "the statement issued by Joseph Burstyn to the effect that the Italian picture *The Bi-*

cycle Thief was banned . . . as part of an attempt to sabotage foreign-language pictures in the United States is utterly false."

Breen pointed out indignantly that many foreign films had been approved under the code. "To suggest that [we were] influenced in any way by factors other than the moral content of the picture is nonsense."

A libertarian brouhaha was building. On March 3, 1950, the National Council on Freedom from Censorship, an organization chaired by playwright Elmer Rice, wrote to Eric Johnston, who had by now replaced Will Hays. In his letter, Rice protested the action of the Hollywood censors in refusing to grant a seal to the prize-winning Italian film. He said the action barred American theaters from providing the public with the chance to judge for themselves whether this film should or should not be seen. Rice continued that this was a shocking demonstration of censorship power. Perhaps Elmer Rice was too preoccupied with the Broadway stage. He seemed surprisingly naive about the operation of movie censorship, which had for twenty-five years been deciding what films "should or should not be seen." Rice concluded that the exercise of censorship must be condemned as a violation of free expression, and that it would present the American democracy in an unfavorable light abroad.

Burstyn's attribution of ulterior motives to Breen continued to rankle. On March 8th, Breen wrote to Burstyn. He coldly informed him that he had the right to carry his case to the appeals board headed by Eric Johnston, and, as to Burstyn's intimations of Breen's motives, the censor shot back:

As to the concluding paragraph of your letter in which you suggest "that there may be motives involved" in our decision in this matter other than those mentioned. . . . I wish to state categorically that such an inference is utterly false. It is a foul and dishonest suggestion that is unworthy of any responsible person.

In my almost twenty years of day-to-day activity in this office, during which time I have had to deal with more than ten thousand feature-length motion pictures, yours is the first and only charge of this nature which has ever been made against me. . . . [Breen's defense was somewhat irrelevant since nearly all of the ten thousand films were American-made and would hardly prompt the charge that Breen was protecting the U.S. market from an invasion of imports. Of course, Breen was guiltless of Burstyn's charge, as he was merely applying to *The Bicycle Thief* the same criterion that he had religiously applied to American product for over two decades.]

Time magazine lent respectability to Burstyn's intemperate insinuation in a story that asked the question: Is there a subtle form of sabotage being used against foreign films? With friends like Henry Luce, Breen needed no enemies. F.S. Harmon, an official of the Code Administration, responded to the Time article with a "Dear Harry" letter to Henry Luce, in defense of Breen:

Under the good taste provisions of the Production Code, several hundred toilet gags are eliminated from scripts and pictures each year. Equality of treatment are the cornerstone upon which the Administration Code rests. [Accordingly] the distributor of *The Bicycle Thief* was requested to remove the toilet gag from his picture. . . .

Similarly we requested removal of a scene showing a scene in an Italian whorehouse. . . .

Unless and until we are convinced that the standards of the rank and file of the American people have lowered to the point where they wish scenes of this kind to become a regular portion of the motion picture entertainment, we shall continue to enforce the good taste provision of the code. . . .

As steam continued to build in the media and the artistic community, Burstyn appealed to the Hays Office's parent body, which had the power to overturn the censors' rulings. Stung and threatened, Joe Breen wrote to the Appeals Board:

In connection with the appeal . . . the following information is respectfully submitted . . . :

With regard to the . . . scene of the little boy about to urinate, it is interesting to note that, in the course of almost twenty years with the Production Code Administration, this is the first time any such scene has been submitted for approval. . . . No American producer has even suggested such a scene for inclusion in a picture. . . . While this scene may appear to be "realistic" or "humorous" or "cute" to certain sophisticated audiences, it is in bad taste per se. . . .

As to the scene in the bawdy house . . . it is because such locales inescapably suggest commercialized vice and human depravity, and to arouse unwholesome interest and curiosity on the part of youth, that such subject matter is not proper for inclusion in motion pictures. . . .

The Appeals Board upheld Breen and the Hays Office.

GENTLEMEN'S AGREEMENT

In adapting Laura Z. Hobson's uncompromising novel of anti-Semitism to the screen, Darryl F. Zanuck was handling social dynamite; yet he managed the transformation well. Zanuck was addressing himself to the immorality of anti-Semitism and the obscenity of racism. The censors chose to focus on the "immorality" of an unmarried couple winding up in bed and the "obscenity" of the leading lady having been divorced.

The American motion picture industry had reason to be proud of turning the Hobson novel into a highly visible film, with its clear indictment that a good portion of the audience were fashionable bigots. The film censors displayed somewhat less courage. The heroics of censorship is usually performed under duress. There were no compromises or evasions in the treatment of bigotry, but there were numerous compromises in the treatment of sex and divorce.

In the spring of 1947, Darryl F. Zanuck, the production chief of 20th Century-Fox, optioned Laura Z. Hobson's bestselling novel Gentlemen's Agreement *and sent a synopsis of the book to Joe Breen at the Hays Office. Breen wasted no time in reporting his reactions to Zanuck. On March 21st he wrote:*

We have read the synopsis of the novel *Gentlemen's Agreement*, which you submitted for our report from the standpoint of the Production Code. . . . In preparing a screenplay, we beg to make the following recommendations:

There must . . . be no suggestion anywhere of an illicit affair between your two sympathetic leads Phil [Gregory Peck] and Kathy [Dorothy McGuire]. While this inference is not absolutely clear in the novel, there seems to be a possible inference of this sort at one spot in the synopsis. This should be omitted in the script.

Also we urge upon you the advisability of not having Kathy being a divorced woman. Possibly the character of her divorced husband could be changed. . . .

By May, Moss Hart had completed a screenplay for the film and Elia Kazan had been hired to direct it. The script was sent to Joe Breen, who responded on May 23rd:

> We have read the script . . . for your proposed production of *Gentlemen's Agreement.* . . . We would like to state . . . that it is regrettable that the sympathetic lead in your story should be a divorced woman. We have steadfastly made a practice of urging that such characterizations be omitted whenever possible for the general good and welfare of the industry.
>
> Our feeling is based upon the fact that, by having your sympathetic lead a divorced woman, your story inevitably carries the flavor of acceptance and a tacit justification of divorce. We have, of course, steadfastly refused to approve stories which contained an outright justification of divorce, and have endeavored to approve divorce in motion pictures only when it was obtained against the wishes and generally over the objection of the sympathetic lead. . . .

THE LOST WEEKEND

Not all movie censorship originated in Hollywood and the state censor boards. Some of the most powerful forces for censorship are pressure groups that represent various special interests. They were a more virulent form of censorship than the Hays Office, because, like the CIA in its palmy days, they tended to work their wiles in clandestine ways. They had no specific code and no specific taboos. The world was their blue pencil, or that part of it that constituted a threat to their members.

The censoring associations may represent the biases of a religious group, an industry, or a profession, but their aim is always to protect the interests of their associates. They have tended to repress artistic liberties to the same extent as any sanctimonious reformer. Industrial pressure groups are particularly potent in that they can focus all their energies on a targeted movie that threatens their welfare.

A splendid example of this pervasive pressure was offered by the liquor industry's lobbyists in attempting to control the damage caused by Paramount's riveting film on the excesses of drink, *The Lost Weekend.* Allied Liquor Industries, a nationwide, industry-wide public relations group, used its formidable powers to influence the production of the film. The instrument of its leverage was the Hays Office—there is a kinship among censors. As the head of the liquor industry group observed, attempting to stimulate a fellow feeling of cooperation, "The liquor industry has public relations problems in many respects not unlike those affecting the motion picture industry."

The Lost Weekend was potentially damaging to the vested interests of the distilleries. It was the screen version of a novel about a dipsomaniac. Its tainted hero becomes a drunkard to balance his frustrations and despair. On a weekend binge he develops D.T.s and decides to kill himself. This stark and terrifying study of the dangers of drink was gruesome enough to send distillery stocks plummeting. Like the novel, the film told the story of a man's abject surrender to his craving for drink, and told it in terms of horrifying damages. Small wonder that the liquor industry's public relations group exerted every effort to soften the grim story.

On February 11, 1944, a story in the Hollywood Reporter, filmland's trade journal, declared: "Jimmy Fidler on his radio broadcast on Sunday stated: 'Paramount Studios, after paying $100,000 for screen rights to The Lost Weekend, must scrap the valuable property and rewrite the story. The Will Hays office banned it because the plot concerns a man who spends a drunken weekend.' "

Reports of the death of The Lost Weekend were highly exaggerated. At most it was suffering a flesh wound. Eight months later, the Will Hays Office had received the first seventy-four pages of a screenplay by Billy Wilder and Charles Brackett, adapting Charles Jackson's controversial novel to the screen. Replied Breen:

> We have read pages 1–74, dated September 11, for your proposed picture *The Lost Weekend*. . . .
>
> The characterization of Gloria as a prostitute is definitely unacceptable. It would be absolutely essential to give her some legitimate occupation.
>
> Perhaps we could define her as a buyer who entertains out-of-town visitors. . . .
>
> *Page 8–11:* We presume no toilet will be shown in Scene 87. There must be nothing vulgar in this scene in which the ladies are described as "curbing the dog."

As *The Lost Weekend* went before the camera, the wheels of special interest began to turn. Paramount Pictures received a letter from the head of Allied Liquor Industries. The letter, from Stanley Bear, executive vice president of the organization, expressed serious concern about the "adverse effect on the liquor industry" of *The Lost Weekend*, which was already in production. Bear pointed out that the liquor industry had an image problem similar to that of the movie business—the public was quick to indict them unjustly. Bear dropped a name, none too subtly, pointing out that Will Hays on several occasions had discussed with him the work he was trying to do; that is, keep liquor from getting a bad name.

Bear pointed out that the American people, by an overwhelming mandate, had repudiated the principles of Prohibition. They had embraced the freedom to imbibe. Since then, said the lobbyist, the liquor industry had strived to live up to its obligations to the public.

But all was not well, said Bear. Obviously the careful study of this whole matter is warranted, to the end that the liquor industry was engaged in a long twilight struggle to maintain its good standing. Then came the commercial. That standing, said Bear, was too valuable to be placed at risk by a movie about dipsomania—"a problem that lends itself so easily to abuse and misrepresentation."

The Other Censors

The Pennsylvania Board of Censors issued a memorandum of deletions headlined: "A Memorandum of Changes and Views, Subtitles and Language Suggested to Remove Objections to the Picture and Enable it to be Passed." There followed a voluminous document of deletion that included: Eliminating all views of cat killing mouse (as part of D.T.'s) and blood running down the wall; reducing views of din in alcoholic ward; eliminating medium shot of beetle.

DR. EHRLICH'S MAGIC BULLET

When Walter Mirisch brought *West Side Story* to the screen, there was a line in Stephen Sondheim's song "Gee, Officer

Krupke" that was quickly striken from the score: "No one wants a fella with a social disease." Like many other subjects, venereal disease could not be the subject of levity under the code. Neither could it be a serious element in a dramatic story, and so, Humphrey Bogart's old flame in *Dead End* finds herself suffering from tuberculosis, instead of syphilis.

When Warner Brothers set out to tell the life story of bacteriologist Paul Ehrlich, the man who found a cure for venereal disease, it raised a fine point. Here was no minor character out of Sidney Kingsley or a double entendre out of Stephen Sondheim. Here was a life story of a major scientific figure.

This dilemma produced a letter from the Honorable Will Hays to his censorship chief that drew attention to the problem and its ambivalence. Hays's letter had about it the whiff of hypocrisy. Hays started out by expressing respect and tolerance for a film about the Jonas Salk of social disease, and ended by suggesting that theater owners all over America were just waiting to turn it into cash.

On August 22, 1939, Will H. Hays wrote a confidential letter to Joe Breen at his Hollywood Boulevard office. Said Hays of Warner Brothers's plans to produce Dr. Ehrlich's Magic Bullet:

. . . In my opinion there is a distinction between a picture in which a venereal disease is the subject and a picture in which the discovery of a cure for venereal disease is an incident. There is a difference, too, between an incident, as in *Dead End*, where the girl [Claire Trevor] had syphilis, and the inability of her lover [Humphrey Bogart] to kiss her was a dramatic piece of business, and a picture about the life of a great bacteriologist, whose many great discoveries and contributions to society happen to include the discovery of a cure for a venereal disease. . . .

To make a dramatic picture of the life of Dr. Ehrlich and not include this discovery among his great achievements would be unfair to the record; to omit the reference to syphilis in the fictional picture, *Dead End*, with its great basic theme, was no such disservice.

Obviously our careful study of this whole matter is warranted to the end that, if possible, an accurate picture may be made of the life of this renowned scientist, showing his great service, true to historical record and yet being strictly within the code. . . .

We remember, too, that all the arguments and the facts relative to the value of the great humanitarian service that might be the result of a public campaign against syphilis do not prove that a motion picture producer making an entertainment picture on the subject of syphilis is not influenced by the profit motive.

It must be that, regardless of our sympathy with the objectives of the campaign against syphilis, we cannot avoid the responsibility of starting that which results in the opportunity for 16,000 exhibitors to exploit the disease in their neighborhood theaters, where the shock and profit purpose obtain.

Hal B. Wallis, the producer of Dr. Ehrlich's Magic Bullet, *reached an agreement with the Hays Office not to send out any advertising, promotion, or publicity material dealing with venereal disease, and promised that all advertising matter would be submitted to the censors for their approval. Wallis further agreed to revise the script to reduce all references to venereal disease to a minimum, and to eliminate any scenes dealing either with syphilis patients or the treatment of the disease.*

KING'S ROW

It is difficult to picture Ronald Reagan, a man of wholesome tastes, watching the diverse couplings of *Dynasty*. It is harder still to picture him appearing in it. Yet the gem in the crown of Ronald Reagan's movie career was a film that brings *Dynasty* immediately to mind.

King's Row is a film based on a best-selling novel that was censorable in every respect. The hero learns that his girl has been having incestuous relations with her father. The father is a sadistic doctor who amputates legs and willfully disfigures people. (Hence Ronald Reagan's famous line, "Where's the rest of me?") There is a host of moronic and mentally retarded characters, a lunatic asylum, suicides, and people dying of cancer. For a touch of *Dallas*, there is even a banker who steals trust funds and connives in real estate swindles. This, then, was the quintessence of the book and the film that was the zenith of Ronald Reagan's dramatic career.

On April 13, 1941, Jack L. Warner sent Joe Breen a copy of the final script for King's Row. *Breen sighed ponderously and replied:*

We have read with great care the final script . . . for your proposed production titled *King's Row*, and I regret to be compelled to advise you that the material, in our judgment, is quite definitely unacceptable under the provisions of the Production Code and cannot be approved. A picture following along the lines of this script would necessarily have to be rejected. . . .

Before this picture can be approved . . . *all the illicit sex will have to be entirely removed;* . . . the mercy killing will have to be deleted; and the several suggestions of loose sex, chiefly in the attitude of Drake [Ronald Reagan] with reference to the Ross girls, will have to be *entirely eliminated*. In addition, the suggestion that Dr. Gordon's nefarious practices are prompted by a kind of sadism will have to be *completely removed from the story*.

You will have in mind, also, I am sure, that a picture of this kind could not be released in Britain, where *any* suggestion of insanity is always entirely eliminated from films.

In this same connection, I throw out for consideration the very important question of industry policy, which is involved in an undertaking of this kind. Here is a story based upon a so-called best-selling novel, which is identified in the public mind as a definitely repellent story, the telling of which is certain to give pause to seriously thinking persons everywhere. . . . To attempt to translate such a story to the screen, *even though it be rewritten to conform to the provisions of the Production Code,* is in our judgment a very questionable undertaking from the standpoint of the good and welfare of this industry. Such a production may well be a definite *disservice* to the motion picture industry for, no matter how well the screenplay is done, the fact that it stems from so thoroughly questionable a novel is likely to bring down upon the industry, as a whole, the condemnation of decent people everywhere.

Because this story suggests an important question of industry policy, we are referring that phase of the undertaking to Mr. [Will] Hays for a decision as to the acceptability of *any* production based upon the novel *King's Row*. This means that, even though your present script is rewritten to bring it within the provisions of the Production Code, it will still be necessary, before approval can be given to the script, that a decision as to its acceptability, from the standpoint of industry policy, be rendered by the board of directors of this association in New York.

I am sending a copy of this letter to Mr. Hays for such comment, or observation, as he may care to make. . . .

Two days later, after a meeting with producer Hal Wallis, his screenwriter, and his assistant, Joe Breen again wrote to Jack Warner:

This goes to you in confirmation of our conference yesterday with Mr. Wallis, Mr. [Casey] Robinson, and Mr. [David] Lewis, with regard to your proposed picture *King's Row*, and our letter of April 22nd covering the same.

With a view to bringing the proposed picture within the requirements of the Production Code, and also of avoiding any possible danger of a seriously adverse audience reaction to the finished picture, the following changes in the script were agreed upon.

Mr. Wallis assured us that there would be absolutely no suggestion or inference whatever of nymphomania on the part of Cassandra. To this end, her illness will be definitely identified as something else, possibly dementia praecox, and certain lines in the picture which might possibly be interpreted as referring to nymphomania will be changed, so as to remove any possibility of this flavor persisting. . . .

It was agreed that, while it is necessary for the proper telling of your story, that there be an indication of one sex affair between Cassie and Parris [Robert Cummings], Mr. Robinson will inject a new scene into the picture, probably between Parris and Drake, in which Parris will definitely condemn himself for this affair, condemning the affair as wrong, and will indicate his feelings of impending tragedy. This will tie in directly with the later scene in which they learn that Cassie has been killed by her father, Dr. Tower [Claude Rains].

The suggestion of a sex affair between Randy [Ann Sheridan] and Drake will be eliminated entirely.

The suggestion of a mercy killing of the grandmother [Maria Ouspenskaya] by Parris will be eliminated entirely.

We list below the various lines and scenes which seem to us to give the unacceptable flavor . . . :

Page 3: There must be no suggestion of nude bathing on the part of these children. . . .

Pages 48–49: We suggest a careful rewriting of this scene, to delete any lines which might give an objectionable flavor to Cassie's characterization. Specifically, we mention the following: "Then other times she's so different she scares me. She's so wild—as if all she wanted—When's she's like that she's—just a kind of excitement that I dread and wish for at the same time"; "Sure,

Bo—like me and Poppy Ross. Times I could eat her alive, and times I could throw her out on her ear." "Funny she keeps after you. Generally, nice girls—you know what I mean. I think Cassie's nice all right, but generally—well, the ones I've known, like Louise—gosh, you just look at them and they act as if you're yanking their clothes off. Maybe old Cass is cooped up so much that when she does get loose she's all the way loose."

In addition to being very questionable from the standpoint of characterization, the above dialog is absolutely impossible from the standpoint of censorship, and will be eliminated elsewhere. . . .

Page 83: It was agreed in this scene that it would be definitely indicated that Dr. Tower knew about the affair between Cassie and Parris, and that this had something to do with the killing of the girl. . . .

Page 120: This action by Dr. Gordon [Charles Coburn] striking Louise should be masked [unseen by audience].

Page 166: In order to clear up the relationship between Randy and Drake, please omit the line "I had given him everything with gladness."

All the above demands were fulfilled in the final draft of the screenplay.

Chapter 17

DRAMAS FROM BROADWAY

TEA AND SYMPATHY

Homosexuality was a subject that the Hays Office handled most gingerly. The Production Code called it "sex perversion" and said that any inference of it was forbidden. By 1961, the censors had grown so liberal they stopped calling homosexuality perverse. They amended the code to permit movies to display "sex aberration," so long as it was treated with discretion. The gay life was repellent to the movie censors, though it was the chosen lifestyle of some of Hollywood's most distinguished actors, directors, and composers. Whenever the censors encountered homosexuality in a script—what they referred to in their prim lexicon as "a pansy flavor"—they reached for the scalpel. When MGM brought Tennessee Williams' *Cat on a Hot Tin Roof* to the screen, they turned the lead's homosexuality into hero worship. The censors tiptoed around the subject in another hit borrowed from the stage, *Tea and Sympathy*. Playwright Robert Anderson had to struggle with both the censors and his conscience in turning out a screenplay that did not severely compromise his play. In the famous drama, the wife of a boys' school headmaster gives herself to a tormented student to save him from the mistaken belief that he is a homosexual. In adapting his play to the screen, the issue of homosexuality is skirted. It is somewhat like producing *Macbeth* without the murder. On the screen, the wife (Deborah Kerr) gives herself to the boy so that he will know he is a man.

In addition, the censors required that the wife suffer for her sin. Some observer with decadent instincts might feel that her

187

sin was mitigated in that she prevented the boy from committing suicide, but, like Sweeney Todd, the censors served a vengeful God. So the playwright was required to add a new ending to the film: The boy returns to his school and learns in a letter from the wife that her adultery has ruined her life. One New York critic advised his readers to leave the movie theater before the last scene.

It was quite a step that *Tea and Sympathy* reached the screen at all. The implications of homosexuality were crystal clear, and the wife's adultery would have been obstructed a few years before. By 1953, when MGM released *Tea and Sympathy*, the formidable obstacles raised by the Hays Office to any objectionable materials were being loosened. Reflecting a liberalization in social attitudes and a closing of the chasm between life and popular art, the movie industry was quietly exposing itself to truth. The censors and the filmmakers rarely talked about it, fearing that they might alarm the public and frighten the children, but with movies like *Tea and Sympathy*, Hollywood was reconsidering the consequences of its repressive code. Some of the more unrealistic forbidden zones—like homosexuality and adultery—were being explored, and some of the old pieties were given some pitiless glances. Joe Breen was allowing the movies to deal with problems that were taboo a few short years before.

In *Tea and Sympathy*, the woman's adultery is motivated by a most touching compassion for the boy's anguish; but adultery is adultery and must be punished, and so, the guardian of the Hays Office winked at compensatory damages. It was doubtless a bone in playwright Anderson's throat when he had to show the woman suffering for her sin—when he had to append the thought that the boy would have found a way out of his youthful angst by himself without the woman's tender gift. The fact was that the preachy platitudes come as an irrelevant epilogue to a movingly honest story.

On October 14, 1953, in a memo for the files, Geoffrey Shurlock wrote:

Re *Tea and Sympathy*—Paramount
   Mr. [Luigi] Luraschi [of Paramount] called today and asked if we were acquainted with this New York play and asked us to give a code opinion on it. I indicated that, from the reviews, it

was obvious that there were two serious code violations. The first is that the story revolves around a false accusation of homosexuality leveled against a schoolboy.

The second is that the boy's psychological problem is solved by having the wife of the headmaster give herself to him sexually. This treatment of adultery is also a definite code violation. Mr. Luraschi indicated that he would transmit this report to his New York office, who were making this original inquiry.

Paramount hastily lost interest in Tea and Sympathy. *At about the same time, Columbia's Harry Cohn sent a synopsis of the play to the Hays Office and evoked this reply from Joe Breen:*

We have read the synopsis of the play *Tea and Sympathy*, which you have submitted for our consideration . . . and regret to have to report that it contains some serious code violations. . . .

Breen reiterated the two major objections cited by Shurlock in his memo to the files. He added a third objectionable element:

Third, the element of the boy's attempt to sleep with the prostitute is thoroughly unacceptable.

We regret having to report unfavorably on this play, but you will understand that, under the requirements of the code, it is the only opinion we can render.

Columbia's interest in Tea and Sympathy *went the way of Paramount's. Hollywood's attention to the riveting Broadway play waned for two years. Then in 1955, Dore Schary, the young production chief at MGM, sent a treatment for a motion picture based on* Tea and Sympathy *to the censors of the Hays Office. Breen replied:*

We have read the treatment . . . of the play *Tea and Sympathy* and note the changes and improvements made therein. We regret that we have to say that, in spite of the work that has been done in an effort to remove the cause of objections, the present version still appears to be in violation [of the code].

It seems to us that, in spite of the rewriting, the problem of the boy is still his fear that he may be homosexual.

And the wife's giving herself to him in adultery, still appears to be a violation of the code, inasmuch as her adultery would seem to be justified in view of the fact that it solves the boy's problem. . . .

MGM's interest was not so perishable, especially when that es-
timable showman, Samuel Goldwyn, entered the picture with
an effort to cut the Gordian knot. The situation was described
by Jack Vizzard, a Hays Office censor, in a September 9, 1953
memo for the files:

> At the request of MGM, Mr. Shurlock and Mr. Vizzard left for
> New York on Thursday to see *[Tea and Sympathy]*. While we
> were there, Mr. Sam Goldwyn discovered the purpose of our trip
> and insisted we confer with him on the subject, since he also
> was vitally interested. He arranged for a conference at his Wal-
> dorf Astoria suite on the morning of October 29th with Elia Ka-
> zan, director of the stage play, Robert Anderson, the author, and
> Mrs. [Frances] Goldwyn present.
>
> We thoroughly and unequivocally discouraged Mr. Goldwyn
> from going into this project. We also secured from Mr. Kazan a
> statement that, in his opinion this play should never be made
> into a motion picture, and that, as far as he was concerned, it
> would not be. The author did not come out so flat-footedly.
>
> An important item consisted of the note which the author had
> typed up for Mr. Goldwyn, in which he set forth his minimum
> requirements as to what any screenplay based on this stage play
> should contain. Mr. Goldwyn gave us a brief glance at the note.
> Relying on memory, it contained the following significant items:
>
> 1. It was a *sine qua non* that the leading lady solve the boy's
> problem by giving herself to him sexually. It would be *unaccept-*
> *able* to the author that she merely offered him her *love.*
>
> 2. It would be essential that the boy's problem spring from
> the malicious charge of homosexuality against him; a charge that
> assumes such proportions that the boy begins to doubt his own
> manhood and is driven to the brink of suicide. It would be *un-*
> *acceptable* to the author that the charge be tampered with or
> compromised so that the boy be accused of being a "sissy." . . .
>
> 3. The proper telling of the story *requires* the sequence in
> which the boy, egged on by a companion who wishes to help
> him out of his dilemma, goes to what the note refers to as "the
> town whore." . . .

MGM persevered with the production of the film, with Robert
Anderson adapting his play to the screen, assured by Schary
that he would be allowed to keep the core of the story. As An-
derson wrote and casting proceeded—Deborah Kerr as the wife,
John Kerr as the boy—Nicholas Schenck, the president of Loews
Incorporated, MGM's parent company, received a letter from the

Very Reverend Monsignor Thomas P. Little of the Legion of Decency. The Monsignor was alarmed. He had read in both the
trade and secular press of MGM's planned production of *Tea
and Sympathy*. He observed that the Legion of Decency normally confined itself to examining completed films, but the
Monsignor wanted Loews to know in advance that two elements of the stage play would be "gravely offensive" to American Catholics—the homosexuality of the boy and the wife
sleeping with him. The churchman's letter, added to the weight
of the Hays Office admonitions, led MGM to soften the edges of
these two crucial points. In the film, the boy is not charged with
homosexuality as in the stage version, but with being interested
in classical music rather than physical sports. He agrees to play
a female role in a school play, sings folk songs, and has learned
to cook and sew during his lonely childhood days. Small wonder Robert Anderson recalls the film with bitterness, saying, "I
will never again give in. You become convinced you're saving
the story, but you're not."

THE CHILDREN'S HOUR

Censorship has had as destructive an effect on the life of Lillian
Hellman as the lies of a malicious child had on the lives of the
women in her famous play, *The Children's Hour*. Political censorship and the Joe McCarthy witchhunts of the fifties placed
great strains on her and sent her longtime companion Dashiell
Hammett to prison. State censorship caused problems for *The
Children's Hour* during the melodrama's lengthy Broadway run
in 1934 and 1935. Opening night, there were threats of injunc-
tions and interference by the New York Police Department.
(Ironically, the play was revived in 1952, when Miss Hellman
was being harassed by the McCarthy committee.) When Sam
Goldwyn filmed the play in 1936, the movie censors required
that he change the story somewhat. In the Hellman play, a young
doctor loves a female teacher and so does another woman. The
censor's version: The two women both love the young doctor.
The alteration was so destructive to the Hellman story, that
Goldwyn changed the name of the movie to *These Three*, and
director William Wyler said at the time, "Miss Hellman's play
has not yet been filmed."

The censors continued to beset Miss Hellman's classic drama. When United Artists set out to make the film in 1961, the censorship code still forbade the screen dealing with the subject of lesbianism and produced its own quota of complaints and recriminations. In the sixties version, the word "lesbian" is never spoken—just as all through the fifties, the word "pregnant" was never allowed to defile our TV sets. Miss Hellman's basic triangle is preserved in reasonably adult fashion. It became customary in the dying days of movie censorship to praise Hollywood for being "reasonably adult," much as one praises an unruly three-year-old for not spilling too much of his oatmeal. William Wyler directed the sixties version as though walking on intellectual eggs, sparing the audience's sensibilities to a dismaying degree.

The problem is triggered by a clever, obnoxious little girl, sulking over her schoolroom punishment, whose instincts lead her to assert a destructive lie that holds a grain of truth. She declares that she has seen her two teachers embracing. In 1930, when Miss Hellman was twenty-six years old, she had read a book called *Bad Companions*, about a scandal caused by a sulky child who said her headmistresses had a deep fondness for one another. The villainy of *The Children's Hour* seems to be less with the nasty child who saw lesbianism where it did not exist, than with the ubiquitous censors who saw obscenity where *it* did not exist.

In 1961, Geoffrey Shurlock wrote to William Wyler about the new screen adaptation of The Children's Hour, *written by John Michael Hayes. The censor chief wrote:*

> Confirming our telephone conversation about your script *The Infamous*, inasmuch as the story deals with the false charge of homosexuality between your two female leads, we could not approve it under the present code regulations, which read "sex perversion or any inference of it is forbidden." As I further indicated, your problem stems from the subject matter; we found nothing in the treatment of this subject in the script we felt would seem to be offensive. . . .

United Artists, the producing and releasing company for the proposed film, was increasingly impatient with the intransigence of the censors on *The Children's Hour* in particular, and on the subject of homosexuality in general, since UA had a few important films in preparation that reflected this theme. With some apprehension, Arthur Krim, the president of United Artists, wrote to Eric Johnston, head of the Motion Picture Association of America. United Artists, he said, was contemplating several films in which the subject of homosexuality was prominent. These pictures were *The Best Man*, from Gore Vidal's witty political play; *Advise and Consent*, from the bestselling Allen Drury novel; and *The Children's Hour*, which was to be produced by the Mirisch Brothers and directed by William Wyler. The Hellman film was to start shooting in six weeks, said Krim. The screenplay had been submitted to the Hays Office's Geoffrey Shurlock, and Shurlock had written back that the script could not be approved. Krim pointed out that Shurlock had found nothing offensive in the scenario. Actually, said Krim, all reference to homosexuality in *The Children's Hour* was from a false charge. There would be no acts or suggestion of homosexuality on the screen. With a mixture of impatience and importunity, Krim declared that he was anxious to distribute these three pictures with a code seal. The implication was that the alternative was to release them *without* a seal rather than to shelve or emasculate them. Krim proposed that the censors initiate steps for an amendment to the code that would permit such a release. Krim's persistence was rewarded on October 3, 1961, when the Production Code was amended to permit the prudent treatment of homosexuality—which it called "sexual aberration." The times they were a-changin'.

INHERIT THE WIND

Stanley Kramer's film version of *Inherit the Wind*, the play about the Scopes Monkey Trial, demonstrated that censorship does not need a sexual theme as its target. The censors can become equally perturbed with a movie of ideas. *Inherit the Wind* told in dramatic fashion the explosive highlights of the trial at which William Jennings Bryan and Clarence Darrow fought over a teacher's rights to discuss Darwin's theory of evolution. The names were changed, but the ideas were the same, and they flashed like summer lightning. The censors felt that the lightning was striking some innocent bystanders.

To the Hays Office, *Inherit the Wind* presented religious people in a very unfavorable light. The playwrights, Jerome Lawrence and Robert E. Lee—who, on another occasion had transferred the corruption of the Harding Administration to the stage— were portraying Christians as fanatical in their beliefs.

Inherit the Wind offered a good example of the scope and limits of censorship. Though the changes they exacted damaged the film, they did not cripple it. *Inherit the Wind*, in the manner of all Stanley Kramer's films, was a movie of strong ideas and opinions. Despite the censors' adjustments, the ideas were presented with a boldness that reflected the censors' declining powers in the year 1959. There was bitterness, mordant humor, and the violence of clashing ideas. Movies—and movie audiences—were slowly coming of age.

On March 21, 1955, Frank McCarthy sent a copy of the Lawrence and Lee play, plus a synopsis, to Geoffrey Shurlock at the Hays Office. He responded:

> We have read the synopsis of the play titled *Inherit the Wind*. . . . We regret to inform you that this basic story is unacceptable . . . and that a picture based on this material could not be approved by this office.
>
> A story such as this violates that portion of the code which states that "no film . . . may throw ridicule on any religious faith."
>
> The material contains an attack on Christian doctrines and in general presents religious-thinking people in an extremely unfavorable light. Moreover, this material contains serious misrepresentations of facts regarding the basic principles of Christianity. We regret the necessity of this unfavorable judgment. However, you will realize that the proper dispensation of our responsibilities [gives us] no alternative.

In June of 1955, Hecht-Lancaster Productions, a company comprised of Harold Hecht and Burt Lancaster that had dealt with other controversial themes behind the facade of fiction, took an interest in Inherit the Wind. *On June 10th, Shurlock wrote a private memo to the files:*

> On Wednesday June 1 . . . met with Mr. Bernard Smith of Hecht-Lancaster Productions. The subject of discussion was the play script of [*Inherit the Wind*] which was submitted to this office. . . .

Mr. Smith was informed that this play contained certain code "violations," which would have had to be corrected if this office was to give its approval to a film based on this material.

This play seems to contain an unfair portrayal of religious-thinking people, i.e., those of the Christian faith. Nearly all of the Christians portrayed in this story seem to be described as near-fanatic, Old Testament fundamentalists. In addition, there is a tendency to create a considerable amount of sympathy against the Christian Bible and to misrepresent certain facts regarding Christian dogma. This all adds up to the ridicule of a religious faith, thus rendering this story unacceptable. . . .

It was mutually agreed that the problem could be overcome by differentiating between the extreme fundamentalism presented in this play and the true Christian faith. . . . Mr. Smith said it was already a desire of his organization to make this distinction when developing this material into a screenplay. He agreed that observations along this line should come from one of the important characters, such as the newspaper correspondent [played by Gene Kelly, portraying H. L. Mencken] or the lawyer Drummond [Spencer Tracy, portraying Clarence Darrow], or possibly the young professor [Dick York]. It is our understanding that these observations will clearly distinguish this one narrow-minded community from the Christian world as a whole. Also, Mr. Smith pointed out that it was his feeling that it would be well to indicate that the attack led by Drummond was not on the Christian Bible per se, but rather on the obtuse literal interpretation of the Old Testament clung to by the citizens of this town. . . .

Finally, we observed that the characterization of Reverend Breen [Claude Akins] amounted to that of a villain, and, as such, constituted a code violation. It was agreed that a good solution to this problem would be to change him to some sort of civic leader. . . .

GOLDEN BOY

Clifford Odets was not quite a Shaw or an Ibsen, but, among American playwrights, he had the ability to celebrate life in the bleak Depression. He was at heart a romantic, and alive to the sensual joys of life. He presented them with his great gift for naturalistic speech. There was great authenticity to his characters and their hungers both carnal and financial. Odets intoxicated his Broadway audiences with the bittersweet aroma of hope and frustration. Nowhere did he succeed more than in his play *Golden Boy*.

Unfortunately for Odets and Columbia Pictures, which bought the screen rights to Odets's story of a sensitive boxer, the preoccupation of the Hays Office was to suppress a candid presentation of life's sensual pleasures and erotic desires, life's earthy language and coarse encounters. The censor's job was to keep reality off the screen, and, in its place, to present life as the moral guardians would like it to be. Their goal was unassailable: to protect the filmgoer from confronting a harsh reality that he had come to the movie house to escape. At least, that was the rationale that motivated the Hays Office.

In the case of *Golden Boy*, what suffered, along with the soaring prose of Clifford Odets, was truth, and life generally teaches that we pay a price when we choose comfortable illusions in place of untidy reality.

Golden Boy's inherent truths ran into trouble with the Production Code—its earthy language; its melting pot of Italians, Jews, and Irish; its sex, both illicit and marital. It is the story of Joe Bonaparte, who would have made a superlative boxer if he had been a less sensitive man. So, in quest of things pecuniary, he is thrust into the prize ring, and his musician's hands are placed at risk. Two things are unattainable in the ring: his father's forgiveness and the love of his manager's woman.

Twenty years after its film premiere, Sammy Davis Jr. brought *Golden Boy* to Broadway in musical form. Times had changed, and the theater audience hardly blinked when the new Golden Boy turned to his manager and snapped, "You gave me shit."

In October 1938, Harry Cohn of Columbia Pictures sent a copy of Clifford Odets's play Golden Boy *to the Hays Office to test the water. Joe Breen replied:*

We have received and read the play script *Golden Boy* submitted for your consideration. This play contains two elements which are basically unacceptable from the standpoint of the Production Code.

The adulterous relationship between Moody [Adolphe Menjou] a married man, and your sympathetic female lead, Lorna [Barbara Stanwyck].

Second . . . there is a suggestion of a sexual affair between Lorna and Joe. These should be changed.

Also, the characterizations of several of the personages as Italians may cause you trouble with your release in that country.

In preparing the screen version it will . . . be necessary to omit all profanity. Let me also call your attention to a number of other lines which are unacceptable:

Page 1-1-10: Omit "Is that crap?" . . .

Page 1-2-13: Omit ". . . the comedy of reproduction."

Page 1-2-15: Omit "What the hell's so special in bed?"

Page 1-3-25: Omit "Because a woman's place is in the hay."

Page 1-3-31: Omit "I feel like the Resurrection."

Page 1-3-34: Omit "I don't like this seduction scene."

Page 1-3-37: Omit "I'm a tramp from Newark, Tom, I know a dozen ways."

Page 2-1-10: Omit "In the first year give her a baby."

Page 2-1-11: Omit "You expect me to sleep with that boy?"

Page 2-2-16: Modify the line "He picked me up in Friskin's Hotel."

Page 2-3-29: Omit the line "Because he's a queer?"

Page 2-3-36: Omit the line "This isn't a hotel bedroom."

Page 2-4-38: Omit the line, "Stop looking down her dress."

By December, a screenplay had been written based on the Odets play and dispatched to the Hays Office. Breen wrote to Harry Cohn:

We have read the first draft script . . . for your proposed production titled *Golden Boy.* . . . There are a number of important details . . . which are not acceptable. . . .

The most important of these . . . is suggested by the relationship of Moody, a married man, and Lorna. To us it is inescapable that Lorna is a "kept woman," and . . . in our judgment [this] is not necessary to a proper telling of the story. . . .

The second major difficulty . . . is suggested by the several scenes of physical contact between Moody, a married man, and Lorna.

In addition, there are a number of expressions used by the characters in this story which are quite definitely not acceptable and all of which will have to be changed.

Going through the script page by page, we respectfully direct your attention to the following . . . :

Page 24: The gag which is suggested here and throughout the script of Siggie [Sam Levene] and Anna, about their going to bed, and Anna's embarrassment to the suggestion, should be entirely deleted.

Page 25: The business of Siggie smacking his wife should not be played seriously. If it is done so, it will be deleted by a number of [state] censor boards.

Page 35: The action of Lorna pointing the scissors toward Joe's posterior should not be offensively suggestive. . . .

Page 74: The conversation between Joe and Lorna about their respective anatomies is likewise questionable. . . .

Page 75: Please delete Joe's question "Moody lives here too, doesn't he? Do you have the same room?"

Page 97: We suggest you substitute the word "fiancée" for the word "friend" in the speech by Lorna, "No—I'm his manager's friend."

Page 138: Please eliminate the expression by Moody, "In your hat."

WHO'S AFRAID OF VIRGINIA WOOLF

When Edward Albee's brutally funny explosion of black humor—a play about a married couple who claw away at one another—was converted to the movie screen, it received only the reluctant blessings of the censors. The Hays Office had refused to issue its Seal of Approval, and Warner Brothers had appealed for an exemption to the code regulations on profanity. The review board granted the exemption, declaring that the movie was not designed to be prurient and had, after all, won the New York Drama Critics Award. There was a whiff of hypocrisy to this reasoning, since many other plays that had received the plaudits of Broadway critics—such as *Tea and Sympathy, The Children's Hour,* and *Golden Boy*—had been hampered or harassed in receiving faithful reproduction on the screen.

Virginia Woolf actually flourished in the furnace of censorship. The effect of the Catholic press might almost be described as beneficent, since their outrage at the film's obscene language gave the movie more publicity than any Hollywood production had received since *The Outlaw.* It was a pity that the element of Albee's work that received the most attention was its earthy language. It is true that the saga of George and Martha is redolent with imaginative vulgarity, but it also contains a quality that is rarer still: searing honesty. If *Virginia Woolf* brimmed over with vulgarity and barely suppressed violence, "it is inescapable," as Joe Breen would express it, that so does life.

As with half a century of films that clerical critics found objectionable, the most outraged reaction seemed to come from churchmen who had not actually seen the picture—but they knew what they wouldn't have liked had they seen it. Censors were fond of asserting that movies should present life as it should be rather than as it is. This theory was falling increasingly into disrepute, as was the belief that exposure to anything shocking on the screen had a disposition to encourage ugly deeds.

In March of 1963, Jack L. Warner met with chief censor Geoffrey Shurlock and then sent a copy of Edward Albee's play, Who's Afraid of Virginia Woolf, *to the office of the Production Code Administration. This was to be a highly visible production for Warners. It would star Elizabeth Taylor and Richard Burton and would be directed by Broadway wunderkind Mike Nichols. Geoff Shurlock's reply was thorough in its delineation of Albee's profane prose. Wrote the censor:*

This is pursuant to our conference of March 25, 1963, regarding the play *Who's Afraid of Virginia Woolf.* . . . We are setting forth the details of this play which we consider unacceptable under the code:
 Page 1: "Jesus H. Christ . . ."
 Page 4: "For Christ's sake . . ."
 Page 7: "God damn."
 Page 15: ". . . on the living room rug."
 Page 23: "Screw, Sweety."
 Page 28: "The sacrifice is usually of a somewhat more private portion of the anatomy."
 Page 39: "Son of a bitch."
 Page 47: "Right ball."
 Page 58: "Bastard." (twice)
 Page 59: Stageside breast. (Stage directions.)
 Page 66: "Underside of the scrotum . . ."
 Page 70: "Bugger." (three times)
 Page 78: ". . . you can't get an annulment if there's entrance."
 Page 106: ". . . what they say about Chinese women."
 Page 112–113: ". . . plowing pertinent wives . . ."
 Page 114: ". . . plow 'em all."
 Page 117: "Up yours."
 Page 120: ". . . fiddling at him all the time."
 Page 129: "Angel tits."
 Page 130: "Monkey nipples."

Page 139: "Hump the Hostess." (four times) ". . . mount her like a goddamn dog."

Page 152: ". . . your melons bobbing."

Page 163: . . . she slips her hand between his legs somewhere between the knee and the crotch. . . . Her hand is moving up his leg. (Stage directions.)

Page 165: . . . already had his hand on Martha's breast. Now puts his hand inside her dress. (Stage directions.)

Page 177: "Apple jelly."

Page 189: ". . . sits there with her dress over her head. . . . Don't you know how stuffy it is with your dress up over your head . . ."

Page 193: ". . . Can't you get the latch up either?"

Page 204: ". . . protect your plough."

Warner Brother's film Virginia Woolf *held faithful to the Albee play. The Production Code Administration denied the film its Seal of Approval and Warners appealed to the MPAA board, as was its right. The board met at the St. Regis Hotel in New York under the chairmanship of Jack Valenti, and, as a result of their cogitations, issued a press release which stated:*

As a result of the appeal made by the producer, Warner Brothers, the Production Code review board today granted an exemption from existing code regulations for *Who's Afraid of Virginia Woolf.* This decision followed a hearing at which the picture was screened and discussed by members of the review board.

Following the meeting, the review board issued the following statement: Granting of an exception to *Who's Afraid of Virginia Woolf* was done for the following reasons:

1. The film was not designed to be prurient. This film document dealing with the tragic realism of life is largely a reproduction of the Edward Albee play, which won the New York Drama Critics Award in 1963 and has played throughout the country.

2. Warner Brothers has taken the position that no person under eighteen will be admitted unless accompanied by a parent. . . .

3. . . . This exemption does not mean that the floodgates are open for language or other material. The exemption means precisely the opposite. . . . Whenever films go beyond rational measures of community standards [they will be denied approval].

A STREETCAR NAMED DESIRE

If there were ingredients in the plays of Lillian Hellman, Robert Anderson, and Bernard Shaw that raised censorial hackles at the Hays Office, no playwright wrinkled more brows and provoked more opposition than Tennessee Williams. A catalogue of perversities filled his sex-haunted work in plays like *Cat on a Hot Tin Roof*, *The Glass Menagerie*, *Baby Doll*, *Summer and Smoke*, and *Sweet Bird of Youth*, and moviemakers seemed drawn to his plays, ignoring the warnings of the censors.

The Tennessee Williams play that produced the greatest fulminations of the Hays Office and the most violent conflict between censors and creators, was *A Streetcar Named Desire*. Chief administrator Joe Breen had admonished Warner Brothers that were would be serious problems in bringing the steamy story to the screen. Charles Feldman was an independent producer who had optioned the play for the screen and arranged with Warners to finance and distribute the movie. Breen turned the full force of his persuasion on the packager. Breen advised Feldman that the play posed insuperable problems. Feldman was undeterred.

Equally devoted to the play was Elia Kazan who had directed Williams's play on Broadway and had agreed to direct the film, with Marlon Brando repeating his brutish portrayal of Stanley Kowalski and Vivien Leigh as the vulnerable Blanche DuBois. Kazan and Williams were worldly men who had long ago discarded their belief in the tooth fairy. Yet both were convinced they could make a movie from *Streetcar* that would satisfy the censors. Like the lady who rode the tiger, Kazan and Williams returned inside. The director learned to his grief that Warner Brothers had agreed to make various deletions in the finished film requested by the Legion of Decency. What particularly enraged Kazen was the fact that the changes were made without his knowledge. The cuts were made to avoid a "Condemned" rating that would mean Catholics would be directed to shun the film. The dreaded rating would also trigger boycotts in theater lobbies and vituperation from state censor boards everywhere.

The cuts prompted by the Legion amounted to four minutes of film. As Kazan described them, they included the last three words of the line, "I would like to kiss you softly and sweetly on the mouth," and cuts in a staircase scene between Stanley and his wife which, to the Legion, carried the suggestion of carnality. Four minutes is not an inordinate amount of film for a work dealing with homosexuality, nymphomania, and rape, but to Kazan and Williams, there was no such thing as a little garlic, and no such thing as a little censorship.

After reading the play script for A Streetcar Named Desire, on April 28, 1950, Joe Breen sent a memo to Warner Brothers:

[We] set forth the following three points as representing the three principal problems posed by this material under the code.

1. The script contains an inference of sex perversion. This principally has reference to the character of Blanche's young husband. . . . There seems little doubt that this young man was a homosexual.

2. There seems to be an inference of a type of nymphomania with regards to the character of Blanche herself. Her peculiar and neurotic attitude towards sex, and particularly to sex attraction for young boys, has about it an erotic flavor that seems to verge on perversion of a sort.

3. The third problem has reference to the rape which is both justified and unpunished.

With reference to the first point, the solution lies in affirmatively establishing some other reason for suicide, which will get away entirely from sex perversion, which is absolutely forbidden by the code. It was felt that this could be achieved simply by eliminating dialogue: that something else would have to be added which would effectively establish that this boy's problem was not one of homosexuality.

With reference to the second problem, it was felt, from a standpoint of the code, that Blanche's problem be more on an emotional basis and not from a standpoint of sexual promiscuity. The suggestion was offered that, in her approaches to the various men referred to in the course of the story, she would be searching for romance and security, and not for gross sex. It would be indicated that this was the reason that she had been asked to leave the hotel; and this point would be further emphasized by the way her scenes were played with the young newspaper collector and with Mitch [Karl Malden]. We felt that this could be achieved with a minimum of rewriting. In any scenes in which Blanche approaches men, she, at some time during the conversation, calls the man, Allan, the name of her first husband. This will carry the inference that Blanche is seeking for the husband she has lost in any man she approaches.

With regards to the problem of the rape, the following suggestion was made: the big scene of the assault on Blanche by Stanley would be kept relatively intact as now written. In the sequences which follow, in which we find Blanche now completely demented, we also find that she is hinting that Stanley actually raped her. On the other hand, Stanley, when this accusation comes to his attention, violently denies this and proves positively that he did not rape her. The device by which he proves himself is yet to be invented.

The point of this suggestion is that Blanche in her pitiable state is making one last effort to assault the security and well-being of her sister, Stella, of whom she is so envious; that even with her broken mind she is endeavoring to achieve her objective—which was her goal through the entire play—of wrecking her sister's home with a lie.

[It seems] that this would very likely be a solution to the rape as now written. . . . An alternate suggestion [would be] that it is clearly established to the audience during the course of the rape scene, that Blanche is, at this time, demented. She calls Stanley by the name Allan. She imagines the rape; the rape does not actually take place, and this is known by the audience. Another suggestion [is] that the scene could be told from Stanley's point of view, and that, although he contemplates rape, he does not go through with the act and leaves the room when he realizes that Blanche is demented. . . . This would be [by] far the most satisfactory solution to this difficult problem. . . .

Chapter 18

AFTER THE HAYS OFFICE

When the Hays Office was formed in the thirties, it was a desperate attempt to stave off censorship legislation by the U.S. Congress. The attempt was successful. Congress withheld its hand. Though some would say the price was heavy, in the suffocation of film freedom, Washington stayed out of the censorship business. However stringently, Hollywood regulated itself. Censorship stayed in the family.

Today filmmakers enjoy far more freedom than they did half a century ago; yet, there is truth to the observation that the more things change, the more they remain the same. When the Hays Office expired in 1968, it was replaced by the rating system we know today. The reason censorship was not replaced by a free market was the same fear that drove the movie moguls to summon Mr. Hays—the fear of possible censorship legislation.

Of course, the rating system, by which a rating board classifies films as G, PG, PG-13, R, or X, is more resilient than the loathsome censorship code in which cleavage and kisses were measured by tape measure and stopwatch. Theoretically, the current classification system permits moviemakers to make the films they wish. There are no strict limits on creative expression, but to be just, one must acknowledge that the rating—though it does not limit the length of the clinch—does limit the size of the audience, and, therefore prompts the artist to tailor his vision to a particular target. Drop an expletive and avoid an R, or add some nudity and escape a G.

Our society has changed dramatically since the days when "a glimpse of stocking was looked on as something shocking," as Cole Porter expressed it. Yet despite this vastly more sophisticated and permissive audience, self-regulation remains to mock
204

our pretensions of film freedom. There is a persuasive case to
be made for jettisoning the rating system as without justification. Let the marketplace rule, say some observers. Boredom will
drive out the smut, as it did in the pornography stalls of Copen-
hagen.

It is a tribute to the vaunted power of the cinema that self-
regulation has not been totally abandoned for the possible excesses of liberty and license. The movie industry and the public
evidently fear the potency of movies if they were to be entirely
untrammeled, and it must be noted that, whatever the limits
placed on filmmakers by the rating system, today Hollywood is
producing films of an honesty and impact that could never be
imagined in the days of Mayer, Cohn, and Goldwyn.

Truth and money are a powerful tandem, and they led to the
death of the Hays Code. First there was the pressure of moviemakers wanting more freedom of expression; second, the pecuniary inroads of television. Together they sounded the death
knell of screen censorship.

The Classification and Rating Administration, which replaced
the Production Code Administration, must have started Joe Breen
spinning in his grave. In substance, it allowed the writer or director to make exactly the movie he wanted. He did not pay the
price of damnation, boycott, or harassment. The only cost was
the rating he received and the limits it placed on his box office
potential.

Filmmakers could make any film up to the level of an X. The
operation of the rating system was not unlike that of the Hays
Office in that raters would read screenplays and react to them,
but, instead of responding with papal pronouncements about
mild profanities and innocuous gestures, the rating people merely
suggested what rating the film was likely to receive. Commonly,
the moviemaker tells the board what rating he wishes, and the
correspondence and conversation centers on how to alter the
script to produce that classification.

The producer may appeal a rating with which he is dissatis-
fied, much as Howard Hughes and Jack Warner used to appeal
the withholding of a Seal of Approval. The appeals are more
numerous than they were under the rigid Hays system, and more
often successful.

After one has drawn a sweet breath of freedom at leaving the
stifling air of Breen's repressions, one has to admit that the rat-

ing system, for all its tolerance and for all the erudition and liberality of its leaders, is still a kind of censorship—and a pre-censorship at that. It compels the filmmaker to trim his vision to the ratings. To the man who lied about him in court in order to gain a petty appointment, Thomas More said that it was a pity to lose one's soul to gain riches, but to do it for Wales! It was a pity to lose one's virtue to get a movie released, but to do it for an R!

Critics of the rating system point out that today's auteurs alter their film to bow acquiescently to a system that is obsolete and destructive. Yet to those who defend the system as a prudent way to protect the sensibilities of the young—which is its chief reason for being—it is not easy to dismiss their concern. Anyone who has seen the impact of sex and violence in some explosive and expoitive films, cannot declare with absolute confidence that movies could do little injury to young minds. The power of the screen is such, and the impressionability of adolescents is such, that to strip away even the modest signposts of the rating system, might have its dangers.

It is said that those who do not learn from history are condemned to repeat it. Movies have grown so horrific and sadistic in recent years, that a trend to conservatism, which has been visible in America's politics, may well invade its movies. If the sexual candor of films triggers a backlash that imposes a new censorship on our filmmakers, they need only look back to the seeds of cinema to see the phenomenon that their excesses are producing. Back in the twenties it was the exploitive instincts of the early filmmakers—pushing the "Sex" button—that enraged the public and produced the censors. It would be tragic if history were to repeat itself, in a rebirth of censorship, with a new Will Hays and his horrendous code rising Phoenix-like from the ashes of today's freedoms.

THE MOTION PICTURE PRODUCTION CODE

Foreword

Motion picture producers recognize the high trust and confidence that have been placed in them by the people of the world and that have made motion pictures a universal form of entertainment.

They recognize their responsibility to the public because of this trust and because entertainment and art are important influences in the life of a nation.

Hence, though regarding motion pictures primarily as entertainment without any explicit purposes of teaching or propaganda, they know that the motion picture within its own field of entertainment may be directly responsible for spiritual or moral progress, for higher types of social life, and for much correct thinking.

On their part, they ask from the public and from public leaders a sympathetic understanding of the problems inherent in motion picture production and a spirit of cooperation that will allow the opportunity necessary to bring the motion picture to a still higher level of wholesome entertainment for all concerned.

THE PRODUCTION CODE

General Principles

1. No picture shall be produced which will lower the moral standards of those who see it. Hence the sympathy of the audi-

ence shall never be thrown to the side of crime, wrongdoing, evil, or sin.

2. Correct standards of life, subject only to the requirements of drama and entertainment, shall be presented.

3. Law—divine, natural, or human—shall not be ridiculed, nor shall sympathy be created for its violation.

Particular Applications:
1. Crime
   1. Crime shall never be presented in such a way as to throw sympathy with the crime as against law and justice, or to inspire others with a desire for imitation.
   2. Methods of crime shall not be explicitly presented or detailed in a manner calculated to glamorize crime or inspire imitation.
   3. Action showing the taking of human life is to be held to the minimum. Its frequent presentation tends to lessen regard for the sacredness of life.
   4. Suicide, as a solution of problems occurring in the development of screen drama, is to be discouraged unless absolutely necessary for the development of the plot, and shall never be justified, or glorified, or used specifically to defeat the ends of justice.
   5. Excessive flaunting of weapons by criminals shall not be permitted.
   6. There shall be no scenes of law-enforcing officers dying at the hands of criminals, unless such scenes are absolutely necessary to the plot.
   7. Pictures dealing with criminal activities in which minors participate, or to which minors are related, shall not be approved if they tend to incite demoralizing imitation on the part of youth.
   8. Murder:
      a. The technique of murder must not be presented in a way that will inspire imitation.
      b. Brutal killings are not to be presented in detail.
      c. Revenge in modern times shall not be justified.
      d. Mercy killing shall never be made to seem right or permissible.

9. Drug addiction or the illicit traffic in addition-producing drugs shall not be shown if the portrayal:

    a. Tends in any manner to encourage, stimulate, or justify the use of such drugs; or

    b. Stresses, visually or by dialog, their temporarily attractive effects; or

    c. Suggests that the drug habit may be quickly or easily broken; or

    d. Shows details of drug procurement or of the taking of drugs in any manner; or

    e. Emphasizes the profits of the drug traffic; or

    f. Involves children who are shown knowingly to use or traffic in drugs.

10. Stories on the kidnapping or illegal abduction of children are acceptable under the code only

    a. when the subject is handled with restraint and discretion and avoids details, gruesomeness and undue horror; and

    b. the child is returned unharmed.

2. Brutality

Excessive and inhuman acts of cruelty and brutality shall not be presented. This includes all detailed and protracted presentation of physical violence, torture, and abuse.

3. Sex

The sanctity of the institution of marriage and home shall be upheld. No film shall infer that casual or promiscuous sex relationships are the accepted or common thing.

1. Adultery and illicit sex, sometimes necessary plot material, shall not be explicitly treated, nor shall they be justified or made to seem right and permissible.

2. Scenes of passion:

    a. These should not be introduced except where they are definitely essential to the plot.

    b. Lustful and open-mouthed kissing, lustful embraces, suggestive posture and gestures are not to be shown.

    c. In general, passion should be treated in such manner as not to stimulate the baser emotions.

3. Seduction or rape:

    a. These should never be more than suggested, and then

only when essential to the plot. They should never be shown explicitly.
  b. They are never acceptable subject matter for comedy.
  c. They should never be made to seem right and permissible.
4. The subject of abortion shall be discouraged, shall never be more than suggested, and when referred to shall be condemned. It must never be treated lightly or made the subject of comedy. Abortion shall never be shown explicitly or by inference, and a story must not indicate that an abortion has been performed. The word "abortion" shall not be used.
5. The methods and techniques of prostitution and white slavery shall never be presented in detail, nor shall the subjects be presented unless shown in contrast as such may not be shown.
6. Sex perversion or any inference of it is forbidden.
7. Sex hygiene and venereal diseases are not acceptable subject matter for theatrical motion pictures.
8. Children's sex organs are never to be exposed. This provision shall not apply to infants.

4. Vulgarity

Vulgar expressions and double meanings having the same effect are forbidden. This shall include, but not be limited to, such words and expressions as chippie, fairy, goose, nuts, pansy, S.O.B., son-of-a. The treatment of low, disgusting, unpleasant, though not necessarily evil, subjects should be guided always by the dictates of good taste and a proper regard for the sensibilities of the audience.

5. Obscenity

  1. Dances suggesting or representing sexual actions or emphasizing indecent movements are to be regarded as obscene.
  2. Obscenity in words, gesture, reference, song, joke, or by suggestion, even when likely to be understood by only part of the audience, is forbidden.

6. Blasphemy and Profanity

  1. Blasphemy is forbidden. Reference to the Deity, God, Lord, Jesus, Christ shall not be irreverent.
  2. Profanity is forbidden. The words "hell" and "damn," while sometimes dramatically valid, will, if used without

moderation, be considered offensive by many members of the audience. Their use shall be governed by the discretion and prudent advice of the Code Administration.

7. Costumes

1. Complete nudity, in fact or in silhouette, is never permitted, nor shall there by any licentious notice by characters in the film of suggested nudity.

2. Indecent or undue exposure is forbidden.

The foregoing shall not be interpreted to exclude actual scenes photographed in a foreign land of the natives of that land, showing native life, provided:

1. Such scenes are included in a documentary film or travelogue depicting exclusively such land, its customs, and civilization; and

2. Such scenes are not in themselves intrinsically objectionable.

8. Religion

1. No film or episode shall throw ridicule on any religious faith.

2. Ministers of religion, or persons posing as such, shall not be portrayed as comic characters or as villains so as to cast disrespect on religion.

3. Ceremonies of any definite religion shall be carefully and respectfully handled.

9. Special Subjects

The following subjects must be treated with discretion and restraint within the careful limits of good taste:

1. Bedroom scenes.

2. Hangings and electrocutions.

3. Liquor and drinking.

4. Surgical operations and childbirth.

5. Third-degree methods.

10. National Feelings

1. The use of the flag shall be consistently respectful.

2. The history, institutions, prominent people, and citizenry of all nations shall be represented fairly.

3. No picture shall be produced that tends to incite bigotry or hatred among peoples of differing races, religions, or national origins. The use of such offensive words as Chink, Dago, Frog, Greaser, Hunkie, Kike, Nigger, Spic, Wop, Yid should be avoided.

11. Titles

The following titles shall not be used:

    1. Titles which are salacious, indecent, obscene, profane, or vulgar.

    2. Titles which violate any other clause of this code.

12. Cruelty to Animals

In the production of motion pictures involving animals the producer shall consult with the authorized representative of the American Humane Association and invite him to be present during the staging of such animal action. There shall be no use of any contrivance or apparatus for tripping or otherwise treating animals in any unacceptably harsh manner.

Appendix II_____
LIST OF "DONT'S" AND "BE CAREFULS"

[This was the first formulation of what would later become the Production Code. It was adopted by the major film studios in 1927.]

Resolved, that those things which are included in the following list shall not appear in pictures produced by members of this Association, irrespective of the manner in which they are treated:

    1. Pointed profanity—by either title or lip—this includes words "God," "Lord," "Jesus," "Christ" (unless used reverently in connection with proper religious ceremonies), "hell," "damn," "Gawd," and every other profane and vulgar expression, however it may be spelled.

    2. Any licentious or suggestive nudity—in fact or in silhouette; and any lecherous or licentious notice thereof by other characters in the picture.

    3. The illegal traffic in drugs.

    4. Any inference of sex perversion.

    5. White slavery.

    6. Miscegenation (sex relationships between the white and black races).

    7. Sex hygiene and venereal diseases.

    8. Scenes of actual childbirth—in fact or in silhouette.

    9. Children's sex organs.

    10. Ridicule of the clergy.

    11. Willful offense to any nation, race or creed.

And be it further resolved that special care be exercised in the manner in which the following subjects are treated, to the end that vulgarity and suggestiveness may be eliminated and that good taste may be emphasized:

1. The use of the flag.
2. International relations (avoiding picturization in an unfavorable light another country's religion, history, institutions, prominent people, and citizenry).
3. Arson.
4. The use of firearms.
5. Theft, robbery, safecracking, and dynamiting of trains, mines, buildings, etc. (having in mind the effect which a too-detailed description of these may have upon the moron).
6. Brutality and possible gruesomeness.
7. Technique of committing murder by whatever method.
8. Methods of smuggling.
9. Third-degree methods.
10. Actual hangings or electrocutions as legal punishment for crime.
11. Sympathy for criminals.
12. Attitude toward public characters and institutions.
13. Sedition.
14. Apparent cruelty to children and animals.
15. Branding of people or animals.
16. The sale of women, or of a woman selling her virtue.
17. Rape or attempted rape.
18. First-night scenes.
19. Man and woman in bed together.
20. Deliberate seduction of girls.
21. The institution of marriage.
22. Surgical operations.
23. The use of drugs.
24. Titles or scenes having to do with the law enforcement or law-enforcing officers.
25. Excessive or lustful kissing, particularly when one character or the other is a "heavy."

Resolved, that the execution of the purpose of this resolution is a fair trade practice.

Appendix III
REASONS SUPPORTING THE PRODUCTION CODE

[The authors of the censorship code provided this supporting rationale for the clauses and formulations that comprised it.]

I. Theatrical motion pictures, that is, pictures intended for the theatre as distinct from pictures intended for churches, schools, lecture halls, educational movements, social reform movements, etc., are primarily to be regarded as entertainment. Mankind has always recognized the importance of entertainment and its value in rebuilding the bodies and souls of human beings. But it has always recognized that entertainment can be of a character either helpful or harmful to the human race, and in consequence has clearly distinguished between:

    a. Entertainment which tends to improve the race, or at least to recreate and rebuild human beings exhausted of life; and

    b. Entertainment which tends to degrade beings, or to lower their standards of life and living.

Hence the moral importance of entertainment is something which has been universally recognized. It enters intimately into the lives of men and women and affects them closely; it occupies their minds and affections during leisure hours; and ultimately touches the whole of their lives. A man can be judged by his standard of entertainment as easily as by the standard of his work.

So correct entertainment raises the whole standard of a nation. Wrong entertainment lowers the whole living conditions and moral ideals of a race.

Note, for example, the healthy reactions to healthful sports, like baseball; the unhealthy reactions to sports like cockfighting, bullfighting, bear baiting, etc. Note too, the effect on ancient nations of gladiatorial combats, the obscene plays of Roman times, etc.

II. Motion pictures are very important as art. Though a new art, possibly a combination art, it has the same object as the other arts, the presentation of human thoughts, emotion and experience, in terms of an appeal to the soul through the senses.

Here as in entertainment, Art enters intimately into the lives of human beings. Art can be morally good, lifting men to higher levels. This has been done through good music, great painting, authentic fiction, poetry, drama. Art can be morally evil in its effects. This is the case clearly enough with unclean art, indecent books, suggestive drama. The effect on the lives of men and women is obvious.

Note: It has often been argued that art in itself is unmoral, neither good nor bad. This is perhaps true of the thing which is music, painting, poetry, etc. But the thing is the product of some person's mind, and the intention of that mind was either good or bad morally when it produced the thing. Besides, the thing has its effect upon those who come into contact with it. In both these ways, that is, as a product of a mind and as the cause of definite effects, it has a deep moral significance and an unmistakable moral quality.

Hence: The motion pictures, which are the most popular of modern arts for the masses, have their moral quality from the intention of the minds which produce them and from their effects on the moral lives and reactions of their audiences. This gives them a most important morality.

1. They reproduce the morality of the men who use the pictures as a medium for the expression of their ideas and ideals.

2. They affect the moral standards of those who, through the screen, take in these ideas and ideals.

In the case of the motion picture, this effect may be particularly emphasized because no art has so quick and so widespread an appeal to the masses. It has become, in an incredibly short period, the art of the multitudes.

III. The motion picture, because of its importance as entertainment and because of the trust placed in it by the peoples of the world, has special moral obligations.

A. Most arts appeal to the mature. This art appeals at once to every class: mature, immature, developed, undeveloped, law abiding, criminal. Music has its grades for different classes; so have literature and drama. This art of the motion picture, combining as it does the two fundamental appeals of looking at a picture and listening to a story, at once reaches every class of society.

B. By reason of the mobility of a film and the ease of picture distribution, and because of the possibility of duplicating positives in large quantities, this art reaches places unpenetrated by other forms of art.

C. Because of these two facts, it is difficult to produce films intended for only certain classes of people. The exhibitors' theatres are built for the masses, for the cultivated and the rude, the mature and the immature, the self-respecting and the criminal. Films, unlike books and music, can with difficulty be confined to certain selected groups.

D. The latitude given to film material cannot, in consequence, be as wide as the latitude given to book material. In addition:

    a. A book describes, a film vividly presents. One presents on a cold page; the other by apparently living people.

    b. A book reaches the mind through words merely; a film reaches the eyes and ears through the reproduction of actual events.

    c. The reaction of a reader to a book depends largely on the keenness of the reader's imagination; the reaction to a film depends on the vividness of presentation. Hence many things which might be described or suggested in a book could not possibly be presented in a film.

E. This is also true when comparing the film with the newspaper.

    a. Newspapers present by description, films by actual presentation.

    b. Newspapers are after the fact and present things as having taken place; the film gives the events in the process of enactment and with the apparent reality of life.

F. Everything possible in a play is not possible in a film:

    a. Because of the larger audience of the film, and its consequential mixed character. Psychologically, the larger the audience, the lower the moral mass resistance to suggestion.

b. Because through light, enlargement of character, presentation, scenic emphasis, etc., the screen story is brought closer to the audience than the play.

c. The enthusiasm for and interest in the film actors and actresses, developed beyond anything of the sort in history, makes the audience largely sympathetic toward the characters they portray and the stories in which they figure. Hence the audience is more ready to confuse actor and actress and the characters they portray, and it is most receptive of the emotions and ideals presented by its favorite stars.

G. Small communities, remote from sophistication and from the hardening process which often takes place in the ethical and moral standards of groups in large cities, are easily and readily reached by any sort of film.

H. The grandeur of mass settings, large scenes, spectacular features, etc., affects and arouses more intensely the emotional side of the audience.

In general, the mobility, popularity, accessibility, emotional appeal, vividness, straightforward presentation of fact in the film make for more intimate contact with a larger audience and for greater emotional appeal.

Hence the larger moral responsibilities of the motion pictures.

INDEX